Global Diversities

In collaboration with the Max Planck Institute for the Study of Ethnic and Religious Diversity

Series Editors: **Steven Vertovec**, Max Planck Institute for the Study of Religious and Ethnic Diversity and University of Gottingen, Germany; **Peter van der Veer**, Max Planck Institute for the Study of Religious and Ethnic Diversity and Utrecht University, The Netherlands; **Ayelet Shachar**, Max Planck Institute for the Study of Religious and Ethnic Diversity

Over the past decade, the concept of 'diversity' has gained a leading place in academic thought, business practice, politics, and public policy across the world. However, local conditions and meanings of 'diversity' are highly dissimilar and changing. For these reasons, deeper and more comparative understandings of pertinent concepts, processes, and phenomena are in great demand. This series will examine multiple forms and configurations of diversity, how these have been conceived, imagined, and represented, how they have been or could be regulated or governed, how different processes of inter-ethnic or inter-religious encounter unfold, how conflicts arise and how political solutions are negotiated and practiced, and what truly convivial societies might actually look like. By comparatively examining a range of conditions, processes, and cases revealing the contemporary meanings and dynamics of 'diversity', this series will be a key resource for students and professional social scientists. It will represent a landmark within a field that has become, and will continue to be, one of the foremost topics of global concern throughout the twenty-first century. Reflecting this multi-disciplinary field, the series will include works from Anthropology, Political Science, Sociology, Law, Geography, and Religious Studies. The series publishes standard monographs, edited collections, and Palgrave Pivot titles, for shorter works that are between 25-50,000 words.

Titles include:

Jin-Heon Jung
MIGRATION AND RELIGION IN EAST ASIA
North Korean Migrants' Evangelical Encounters

Tam T. T. Ngo and Justine B. Quijada
ATHEIST SECULARISM AND ITS DISCONTENTS
A Comparative Study of Religion and Communism in Eurasia

Steven Vertovec
DIVERSITIES OLD AND NEW
Migration and Socio-Spatial Patterns in New York, Singapore and Johannesburg

Susanne Wessendorf
COMMONPLACE DIVERSITY
Social Relations in a Super-Diverse Context

Forthcoming titles:

Laavanya Kathiravelu
MIGRANT DUBAI
Building a Global City

Tatiana Matejskova and Marco Antonsich
GOVERNING THROUGH DIVERSITY
Migration Societies in Post-Multiculturalist Times

Fran Meissner
SOCIALISING WITH DIVERSITY
Making Sense of Urban Superdiversity

Monika Palmberger
HOW GENERATIONS REMEMBER
Contested Memories in Post-War Bosnia and Herzegovina

Maria Schiller
EUROPEAN CITIES, MUNICIPAL ORGANIZATIONS AND DIVERSITY
The New Politics of Difference

Junjia Ye
INEQUALITY IN THE GLOBAL CITY
Division of Labour and the Politics of Cosmopolitanism

Global Diversities
Series Standing Order ISBN 978–1–137–37750–0 (hardback) and
978–1–137–37751–7 (paperback)
(*outside North America only*)

You can receive future titles in this series as they are published by placing a standing order. Please contact your bookseller or, in case of difficulty, write to us at the address below with your name and address, the title of the series and the ISBN quoted above.

Customer Services Department, Macmillan Distribution Ltd, Houndmills, Basingstoke, Hampshire RG21 6XS, England

Migration and Religion in East Asia

North Korean Migrants' Evangelical Encounters

Jin-Heon Jung

Research Fellow, Max Planck Institute for the Study of Religious and Ethnic Diversity, Germany

First published 2015 by
PALGRAVE MACMILLAN

Palgrave Macmillan in the UK is an imprint of Macmillan Publishers Limited, registered in England, company number 785998, of Houndmills, Basingstoke, Hampshire RG21 6XS.

Palgrave Macmillan in the US is a division of St Martin's Press LLC, 175 Fifth Avenue, New York, NY 10010.

Palgrave Macmillan is the global academic imprint of the above companies and has companies and representatives throughout the world.

Palgrave® and Macmillan® are registered trademarks in the United States, the United Kingdom, Europe and other countries.

ISBN 978–1–137–45038–8

This book is printed on paper suitable for recycling and made from fully managed and sustained forest sources. Logging, pulping and manufacturing processes are expected to conform to the environmental regulations of the country of origin.

A catalogue record for this book is available from the British Library.

Library of Congress Cataloging-in-Publication Data
Jung, Jin-Heon, 1969– author.
   Migration and religion in East Asia : North Korean migrants' evangelical encounters / Jin-Heon Jung, Research Fellow, Max Planck Institute for the Study of Religious and Ethnic Diversity, Germany.
      pages   cm
   Summary: "Since the mid-1990s when North Korea was gripped by a devastating famine, increasing numbers of North Korean migrants have been crossing the Sino-North Korean border en route to Seoul, South Korea, in search of a better life. Based on fieldwork conducted in Seoul and Northeast China, Migration and Religion in East Asia sheds light on North Korean migrants' Christian encounters and conversions throughout the process of migration and settlement. Focusing on churches as primary contact zones, it highlights the ways in which the migrants and their evangelical counterparts both draw on and contest each others' envisioning of a reunified Christianized nation-state. Analysing the intersections between religious and political conversion and physical migration, it scrutinises cultural understandings of identity politics, religio-political aspirations, competing discourses on humanitarianism, and freedom in both religious and national terms in the context of late-Cold War Korea" — Provided by publisher.
   ISBN 978–1–137–45038–8 (hardback)
   1. Christianity—Korea.   2. Evangelicalism—Korea.   3. Korea—Church history—21st century.   4. Emigration and immigration—Religious aspects—Christianity—History—21st century.   5. Korea—Emigration and immigration—History—21st century.   6. Emigration and immigration—Political aspects—History—21st century.   I. Title.
   BR1329.J86 2015
   275.19′08308691—dc23   2015015582

To Sumi and Julian Doyeon

Contents

Figures and Tables

Figures

Tables

Preface

This book documents the meeting of North Korean migrants and the South Korean evangelical church at a pivotal historical moment: when the prevailing cultural logic of the anti-North Korean Cold War ideology waned, and the public standing of the South Korean evangelical churches faltered. The era of my research, however, is historical in that today the quite conservative South Korean presidents Lee Myung-bak (2008–2013) and current incumbent Park Keun-hye (2013–present) have arguably reinstated a regime with both authoritarian and evangelical accents. The term *ch'ongbuk*, or pro-North Korean stance, appears to legitimize control over those who oppose the ruling government, claim freedom of expression, work for lesbian, gay, bisexual, and transgender rights, labor rights, and so on. The encounter I document here is one that I think speaks to the present situation and contains ethnographic truth.

I carried out ethnographic research in Seoul, South Korea, and Yanji, on the Sino–North Korean border in northeast China from August 2006 to December 2007, and a series of follow-up researches in Seoul by 2013. My research also draws on my previous experiences from 1999 to 2002, working with the Center for Cultural Integration, a South Korean non-government organization, on a North Korean famine relief project in China and with North Korean migrant youth education programs in South Korea. These experiences helped me to establish good relations with North Korean migrants, to receive substantial help from local agents in China, and to gain a better understanding of the trends in North Korean migration patterns and South Korean policies towards migrants over time. In this regard, this book is a product of both my previous activities and fieldwork.

In 2002, while developing alternative education programs for North Korean migrant youth in South Korea, I became aware of the importance of anthropological approaches in developing culturally relativistic programs. Although the number of migrant youth arriving in South Korea through China was rising, there were no specific care programs for them at Hanawon, the primary government-run integration center for new arrivals. I helped to set up and run an education program at this facility and later in Seoul. In the same period of time, I co-authored the book *Pukhanesŏ on nae ch'ingu* (A Friend from North Korea) for South

Korean elementary school teachers to use for unification education classes. My co-authors were a South Korean professor of psychology, Chung Jean-kyung, and two North Korean migrants, Kim Sung-min and Choi Jin-yi, who had been writers in the North. These activities gave me a chance to witness the cultural differences South and North Koreans experience in interacting together. Anthropological approaches, which value "historicity" and "particularity" (Boas 1896 [1940]) as a means of understanding culture as a whole, thus emerged as a best practice for organizing activities, influencing policy making, and understanding rapid changes in the field.

In January 2002, I was in the first year of my doctoral program in the Department of Anthropology at the University of Illinois, when President Bush, one year before the outbreak of the Iraq War, spread the notion of an "axis of evil" naming Iran, Iraq, and North Korea as key offenders in the "War on Terror." Until then, the issue of North Korean migrants (called defectors by the South Korean media) had drawn relatively little scholarly attention in the United States and in Korean studies circles. Even in 2008, Chung (2008: 3–4) noted that journal articles had largely focused on desperate living conditions, and assigned blame to both the Chinese government and the North Korean regime for human rights violations, suggesting rescue activities without detailed concern for either local specificities or global implications.

Since then, I have witnessed anticommunist discourses and narratives as they have begun to emerge among newly arrived North Korean migrants. I consider this a starting point in the formation of a canonical language aimed at the North Korean regime. My experience working for an organization I helped found to establish friendship between young North and South Koreans helps to illustrate this. In early 2002, the organization's website was unique because it featured stories about North Korean individuals that gave a sense of how they lived in the North. The stories somewhat romanticized their lives in pre-famine North Korea, and even stories of immense suffering—family loss, separation, death, and hardship caused by the 1995–1998 famine—were described as merely being the vicissitudes of life. They did not ascribe blame to the North Korean state or system. However, in late 2002, when the phrase "axis of evil" came to imply a potential war against North Korea after Iraq, I noticed a dramatic change in the comments that members left on a free on-line bulletin board. The relatively apolitical writings of previous contributors were replaced by anti-North Korean slogans and stories of revenge from a host of new contributors. The purpose of the site had shifted from that of building friendship between North and South Korean young generations to that of serving anti-North Korean activism. Subsequently, some North Korean migrants whom I had known began to actively cooperate with the Bush administration and South Korean conservative organizations, testifying about the conditions in labor camps and gulags in cases citing North Korean human rights violations. These testimonies contributed directly and indirectly to the enactment of the North Korean Human Rights Act of 2004. This bill secured funding for non-governmental organizations and research institutes working with North Korean refugees and on humanitarian needs. This showed how anti-North Korean sentiment was being reproduced at the civil and transnational level through networking and support between North Korean migrant organizations and conservative South Korean organizations as well as international organizations. Note that concurrently, Kim Dae-jung's administration was promoting a Sunshine Policy toward North Korea, with increasing inter-Korean contact and socio-economic exchange (1998–2007). In other words, the state-led inter-Korean normalization policy and process came to encounter a backlash from right-wing conservatism.

In the summer of 2004, I went to South Korea to get a feeling for the changes that were taking place in the experiences of North Korean migrants and in their relationship with South Koreans. While observing their daily lives at work or at college, I became interested in the fact that the majority of North Korean migrants were attending church services, religious meetings such as Sunday Bible study, intensive training programs, and church picnics, and receiving a monthly stipend from the church. This led me to recall my first fieldwork experience in China in the summer of 2000, when I met with migrant children through a local church network. At the time, all the secret shelters I visited there were run by Korean-Chinese who had been trained as missionaries at missionary schools that were directly or indirectly established and run by South Korean churches or missionary organizations.

Meanwhile, I became more interested in the significance of Christian conversion for both North Korean migrants and the South Korean church in an era in which reunification was growing more plausible. Thus, it became apparent that more research was needed on the role of the church as a contact zone for North Korean migrants and South Korean Christians.

In 2005, I engaged in several training programs run by megachurches and interviewed both North and South Korean participants. I chose the Freedom School (FS) as my main ethnographic research site because I considered it to be a model training program entailing all the activities that other church programs could only selectively carry out due to budget restrictions and limited human resources. Organizations working with and caring for migrants typically protect migrants' identities and those of their families back in North Korea by prohibiting outsiders from observing and interviewing them. This policy of secrecy also extends to the running of their operations, details that they are not willing to share with other organizations offering similar programs. Nonetheless, I was fortunate enough to receive unlimited access to the FS programs.

From August 2006 to December 2007, I participated in and observed most of the FS programs, including regular classes on Saturdays and Sundays from 9 a.m. to 5 p.m., group Bible studies on Wednesday or Thursday evenings from 7 p.m. to 10 p.m., outdoor activities such as a healing camp, volunteering at a Christian shelter for the disabled, and field trips. While continuing participant observation in FS classes, I conducted open-ended interviews with South Korean Christians and North Korean migrants, and accompanied them on various occasions including to a village office, other theological training programs, and other churches.

My interview data with North and South Koreans suggests that *Pukhan baro algi undong*, or the North Korea awareness campaign promoted by the South Korean government and civil society since the late 1990s, has failed to raise both knowledge and a culturally relative view of North Korean culture in South Korea. Meanwhile, South Korean Christians, whose view on the migrants is ambivalent, try to inculcate "proper" (South Korean) manners in them such as speaking standard South Korean, observing proper sexual conduct, upholding marriage ideals, respecting public etiquette, and endorsing certain parenting methods. Here, Christian morality is mixed with South Korean norms, which stratify all Korean persons according to their social background (e.g., economic achievement, education level, and birthplace networks). In this regard, I have found that the relationship between migrants and South Korean Christians represents the ways in which South Korean class, gender, place of origin, and even racial biases come to life.

In 2007, I conducted intensive fieldwork in China twice: once for one week in late April and again for one month from late June to late July. During this time, I participated in and observed Korean-Chinese churches in two villages and interviewed around 30 individuals, comprising Korean-Chinese pastors, South Korean missionaries, a Han Chinese government official, and undocumented North Korean migrants living in China. The trips gave me an opportunity to witness the socio-political circumstances that North Korean migrants navigate, and the ways in which the Protestant church mediates their migration to South Korea and elsewhere. There is no question that North Korean migrants' reactions to and perspectives on Christianity upon their arrival in South Korea are intimately tied to this sort of direct or indirect transnational church support. Combining interview data in China with migrants' narratives in South Korea, part of my book aims to contextualize North Korean underground railways through which they experience and come to adopt the so-called South Korean Dream.

Acknowledgments

First and foremost, I would like to express my special appreciation to the North Korean migrants, Korean-Chinese missionaries, and South Korean Christians whose voices and practices made my research journey possible. At the same time, I have to confess how painful it was to keep a "research distance" from those who were seeking immediate help in China and occasionally in South Korea. This book is still largely an attempt to bring out their issues around the themes of religion and nationalism in the late Cold War era and may not fully elaborate on the various issues at hand.

This project is rooted in an earlier research project for North Korean famine relief (1998–2000), followed by activities for North Korean young migrants in South Korea I was engaged in. My mentor and advisor Byung-Ho Chung deserves my special gratitude for inspiring and training me throughout the projects. I was also fortunate to learn from Bae Ki-dong, Kim Byung-mo, and Lee Hee-soo during my master's program in anthropology at Hanyang University. I extend my appreciation to those who have been and still are involved in the aforementioned activities including Chung Jean-kyung, Hwang Sang-ik, Jang Soo-hyun, Lee Gi-bum, Chung Jean-ung, Jang Nam-su, Kim Joong-tae, Kim Soo-haeng, Park Jin-won, Choi Hye-kyung, Kim Yoon-sun, Park Jin-hwan, Chung Woo-chang, Kim Yoon-young, Kang Ju-won, Ma Seok-hun, Shin Kuk-gyun, Yoon Sang-seok, Yoon Eun-jung, Kang Hee-suk, Park Jung-sook, Ahn Jin-hee, Kang Hyun-jin, Cho Hyun-sang, Nam Bong-im, and numerous volunteers.

This book was developed from my doctoral dissertation at the University of Illinois at Urbana–Champaign, where I received warm-hearted support and intellectual stimulation from my ideal advisor, Nancy Abelmann, and other dissertation committee members, Martin Manalansan IV, Ellen Moodie, Andrew Orta, and Kenneth M. Wells. I have also greatly benefited from other faculty members including Alejandro Lugo, the late William F. Kelleher Jr., Matti Bunzl, and Theodore Hughes. Special thanks as well to colleagues including Andrew Asher, Gregory Blomquist, Seun Ju Chae, John Cho, Hee Jung Choi, Angela Glaros, Alison Goebel, Daniel Gutierrez, Jennifer Hardin, William Hope, Yoonjung Kang, Heejin Kim, Hyunhee Kim, Martin Kowalewski, Shanshan Lan, Kyou Ho Lee, Soo-Jung Lee, Sangsook

Lee-Chung, Soo-kyung Lim, Steven Maas, Noriko Muraki, Teresa Ramos, Jason Ritchie, Sarah Rowe, So Jin Park, Isabel Scarborough, Yoonjeong Shim, Josie Sohn, Batamaka Some, Jesook Song, Elizabeth Spreng, Akiko Takeyama, Kok Tan, Han-sun Yang, and Bernardo Urbani.

Most recently, I have been privileged to receive inspiring intellectual advice and support at the Max Planck Institute for the Study of Religious and Ethnic Diversity in Germany. I extend my wholehearted appreciation to Peter van der Veer whose patient support made this book possible. I have had the luck to work with and learn from my colleagues and postdoctoral and doctoral fellows; I can't list everyone but they include Alexander Horstmann, Vibha Joshi Parkin, Justine Quijada, Weishan Huang, Yuqin Huang, Reza Masoudi Nejad, Jovan Maud, Dan Smyer Yu, Tam Ngo, and David Parkin; and lately Angela Heo, and Naomi Hellmann for valuable feedback on parts of this book. I am also grateful to other colleagues in the institute for amazing administrative support: Christel Albern, Jie Zhang, Julia Müller, Dagmar Recke, Birgitt Sippel, Diana Wagener, Martin Kühn, and Andreas Barz, to name a few.

In October 2011, I began coordinating a team project on urban aspirations in Seoul; this project on religion and megacities in comparative studies has provided me the privilege to work with Doyoung Song, Hyun Mee Kim, Ju Hui Judy Han, Nicholas Harkness, and Angela Heo.

I would like to extend my special appreciation to the Global Diversities series editors at Palgrave Macmillan, Steven Vertovec and Peter van der Veer, who supported the publication of this book. Special thanks to Judith Allan at Palgrave Macmillan for her kind assistance throughout the publication process.

Some parts of this book have been developed through presentations and publications in altered forms. Part of the historical background in Chapter 1 and some ethnographic vignettes included in Chapter 5 appear in "Underground Railroads of Christian Conversion: North Korean Migrants and Evangelical Missionary Networks in Northeast Asia" (*Encounters* 4: 163–188, 2011). Chapter 3 is revised from its earlier version, "North Korean Refugees and the Politics of Evangelical Mission in the Sino-Korean Border Area" (*Journal of Korean Religions*, 4(2): 147–173, 2013); as is Chapter 6, from "Refugee and Religious Narratives: The Conversion of North Koreans from Refugees to God's Warriors" in *Building Noah's Ark for Refugees, Migrants, and Religious Communities* (Alexander Horstmann and Jin-Heon Jung, eds., Palgrave Macmillan, 2015), and its earlier version, "Narrativization of Religious Conversion: 'Christian Passage' of North Korean Refugees in South Korea" (*Journal of Korean Language and Culture*, 50: 269–288, 2013). Part of the autobiographical narrative of the concluding chapter appeared in "The Politics of Desecularization: Christian Churches and North Korean Migrants in Seoul" in the *Handbook of Religion and the Asian City* (Peter van der Veer, ed., University of California Press, 2015). Many thanks to Young-ah Park, Carl Young, Sonia Ryang, Heon-ik Kwon, Laura Kendall, and Don Seeman for valuable comments on these earlier versions. Although any mistakes and limitations are entirely my own responsibility, I should thank Lillian Bertram and, in particular, Wendy Smyer Yu for correcting my English and refining my rough drafts. My gratitude to the Cartographic Research Laboratory at the University of Alabama for allowing me to modify a map of East Asia for this book.

During the latest stage of follow-up research and write-up, this project was supported by the Academy of Korean Studies Grant funded by the Korean government (MEST) (AKS-2011-AAA-2104). Earlier work was funded by the Wenner-Gren Foundation Dissertation Fieldwork Grant, the Graduate College of the University of Illinois at Urbana–Champaign (through a dissertation travel grant and university fellowships), the Department of Anthropology at the University of Illinois fellowships (Summer Research Fund and Summer Fieldwork Grant from the National Science Foundation), and the Max Planck Institute for the Study of Religious and Ethnic Diversity Doctoral Fellowship.

I would like to extend my special gratitude to Kim Yong-beom who first inspired me about Korean diaspora issues and above all suggested I study cultural anthropology. He and Shin Dong-ho, Jeon Young-sun, Yoo Byung-soo, Lim Hyung-jae, Yoon Jin-ho, Lim Byung-hee, and Kim Hun-kyoum at T'onghap are still my mentors and research comrades providing ceaseless poetic inspiration. I am also indebted to Nam-soo Hyong, Chang-hyun Lee, Young-hoon Kim, and Myung-joon Kim.

Finally, I'd like to extend my deep appreciation to my family. My wife Sumi Her has sacrificed her career for my study and to care for our son, Julian Doyeon. I thank my mother Lee Gang-soon, and mother-in-law Noh Kyung-ja who love and support me despite my filial impiety. I am also indebted to my siblings and siblings-in-law. I believe my father Jung In-heung and father-in-law Her In-hoy are resting in peace in heaven. To my family, I dedicate this work.

Note on Romanization and Translation

In regard to Korean Romanization, I follow the McCune-Reischauer system that is widely accepted in the academy, except for some official names of people, places, and pronouns. For example, I use Yanbian instead of Yŏnbyŏn for the Korean-Chinese Autonomous Prefecture in northeast China, as this is how it appears in most English media. Similarly, I use *Juche* instead of *Chuch'e* for the North Korean national ruling philosophy as it appears in North Korean official documents and websites. Personal names appear in Korean order by which the surnames come first and the given names are hyphenated (e.g., "Kim Dae-jung"), unless they appear in English publications or the person follows a different order. All translations of North and South Korean texts and narratives are my own unless otherwise noted. My interlocutors and most place names quoted in this book are all referred to by pseudonyms for security reasons.

1
Introduction: North Korean Migrants and Contact Zones

This book examines the life trajectories of North Korean migrants as they interact with South Korean transnational missionary networks along the Sino–North Korean border in China and in South Korea. I investigate the meanings and processes of individual migrants' conversion to Christianity through interactional frameworks, namely, those through which North Korean migrants interact with South Korean and Korean-Chinese (朝鮮族) missionaries, and with state powers, and with God. Churches, including related institutions, communities, and networks, serve as cultural "contact zones" (Pratt 1992) for the human–divine interactions upon which this book is based. Since the mid-1990s, when a famine took approximately one million North Korean lives, escalating numbers of people have crossed the Tumen river in search of food resources, job opportunities, and refuge, risking their lives to make their way to South Korea in hope of a "better life" (Suh 2002; Yoon 2003; Chung 2008). Statistics show that a startling 80–90 percent of North Korean migrants identified themselves as Christian when they arrived in South Korea and around 70 percent continued to rely on church services after they arrived (Jeon 2007). The church then emerges as a primary contact zone in which North Korean migrants are incorporated into the South Korean Christian system of values.

South Korean missionaries and Korean-Chinese missionaries initiated and directly or indirectly operate the underground railroads that secure the migrants' physical and politico-ideological movement, namely, "Christian passage," as I call it. North Korean migrants' conversion entails both personal and national salvation in the South Korean evangelical vision of a Christianized reunified nation and conversion narratives by migrants dramatize the stark differences between the two Koreas. More precisely, in adopting a historical and anthropological

1

perspective, this study stresses that while "defectors" from the North were once celebrated as national heroes and heroines by past authoritarian regimes with an anticommunist stance (1960s–1980s), today it is only within the space of civil organizations—in particular, the Evangelical Protestant Church, and the private media—and in the logic of human rights (which is equivalent to religious conversion) that they are empowered to be born again as evangelists, missionaries, human rights activists, model "free" citizens, and so on in South Korea and transnational contexts as well. Indeed, this book primarily focuses on the church that relies on them in its attempt to revive its own hegemonic position in South Korean politics and to help envision an anticommunist-Christianized unified Korea. I argue that North Korean migrants' conversion to Christianity is a cultural project with political and ideological hues that reveal the key characteristics of South Korean anticommunist evangelicalism.

This cultural project and my resulting ethnography have come into being in an era in which inter-Korean relations have fluctuated as radically as the world's geopolitical climate. Once a normal sentiment, South Korean anticommunism briefly seemed to be a bygone ideology of former authoritarian regimes (Kim S. 2006; Cumings 2007). The historical summit meeting between South Korean President Kim Dae-jung and North Korean Leader Kim Jong-il in 2000, increasing economic and cultural exchanges between North and South Korea, and growing humanitarian aid for North Korea from the South made national reconciliation seem realistic for a time. In recent years, however, anticommunism has been on the rise. US–North Korea military tensions and the global economic recession, not to mention China's influence on geopolitics, have facilitated South Korean evangelical churches' role as a holding ground at the center of South Korea's right-wing movement (Ryu 2009). Indeed, right-wing churches have played a crucial role in the shift of power to more conservative administrations led by Lee Myung-bak, an elder of the Somang Presbyterian church (2008–2013), and current President Park Keun-hye, the eldest daughter of former militant dictator, Park Chung-hee (1963–1979).

Due to this rightward drift, economic and cultural exchanges between North and South Korea have nearly stopped. Meanwhile, North Korea's second ruler, Kim Jong-il, transferred power to his youngest son, Kim Jong-un, a hereditary power transfer unheard of in modern nation-states. Contrary to suspicions that assumed the inevitability of internal power conflicts and chaos, this "young General" Kim seems to have stabilized his absolute power. During this power transfer period, North

Korea launched long and short range missiles, proceeded with nuclear tests, and exchanged fire several times with the South.[1] Interestingly, my North Korean migrant interlocutors bear witness to North Korea's increasing economic reliance on China while its relationship with the United States and South Korea deteriorates. In this historical predicament, the number of North Korean migrants arriving in South Korea by way of China continued to increase in the 2000s, averaging 2,000 every year, and dropped to about 1,500 after 2012, when Kim Jong-un took power and the Sino–North Korean border security on both sides increased. No longer expected to serve anticommunist propaganda maneuvers for the South Korean state, North Korean migrants are instead expected to assimilate into South Korea's competitive education system, job market, and social structure. The government's resettlement package, including three months of mandatory "training" at Hanawon, free housing, full healthcare, and incentives for vocational training and higher education, reflects the depoliticization of North Korean migrant issues, since the first civilian President Kim Young-sam took office (1993–1998).

South Korean evangelical churches are second only to the state in providing various services to facilitate migrants' integration into the South Korean capitalist system. In addition, it is significant to note that the churches project ontological overtones with politico-theological hues on the migrants. Hunger, human rights abuses, personal loss and separation, and other forms of suffering are interpreted as signs that God's words can be realized on earth and by them. That is, North Korean migrants become "the chosen" in the Christian community. In the same spirit, however, they also learn to become victim-survivors of the socialist dictatorship and to use the rhetoric of human rights abuse against the North, namely, re-politicizing their subjectivities in the space of the church and in the logic of "universal" freedom and humanitarianism. This book, therefore, pays particular attention to such evangelical efforts as a cultural force that turns North Korean Christians into agents of national (i.e., North and South) evangelization. I approach the Cold War legacy and the politics of global Christianity through the personal trajectories of North Korean migrants. In focusing on the re-subjectification of individual migrants, I am able to demonstrate how the process of Christian conversion is ambiguous and contested.

Much literature, published mostly in Korean, addresses the problems of both governmental and civil support systems for North Korean migrants and the ways in which migrants struggle to adjust to their new society (e.g., Jeon 2000, 2007; Suh 2002; Yoon 2002; Chung 2004, 2008;

Kim Y. 2004; Choo 2006; Chung et al. 2006; Kang 2006; Lankov 2006; Yoon 2007; Kim Y. 2009). In this work, sociologists and anthropologists have found that the difficulties migrants face in adjusting to the South stem from a larger problem—South Korean ethnocentric nationalism. For instance, North Korean migrants are "ethnicized" (Choo 2006) as second class citizens, as was the case between West and East Germans in post-unification Germany; migrants are socially and biologically "stigmatized" (Chung 2000) and viewed as "cultural inferiors" (Kim Y. 2009); and migrants are often discriminated against in schools and on the job market in the South. It is also critical to realize that interactions between South and North Koreans are more dynamic than those typically portrayed in the literature, which posits North Koreans as victims. Kim Yoon-young's thesis (2009) examines the ways in which migrants either strategically conceal or expose their North Korean identities to receive benefits or to justify the receipt of such benefits. Migrants' Christian experiences and reliance on church services remain significant throughout their life. However, they tend to consider Christianity or religion as merely incidental or side issues. When the church is mentioned, it is usually in instrumental terms, as in what services the church does or should provide.

This book regards the church as the primary intra-ethnic "contact zone," areas which Mary Louise Pratt defines as "social spaces where disparate cultures meet, clash, and grapple with each other, often in highly asymmetrical relations of domination and subordination" (1992: 4). I argue that religion serves as a lens through which we can better understand how complex ideological, political, and cultural tensions (e.g., nationalism, imperialism, freedom, human rights) meet in the reconfiguration of migrants' identities. More precisely, for North Korean conversion as a project, this study asserts that the evangelical church renders North Korean migrants as "freed" from the communist regime, and "revives" their religiosity by replacing *Kimilsung-ism* (the ideology of Kim Il-sung, or *Juche* North Korean national ruling philosophy) with Christianity.

In addition to the concept of contact zone, I employ Pierre Bourdieu's notion of "market" and Dorothy Holland et al.'s (1998) "figured world" to better contextualize the conversion project. To avoid any unnecessary confusion, I want to distinguish my use of "market" from religious market theory, since the latter refers to the competition among different religions and denominations, and a person's rational choice of religion as commodity (see Iannaccone 1991). Instead, I use "market" as a metaphor for what Bourdieu calls the "field of power (politics)"[2] in an attempt to better understand competing investments among increasingly diversified actors including faith-based organizations, civil societies, and state governments, all of which are discursively bipolarized in ideological topography in envisioning a national future—a reunified nation. In light of this "imagined" reunification, I use "figured world" (Holland et al. 1998) to discuss migrants' identity reconfiguration in relation to this imagined reunified nation. A "figured world" is defined as "a socially and culturally constructed realm of interpretation in which particular characters and actors are recognized, significance is assigned to certain acts, and particular outcomes are valued over others" (Holland et al. 1998: 52). As I elaborate in the following chapters, it is in the logic of conversion that migrant converts are projected to be "the chosen"—to save the North and revive Korean Christianity "as if" they are already in a reunified nation.

Accordingly, North Korean conversion is dynamic and saturated in meaning in the context of the fashioning of a new national subject. My ethnographic data highlights the veritable contest over what constitutes "true" or authentic Christianity and what Korean-ness should look like in a transforming East Asia. This chapter, then, continues by reviewing the main theoretical concerns in the discussion of conversion as a cultural passage and project; and discusses North and South Korean subjects, arguing that these two cultural "dispositions," in the Bourdieuian sense, have been constructed in a logic of mirrored distinction (i.e., from one another). The main body of the chapter discusses the ways in which North Korean-ness has been shaped by state policies over time, aiming to provide necessary background for further understanding the meaning of the church's interventions in these matters. Finally, I introduce and summarize the remaining chapters (Figures 1.1 and 1.2).

Conversion passage and project

North Korean conversion to Christianity appears to be a cultural passage and project in which each individual transformation is closely linked to broader religious implications (see cf. Nock 1933; Hefner 1993; Austin-Broos 2003). This passage reflects more than a radical shift in consciousness, with each individual completely denying his or her past, but also a series of more complex tensions and changes that accompany the migrants' physical relocation and internal transformation, from following *Juche* or *Kimilsung-ism* to becoming one of God's warriors for the Christianization of the Korean (unified) nation. Conversion intertwined with capitalist citizen making is only comprehensible if

Figure 1.1   The Tumen river flowing between North Korea and China
Source: Courtesy of the Author.

one considers the ways in which churches engineer and mediate the conversion process.

In most societies, it is not surprising to see previously unreligious people take on a new faith or convert from one religion to another. Robert Hefner illuminates conversion as being "influenced by a larger interplay of identity, politics, and morality" (1993: 4). Throughout this book, I shall take into account the structural conditions that push and pull migrants into the terrain of religion. My ethnography asserts that their conversion should not be considered as merely a matter of a liberal individual's ontological transformation without serious consideration of both institutional interventions (i.e., missionary networks) and particular geopolitical conditions (i.e., the Cold War, famine, and globalization).

When Alexander Solzhenitsyn was finally able to make his acceptance speech for the Nobel Prize in literature in 1974, he depicted himself as a writer "from a land without liberty."[3] At the peak of the Cold War period, refugees or exiles from Soviet Russia, East Germany, Vietnam, and Cuba tended to appreciate "freedom" in their new liberal host societies. In comparison to these earlier cases of anticommunist dissidents,

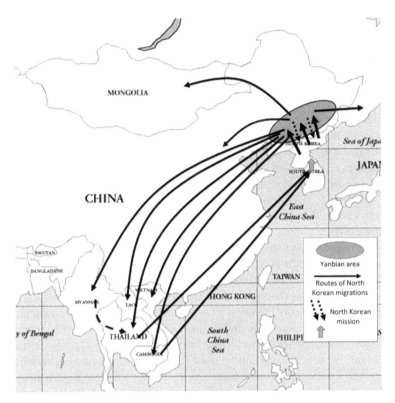

Figure 1.2 A map of underground railways of North Korean migration
Source: Courtesy of Cartographic Research Laboratory, University of Alabama, and modified by the Author.

the Christian conversion of recent North Korean migrants from "the world's most closed socialist country" rings odd or even ironic. Why, people ask, would former socialist subjects "choose" the constraints of "conservative" Christianity in the midst of their newfound freedoms? Longstanding western models of modernity most often posit an individual's submission and devotion to religion as something far from modern and liberal life/society and closer to either "traditional" or non-western societies (van der Veer 1996).

This ethnography of North Korean conversion therefore rests on a large number of anthropological publications on modernity and religion, and considers it in the Cold War context. First, the relationship between nationalism and religion in concert with the state–church relationship has been discussed at length in anthropological literature.

Despite a logical tension between bounded nationalism and transcendent religion, the two mutually rely on each other in the practice of building both a modern nation-state and the Kingdom of God in different ways in different places (van der Veer 1996; van der Veer & Lehmann 1999; Dirks 2001). Second, and similarly, the secularization theory put forth in discussing the relationship between modernity and religion has also been severely criticized (Hefner 1993; Casanova 1994; Keane 2007). Secular modernity in socialism, however, has long been considered as irreconcilable with and antagonistic toward religion. The resurgence of religion after socialism has thus drawn scholarly attention to Christianity, with regard to how Christianity becomes a beacon of democracy, freedom, human rights, and thus universal "truth" (see Rogers 2005; Hann et al. 2006; Wanner 2007; Steinberg & Wanner 2008; Yang 2008).

It is important to study conversion as a joint process and product of the aspirations of individuals and Christian institutions (i.e., churches and missionaries). The history of Christianity is full of tales of individual conversion through either God's calling or the convert's "free will." Without a consideration of power relations, however, this liberal notion of conversion is inevitably suspicious. Scholars of Christian conversion thus consider the particularities of the colonial and post-colonial context, in which Christianity itself has been perceived as a barometer of civilization and modernization in the face of western expansion (Comaroff & Comaroff 1991, 2003; Asad 1993; Burdick 1993; Appadurai 1996; Pels 1997, 1999; Martin 2002; Meyer & Pels 2003; Ong 2003; Orta 2004).

Korean Christianity is no longer a localized foreign religion. After the United States, South Korea is the largest missionary sending country (see Chapter 2), however, many questions remain unexplored regarding Korean Christianity in the global context. In its examination of the Christian encounters of North Korean migrants in the context of the transnational expansion of South Korean churches, this book maintains that conversion is a specific citizen-subject making project in a particular South Korean vision of the Kingdom of God.

My study reveals that North Korean migrants struggle to rationalize such notions as freedom, liberty, love, self, a sense of belonging, sincerity, creationism, and the nation-state, which Christianity introduces and guides them to embrace. Their conversions are not easy and their previous perceptions are not so easily cast aside. For example, some adult migrants seem to have assumed that "free" education, "free" food distribution, and "free" medical care would be guaranteed in the South, similar to what the North Korean socialist system provided before its economy collapsed. Similarly, it is a slow process for them to understand the relationship between South Korean notions of individual/self and society/nation. While South Koreans tend to feel ashamed to depend on public health care, some North Korean migrants value it as a natural state service.[4] In this regard, my ethnography observes the Freedom School, a megachurch-run training program for migrants, in which those norms attributed to being a "productive" citizen—such as self-management, self-discipline, and self-development—are emphasized as Protestant ethics as opposed to "dependent" and submissive North Korean dispositions. My ethnography stresses the ways in which South Korean churches conflate the processes of Christian conversion with the fashioning of "inferior" North Koreans into "superior" South Korean people in a "superior" social system.

In church settings and conversion processes, an established South Korean church hierarchy, ideas of spiritual purity, specific ritual forms, and economic status perpetuate the imbalance of North and South Korean relations. Nonetheless, North Korean migrants rely on churches for various reasons. Why? The answers vary, but some attribute church membership as being like (North Korean) Party membership, allowing for special treatment like that enjoyed by their Worker's Party cadres in the North (Chung 2008). Others seek a social network for better career building; and still others quench the spiritual thirst that followed their disenchantment with *Juche* ideology. Other reasons may be similar to those that can be found in South Korea and around the world. I argue that the question of North Korean conversion brings us to a larger query: what are the limits and potentials of Christianity for migrants' new lives in the South, and further, for the reunification process? I begin to address these questions by providing a brief historical review of human subject making in the context of the divided Koreas, Christianity, and nation-state building.

Making and transcending North/South Korean subjects

As elaborated below, North Korean subjectivities have been shaped in accordance with South Korean power relations. Their identities have been and are always projected in South Korean practices and discourses. National division is not merely a matter of geographical partition. Rather it has separated families, broken kinship ties, led to the creation of enemies, and serves to constantly distinguish the people in the two states. The socio-historical context of this book is large:

the project of politico-religious differentiation entailed in both South Korean and North Korean subject making. This differentiation, however, has stood—if ironically—alongside the shared insistence on Korean ethnic homogeneity (Lee 2006; Shin 2006; Cumings 2007). For South Korea, the human project has Christian humanist hues and is always defined against the logic of North Korea's "secular" socialist subjects. My aim here is not to establish the epistemological truths of these subject projects but to appreciate them as important cultural projects. For example, for North Korea this has entailed defining subjectivity dialectically to the western/American-inflected subject.

Interestingly, the religious and secular distinction serves both to clarify how each Korea has followed different trajectories, and to show how North–South ideological opposition has been arbitrary and absurd. Anticommunism in the South and anti-imperialism in the North are equally religious. Moreover, my North Korean informants are surprised at the fact that Christian elements and the church system are not that different from the ways of North Korean *Kimilsung-ism* and its social management system. Despite claims of cultural similarities and differences between the two societies, it is striking that anything but food culture from the North is degraded and suspected as being inauthentic among the North–South Korean interactions in church settings. In the meantime, as I maintain in this work, North Korean converts challenge and indirectly criticize South Korean religiosity as materialistic and individualistic. I provide the following subsections as an attempt to situate this contestation as it is produced through micro-interactions between South and North Koreans in the context of division projects perpetuated by each regime for more than half a century.

"I hate communists!"

I remember myself as a child in school in South Korea drawing anticommunist posters every year. This activity took place in the name of an "anticommunist poster contest" to which we were all required to submit a poster. Some talented children or those who were the children of "good" parents received awards and the rest were displayed on the school walls for several days. The posters represented how we thought our enemies and their land looked. The dominant image was the one in which "innocent" North Korean people were always suffering from chronic hunger and labor exploitation by red-skinned monsters with guns and tanks. In the northern part of Korea, a giant fat pig (an effigy of Kim Il-sung) and his brutal wolf soldiers were oppressing the people whom we should rescue by destroying the inhuman demons.

Meanwhile, South Korea was a prideful land of normal Koreans being "protected by God, Long Live our country!"—as written in the national anthem which aired every morning and evening; all the vehicles and pedestrians on the street would stop and face towards wherever there was a national flag.

While the war-time stories I begged my mother to tell me for a school assignment made me cry, I already submitted myself to being ready to "smash communists." I was only six or seven years old, but we were encouraged to adopt this attitude by a national "model child," Lee Seung-bok. He became the youngest anticommunist martyr who was reportedly murdered by North Korean commandos in 1968. I was taught that his mouth was torn to shreds as he shouted, "I hate communists!" My school had his statue, which was in front of the Lee Seung-bok Anticommunism Memorial that every major city in South Korea has. I have never forgotten the young boy's statue, in mid-step with one clenched fist held up to the sky evoking in us a decisive and merciless revenge against the "brutal" communists. In addition to Lee, General Ttory, the main character of a South Korean animated film, was also my hero. While Tarzan only defeated small groups of animal smugglers, Ttory, only a teenaged boy, always ridiculed and destroyed the heavily armed communist wolves, and even rescued skinny, "innocent" North Koreans who were exploited in deadly mines or prisons under the personified pig dictator. I also appreciated that the US Army unit stationed in my hometown was there to protect us from the omnipresent provocation of the "Reds."[5]

Today, my childhood experience no longer haunts me. It speaks to a long and intensive history of tensions between Korean communists and evangelicals from the Japanese colonial period (1910–1945). The internal conflicts of that era did not emerge on the surface mainly because Koreans, other than the collaborators, were oppressed by the Japanese (Lee 2010: 62). Ultimately, though, the two groups led various national independence and enlightenment movements against Japan, but it wasn't until shortly after liberation that there emerged large-scale antagonistic clashes between them. Between 1945 and 1953 more than one million people (11–15 percent of the northern population) migrated to the South, including 35–40 percent of the Protestant population in the North (Kang 2007, quoted from Lee 2010: 65). This antagonism finally resulted in evangelical reprisals against communists, with the slaughter of tens of thousands—on Cheju Island in April 1948, in Yŏsu in October 1948, in Sinch'ŏn in October 1950,[6] and so on—led by the Northwest or Sŏbuk Youth, an anticommunism organization formed under evangelical leadership, and the South Korean Army and backed by the US Army Military Government (Lee 2010: 66–69).

The national division and the following Korean War, as Samuel Kim asserts, "for both Koreas... initiated a decisive shift in identity politics from the competition of multiple identities to the dominance of the Cold War identity," which, he continues, "in turn gave birth to an American strategic culture that thrived on a Manichaean vision of global bipolarity and the omnipresent communist threat" (2006: 3). The Cold War identity in the South was conflated with Christian nationalism, which had already played a foundational role in Korean nationalism since the late 19th century, and its "self-reconstruction tradition" (Wells 1990), which influenced the state-led post-war national restoration movements.[7] Different from a western model of modernity in which state–church separation is assumed, South Korea was founded on relatively large-scale evangelical leadership. Syngman Rhee (Yi Sŭngman), a Methodist church elder, served as the first president of South Korea and was supported by the United States. Over 39 percent of the high-ranking officials in his administration were Protestant, compared to 0.6 percent of the population in 1945 (see Yi 2006; Kang 2007; Ryu 2009; Lee 2010 for more discussion about the relationship between the Rhee regime and Protestantism).

With the Korean peninsula remaining at war, anticommunism serves as a stand-in for searching out the "enemy" within "us." Soo-Jung Lee articulates that, "In the case of South Korea, one's ideology was one of the primary criteria for inclusion/exclusion" (2006: 11). With little exception throughout the 1980s and even later, in certain sectors, once a person was labeled as *chwaik* ("leftist"), which was identical to the notion of *ppalgaeng-i* ("Red"), he or she deserved death and family members were socially discriminated against and legally disadvantaged according to the guilt-by-association system. In a century that witnessed some of the bloodiest genocides in human history, the "Reds" were not considered to be humans, but devils deserving extinction to those in the southern part of Korea (Kang 2005).

By the late 1980s in South Korea, Protestants and war refugees from the North had become the driving force behind building new churches out of the ashes through the post-war "economy first" policy of the militant regimes (generals Park Chung Hee and Chun Doo Hwan). At the peak of the intensive modernization period in the 1960s and 1970s, the church population grew explosively, from about 500,000 in 1950 to 623,072 in 1960 (a 24.6 percent increase), and to 3,192,621 in 1970 (a 412.4 percent increase) (Kim B. 2006: 310). Increases of 20–50 percent every five to ten years continued into the early 1990s. Churchgoers attended for various reasons amid rapid social changes, but prosperity theology became central to Korean evangelicalism and spread like wildfire in the context of post-war South Korea. Congregations were told that they deserved this-worldly happiness, physical health, and economic success, and competed to have the largest church building to represent that. Byung-suh Kim argues, "The development psychology, along with industrialization, brought about a 'bigness syndrome': the size of an institution was understood as a measure of success" (Kim B. 2006: 323).

As a consequence, whether it was intended or not, the vast majority of evangelical church leaders and followers were likely to be collaborative and active in the "economy first" policy of the militant regimes. The way that the church supported the political dictatorship was simple, all one needed to fully focus on in church was Jesus Christ as one's savior. In my childhood, church anticommunism was never overtly mentioned and Lee Seung-bok's anticommunist spirit was not a sermon topic. Anticommunism appeared, in the distinct tones of Biblical language, as a result of "God who did not allow the northern communists to conquer this land during the war," and Germany and Japan were ultimately defeated because God was not with them (Han 1987: 27). The church's role as an anticommunist bulwark was instrumental to militant dictators in achieving the Miracle on the Han River, a metonym for 1980s South Korean economic growth. Church and state have hardly been separated; rather they have collaborated and relied on one another in post-war South Korea. In this light, it is problematic to seek a root cause for the rise of Korean Christianity without considering how this local level of the Cold War aura persisted in Korea. It is also noteworthy that it was progressive churches and ministers who provided shelter for political dissidents, led civil and unification movements, and thus fought authoritarian regimes. However, while their sacrificial efforts are appreciated in scholarly works and mass media, the majority of South Korean evangelicals, more than 90 percent of the Protestant population, were not moved by such faith-based social practices for justice. Instead, they were mobilized to bring more people to their churches, or to go abroad for world missionizing.

Thanks to a series of vigorous social movements throughout the 1980s, South Koreans acquired the right to elect their president in 1986 and attention moved on to the unification movement, led largely by college student unions and progressive religious leaders. Meanwhile, the consecutive collapses of former socialist countries triggered a feeling of impending victory over communism, including the North Korean regime, while such radical changes perplexed progressive nationalists. Importantly, the South Korean government relaxed their half-century long anticommunist stance, even though the National Security Law, a brutal means of anticommunism, is still alive. Nevertheless, the South Korean government began to normalize its relationship with the North Korean regime. On the cusp of the 21st century, when two former dissidents Kim Dae-jung (1998–2002) and Roh Moo-hyun (2003–2007) took office consecutively, inter-Korean relations were so normalized that people imagined the reunification of the two Koreas as realistic.

At that historical juncture, evangelical churches stood for anticommunism as a claimed national identity, and even requested that the US' Bush administration destroy the "evil" Kim Jong-il regime. At the same time, some missionary organizations, such as the Durihana Missionary Foundation and Cornerstone, and individual missionaries acting independently helped North Korean migrants escape from the Sino–North Korean border area and settle down in South Korea or western countries, and celebrated them as evidence of God's calling for a Christianized reunified nation. In other words, since the collapse of former communist countries and the 1990s' devastating North Korean famine, Korean evangelicals have felt more empowered and convinced of God's blessing on South Korea versus the cursed North Korea. They moved to brand the former Kim Dae-jung and Roh Moo-hyun regimes as "Red" or "leftist" for having tried to abolish the National Security Law. Evangelical churches have organized street protests and prayer meetings for national salvation, and have tried to strengthen their influence on politics. They put forth enormous effort to elect the conservative President Lee Myung-bak, a megachurch elder, and the current President Park Geun-hye, daughter of the notorious dictator Park Jung-hee who ruled the country for 18 years.

In Jose Casanova's (1994) terms, the church is observed to be a public religious institution in other countries in the west and in East Asia. As previously mentioned, Protestant politicians held power from the beginning of South Korean history under the auspices of the US government. Nevertheless, the political involvement of the South Korean church is unique. They rationalize fervent anticommunism through Biblical language, ritual, and the creation of a projected world. This politicized religious rhetoric has been a driving force in making Christian subjects.

Cold War sentiment and Korean evangelical ritual language, so complicatedly and uncannily interwoven, haunt Korean society. Similar to some of the ideas expressed in Edward Said's *Orientalism* (1978) and in

Daphne Berdahl's *Where the World Ends* (1999) regarding the ideologically inflicted "Manichaean vision"—for example, "Ossi" and "Wessi" differentiation in Germany—"good" South Korea versus "evil" North Korea became a veritable cultural system: wealth and spirituality versus poverty and idolatry; free individuals versus militant collectives; peaceful/humanitarian versus aggressive/inhuman; and so on. This binary opposition between the North and the South continues to serve as a conceptual framework for apprehending North Korean migrants in the South.

"We are happy!"

Both states have engineered a shared myth of ethnic homogeneity for evoking legitimacy in preparation for future reunification, however for the migrants, South Korea is a society where "you need money, which guarantees your social status," said a male North Korean migrant in his early 30s who had been dwelling in Seoul for about three years at the time when he visited a dormitory school. I was participating in establishing and running the school for North Korean young adults who came via China to South Korea without legal guardians in early 2000s. In some migrants' understanding of South Korea, wealth is a barometer of an individual's capability. Nonetheless in the North, immediately following the end of Japanese occupation, material well-being was equally emphasized as a supreme national task. The "Great Supreme Leader" Kim Il-sung promised three meals a day with a bowl of white rice and meat soup (*i pap e koki kuk*, which was only enjoyed by the ruling *yangban* class in feudal times or by the Japanese colonizers and collaborators). *Juche* (self-reliance) ideology was developed as its own ruling philosophy, its own type of anti-imperial nationalist socialism (*Urisik sahoejuǔi*) that proclaimed, "Let's live in our own way!" (see Cumings 1991, 2004).

Under the banner of "our own way!" anti-imperialism in general and anti-Americanism in particular are intrinsically blended in the concept of *Juche*. In a video recorded in 1999 by a non-governmental relief agency at work in Pyongyang, the capital city of North Korea, a six- or seven-year-old boy was asked to say something to South Korean students. In a decisive voice he speaks as if having been prepped: "What I just wanted to say to South Korean friends (*Namjosǒn dongmu-dǔl*) is that let us kick imperial Yankees out of our country as soon as possible and study and play together."[8] At the heart of this young boy's formulaic account is a strong sense of blood purity among ethnic Koreans and North Korean national pride. North Koreans in North Korea "officially" believe that their country is a truly independent state that has never been afraid of, but rather always stands against "imperial" America.

Juche ideology (also called *Juche* or *Juche* Idea) is a core component of *Kimilsung-ism*, the North Korean official system. Since the Soviet Union and China were in a power struggle in the 1950s through the 1980s, Kim Il-sung declared *Juche* as the North Korean form of socialism, different from the forms of socialism in the Soviet Union and China. Kim Il-sung emphasized three principles to clarify what *Juche* meant: "independence in politics" (*chaju*), "self-sustenance in the economy" (*charip*), and "self-defense in national defense" (*chawi*). As for the seed of this ideal, some point to the Christian nationalist movements in the 1920s and 1930s (Wells 1990: 163). It is undeniable that Kim Il-sung, celebrated as the brilliant creator of *Juche*, was influenced by Christianity. He was raised in a devout Christian family, key Christian nationalists joined him in the founding of North Korea, and he respected Reverend Son Jŏng-do as a great benefactor throughout his lifetime. In his autobiography *With the Century* (1993), he reveals that he was impressed with the anti-Japanese Christian movements (see Kim 1993, Vol. 3.1 & Vol. 4.1).

While in South Korea, Christianity and American forms of modernity jointly took the lead in state building, an opposite yet mirror process took place in the North. While numerous people accused as being "leftists" were brutally executed in the South, Christian advocates were excluded by the North's socialist revolution, which began with, and gained popularity through, land reform. It is worth recalling that Christians numbered about 2.1 percent of the population of about ten million in the northern part of the country while their southern counterparts were only 0.6 percent of a population of about 15 million in the early 1940s, before liberation from Japan. Thanks to the 1907 Great Revival that American missionaries proudly presented as the largest revival movement in Asia, Pyongyang was once called the Jerusalem of East Asia.

In September 1945, the Protestant leadership organized the Christian Socialist Democratic Party (*Kidokkyo Sahoe Minjudang*). The party was soon forcibly excluded as they denied participation in a nationwide election that had been scheduled on a Sunday. After that, Reverend Han Kyŏng-jik (Han Kyung-jhik), one of the leaders of the party, migrated south of the 38th parallel and later established the Yongrak Presbyterian Church. Those members of the party who did not migrate to the south were, allegedly, all executed, sent to concentration camps, or "born again" as socialist revolutionary subjects. According to an official record announced by the Korean Church Martyrs Missionary Association in

2001, about 90 percent of Protestant martyrs (of a total 191 martyrs officially recognized as of 2001) were murdered by communists between
1945 and 1953 (see Kang 2007).

These atrocities took place under the banner of "our own way"; *Juche*
ideology also claims to be a human-centric philosophy different from
materialistic Marxism:

> Marxist philosophy raised, as its major task, the clarification of the
> essence of the material world and the general law of its motion,
> whereas the Juche philosophy has raised, as its important task, the
> elucidation of *man's essential characteristics* and the law of social
> movement, man's movement. Therefore, the Juche philosophy is
> an original philosophy which is fundamentally different from the
> preceding philosophy in its task and principles.
>
> (Kim 1996: 2, emphasis added)

The natural entitlement of man as "the best qualified and most powerful being" (Kim 1996: 2) who can dominate and transform the world
is also the model for the *Juche* human. And "man's movement" in the
Korean modern historical context can be characterized as anti-imperial
self-reliant nation-state building. The North Korean *Juche* human is an
individual who serves national sovereignty, represented by the Worker's
Party. The North Korean Constitution, Article 63, says "In the Democratic People's Republic of Korea the rights and duties of citizens are
based on the collectivist principle, 'One for all and all for one'." In order
to maintain their "own" hegemonic spirit of human-centric, anti-
imperial, collective self, ideology education is imperative for nurturing
among the people what is called the socio-political life, an essence of
Juche spirit that appreciates, in principle, not just materialistic rational-
ism but also humanism. Scholars in political science and international
relations have asserted that the North Korean state, as a "weak actor,"
has been and still is surviving by strategically relying on the Great Power
conflicts. For instance, North Korea gained politico-economic benefits
from the Soviet–China rivalries up to the 1980s, and Chinese–US tensions in the post-Cold War era (Armstrong 2013: 3–4). In addition to
this diplomatic strategy, it is crucial to acknowledge the state's *Juche*
citizen-subject making in which ideology itself is a driving force:

> The most serious lesson of the collapse of socialism in several coun-
> tries is that the corruption of socialism begins with ideological
> corruption, and that a break-down on the ideological front results

in the crumbling of all of socialism's fronts and ends in the total ruin of socialism.

(Kim 1995)

The collapse of the Socialist bloc in the early 1990s was, with little doubt, critical to North Korean society. Instead of accommodating this change, the ruling elite in Pyongyang chose to resist it. The *Juche* philosophy that once served to balance the mutual respect and trust between the Supreme Leader and his "beloved" people[9] turned out to be a fundamentalist means to oppress the people for the sake of state sovereignty (Shin 2005). That is to say that just as it emerged and evolved in a particular historical context, *Juche* spirit transformed to support the continuation of the existing power order. The consequences were and still are severe. When floods and droughts occurred consecutively, worsening the economic crisis after the 1990s, people witnessed the failure of the ruling system to stop the increasing death toll; their family members and neighbors died of hunger; the People's Army that previously served to protect the people with pride became hostile thieves, taking food resources away from already deprived people; and the "ideology education" (*sasang haksŭp*) through which they had once come to internalize a strong sense of national pride and self-respect became a means of torture in labor camps, where numerous undocumented border crossers were "treated less than animals," as some of my interlocutors said.

North Korean adult migrants often testify that while in North Korea they were encouraged to consider themselves as extended family cared for by Father Kim Il-sung and to believe that because of their unique revolutionary spirit against imperialists (i.e., the United States and Japan), their country and people are all admired by foreign countries. It is true that Pyongyang continues to broadcast that the world's leaders and anti-imperial advocates keep sending messages and special gifts to "our eternal Supreme Leader" and his successors, including the late Kim Jong-il and current Kim Jong-un, via its national media. It is also true that the country is surviving, anyway, in spite of the radical changes that include the large number and scale of private markets and merchants, the black market economy, the widely yet secretly spread South Korean films and songs that have become popular, and not to mention the large sum of remittances sent by way of brokers from their family escapees in South Korea.

While some western media depict the North as the most closed society in the world and one that is nearly collapsed, as no small number of its people have fled or want to flee, the majority of its population is still surviving and coping with the ever escalating domestic and transnational changes. And its survival has attracted more scholarly attention to the nature and practices of its culture and power structure and their implications. Without a doubt, one of the most heated discussions has been given to the relationship between the Supreme Leader and the people. As is taken into account above, the country's character is often interpreted in terms of an extended socialist-Confucian family where such virtues as benevolence from the Leader and filial piety from the people are mutually circulated (cf. Cumings 2005). Sonia Ryang (2012), however, asserts that it is love, similar to Christian love, rather than neo-Confucian family obligations, that constitutes the North Korean ethos. Similarly yet differently, Heonik Kwon and Byung-Ho Chung (2012) provide vigorous anthropological insights on the ways that North Korean charismatic leadership has been able to persist through varied yet coherent cultural performances, products, and practices. Some observers come to acknowledge the religious aspects, in particular, Protestant characteristics embedded in social structures in the North: the absolute, emotionally fraught, belief in Kim Il-sung and the sacralization of his words and, above all, the organization of social units and activities in ways that are equivalent to church traditions such as confession, group Bible study, and church hierarchy (Kim 2000; Shin 2005; Yi 2011).

The emergence of intellectual and practical interest in the comparison between the North Korean ruling philosophy/system and liberal religion, in particular, Protestant Christianity, enriches not merely the field of North Korean studies and related social theories and methods, but also the people on the move in transnational and inter- and intra-ethnic frameworks and contexts. My North Korean migrant interlocutors took into account the aforementioned similarities between the two institutions. Some parallels include that between the Ten Commandments of Moses and the Ten Point Principle for Solidifying the Party's Monolithic Ideological System; memorizing key speeches and lessons of Kim Il-sung and Kim Jong-il is like reading the Bible; self-criticism is like a religious testimonial; and regular evaluation meetings (*sasangch'onghwa*) before or after work are similar to Bible study sessions. However, they point out a difference, crucial in their accounts: that the self and mutual criticism sessions in the North often result in accusing someone of moral failure or mistakes and inflicting punishment upon the accused at the regular evaluation meeting, while in the words of the church it is rather forgiveness and love that the sinners should end up receiving. They say that the mutual criticism system is the key aspect that makes people watch, distrust, and try to find fault with one another. The everyday competition in human relationships, in their accounts, contrasts with a nostalgic memory of the past when all the people in their home village and nation as a whole lived like an extended family under the care of the Supreme Leader. The "family" metaphor is equally found in South Korea, and probably every modern nation-state, not to mention religious communities.

Encountering sociocultural differences between the two Koreas that were unexpected because of the shared myth of ethnic homogeneity is related to a sense of belonging at the moral, emotional, and rational level. Increasing understanding of cultural differences is not always accompanied with mutual respect, but is often used to enhance cultural biases. Christians who work with migrants often describe the nature of North Korean migrants personalities as an embodiment of *Juche* ideology as if such cultural disposition were fixed and too deeply rooted in their brain and body to purify. They are viewed negatively as being uncivilized and violent, as overly masculine males and relatively docile females, hot tempered, good at lying, and so forth. In this respect, my study also entails ethnographic vignettes elaborating on how North Korean migrants have often struggled to behave and speak in ways that social counterparts want to see and hear, and how their unexpected characteristics such as being humorous, energetic, and independent, surprise people.

Ultimately, as much as the modern world has become "liquidized" across boundaries with the flow of capital, goods, ideas, and people (Appadurai 1996; Bauman 2003), the backlashes, enduring resistances, and controls of local powers are overtly persistent and even absurdly reinforced as well. This book aims to unveil the complex processes of interrelations and contestations among actors that include state powers and institutions, and civil organizations like churches and human agencies. For believers who experience divine intervention, God is also active in how these interrelations and contestations play out. With a historical and anthropological examination of the ways in which North Korean migrant identities have been heavily shaped by South Korean state policy toward North Korea, I have found that while migrants were perceived as anticommunist emblems in the past, they have recently been depoliticized as "regular citizens." Ironically, once stripped of their political value, they are but another "fallen" minority group, and are often described as socially maladjusted losers in South Korean discourses (Kim Y. 2009). In this context, the church, specifically the evangelical church, provides migrants with meanings of existence, vocabularies to interpret the experiences of suffering, and a (hierarchical) sense of belonging, in addition to substantial financial resources and a vision of the future, namely the "capacity to aspire" (Appadurai 2004).

Aspirations for post-division citizenship

With the term aspirations, Arjun Appadurai (2004) invites anthropologists to reconsider the concept of culture, which he argues should incorporate the future-oriented desires and practices in people's everyday life. I view the concept of aspirations as including more than such cognitive actions as hoping, dreaming, anticipating, and so forth. Instead, it suggests the positive ways and processes of designing and making efforts to achieve mutual ends through interactions between peoples, in particular intellectuals and grassroots individuals. I found this conceptualization of aspirations particularly meaningful in weaving together North Korean life trajectories and interactions across places, ideas, and spirits; evangelical passion for North Korean mission; and controls and contestations of state power over the people's transnational movements and mobility. Religious conversion of North Korean migrants to Christianity and their socio-economic assimilation to South Korean capitalist ways of working and behaving are largely perceived as difficult processes, and South Koreans often interpret these difficulties as being rooted in North Koreans' past socialist culture. This may be partly true, but I argue that they are also the result of clashes between the differing expectations and interests that both North and South Korean interlocutors project and negotiate in envisioning the future: for instance, one that includes an aspiring North Korea mission for churches, a family reunion, or socio-economic success for North Korean migrants in the South; or a collapse of the North Korean regime for some North Korean missionaries/human rights activists.

In this spirit, equally significant is contact perspectives in my documentation and analysis of the interactions I took part in and observed at the field sites. As previously mentioned, this project considers churches as primary intra-ethnic contact zones. Contact theory and perspective were first developed by psychologist Gordon W. Allport (1954). For Allport, individual and cultural prejudice causing conflict and discrimination against one another can be resolved or improved through increased everyday contact. It is crucial however to set up such quality conditions as equal status, shared common goals, and broader social support to achieve positive changes. In the context of multiculturalism, transnational migration, super-diversity (Vertovec

2007), and integration, scholars from sociology, geography, psychology, and anthropology alike allude to a nuanced approach to the spaces, conditions, and contexts in which interethnic relations and contacts take place. Markets, district parks, museums (Clifford 1997), schools, and workplaces are a few examples of public spaces in increasingly multiethnic urban cities where researchers carry out empirical field research (e.g., Akins & Pain 2012). While the church in the west has come to be treated as a private realm and while previous studies largely focus on secular settings in discussing contacts, I shed light on the religious spaces, namely churches, secret shelters, and church-run training centers, and the mindful body that migrants experience as corporeal, civil, and cosmic.

Religions are facilitated not only by being in place, but also by moving. Thomas Tweed invites us to conceptualize religions that.

> enable and constrain *terrestrial crossings*, as devotees traverse natural terrain and social space beyond the home and across the homeland; *corporeal crossings*, as the religious fix their attention on the limits of embodied existence; and *cosmic crossings*, as the pious imagine and cross the ultimate horizon of human life.
>
> (2006: 123, emphases in original)

It is crossing and dwelling, or vice versa, that religions intermingle with adherents' life trajectories. In considering physical movement across borders, or the movement of the interlocutors, ideas, religious ideological elements, and material goods, we have to be concerned with particular forms and types of transnational late-Cold War citizenship configurations. North Korean migrants are not just arriving and settling in South Korea, they are also moving to western countries, and sometimes even returning from the South to the North. They hire North Korean brokers, holding South Korean IDs, and Korean-Chinese traders/missionaries to secretly send remittances and South Korean soap operas and films to their family members in the North. The scale, scope, and frequency of such crossings and communication across borders cannot be underestimated. Note that both the North Korean Penal Code and the South Korean National Security Law severely prohibits citizens from soliciting unauthorized contact with people on the other side. Nonetheless, the Sino–North Korean borderline is more porous than the Korean Demilitarized Zone and US economic sanctions against the North have intensified in recent years. It should also be noted that the number of North Koreans moving to other countries by any possible means has increased.

As of 2014, the number of North Koreans granted refugee status in countries like Canada, the United States, the United Kingdom, Belgium, and Germany, for example, was 1,166.[10] Some of them arrived directly in the host country by way of China and its neighboring countries, while others moved to the host country after receiving South Korean ID. Those who had lived in South Korea, hid, but did not throw away, their South Korean passport in the event that their refugee application was denied. In addition, no small number of Korean-Chinese migrants have pretended to be North Korean refugees and joined in this risky journey. Even if western states try to sort out North Koreans from non-North Koreans, the categories of North Korea and North Korean defection still serve ethnic Koreans from Northeast China and North Korea as collateral in the context of the international refugee regime. An economic and political perspective cannot interpret their transnational movements and survival strategies in which feelings of fear and anxiety coexist with belief and aspirations, the emotional toll resulting from the extreme obstacles they encounter as they cross borders serves to challenge them, and so do flexible underground brokering and missionary networks which are elaborated through the migrants' life trajectories in following chapters.

2
Evangelical Nationalism in Divided Korea

> Let us bring as many of our brethren from the North to the
> South as possible so that we can shorten the existence of the
> evil Kim Jong-il regime. At the same time, we all should vote
> for a Christian nominee [Lee Myung-bak, current president of
> South Korea] for our next president. That is the way to rebuild
> the national spirit that has been waning these past ten years,
> and to hasten the date we save the North by replacing Juche
> with Christianity and capitalism!
>
> (Excerpt from Kim Sang-chŏl's speech, January 27, 2007,
> my translation)

One evening in January 2007, Kim Sang-chŏl, the president of the Commission to Help North Korean Refugees (CNKR)[1]—as well as a church
elder, a lawyer, and a former mayor of Seoul—was testifying about God's
call for the Christianization of the two Koreas. This highly political
and religious account was made at a special event hosted by the CNKR
to celebrate the fact that the total number of North Korean refugees
(*Talbuk-nanmin*[2]) who had arrived in South Korea had exceeded 10,000.
Inspired by this speech, a middle-aged South Korean man sitting beside
me began shouting, "Hallelujah!" with a clenched fist. What I was witnessing was a ritual of South Korean evangelical nationalists who aim
to spread the gospel to both Koreas and a telling example of the culture that the majority of North Korean migrants are exposed to and
encounter in their passage from China to the South.

According to Kim's account, regime change in North Korea and social
reform through Christian outreach would result in the salvation of
North Korean individuals who are suffering under an "evil" regime.
In the same vein, South Korea must have an evangelical president in

order to accelerate these goals and to lead the country, which had been misled by what he called "leftist Red regimes" (i.e., the presidencies of Kim Dae-jung and Roh Moo-hyun), back in the "right" direction, and thus hasten a reunified Christian Korea. This event in its forms and narratives represented the right-wing values of Korean evangelical nationalism, demonstrating its calling as an anticommunist bulwark.

More importantly, these series of evangelical meetings and campaigns have varied and increased in the context of particular historical junctures. In South Korea these junctures include the economic slowdown since the 1997 Asian financial crisis (best known as the IMF (International Monetary Fund) crisis in Korea), and the elections that followed and their aftermath: the pro-North Korean regimes that promoted the normalization of inter-Korea relations, and the multicultural trends in values and ethnic make-up. Outside the country, the US' Bush administration's war on terrorism in the post-9/11 context stimulated Korean evangelicals to hold anticommunist and exclusive soteriological beliefs and to strengthen their calling in the name of God. Lastly, within the Korean Protestant Church, the slowdown of the growth of the Christian population and increasing criticism from the public since the 1990s has had a significant impact.

A general definition of evangelicalism is a Protestant movement that emphasizes: conversion experiences in which one accepts Jesus Christ as one's sole savior and lives according to the gospel; the Bible as one's ground of faith; and ardent evangelism at home and abroad. But in order to better understand the meaning of increasing Korean evangelical activities in these manifold geopolitical predicaments, I intend to pay particular attention to evangelical discourses and practices around the themes of suffering and the healing/salvation of Korean individuals and the nation-state. These themes reveal the nature of Korean Protestantism and its relation to ideas of human dignity and a Christian "imagined community" (Anderson 1991(1983)) in South Korea. Drawing on the anthropology of religion's attention to the interrelations of Christianity, modernity, individual/collective subject-making, and nation-state building, briefly reviewed in Chapter 1, this chapter attempts to provide a general overview of evangelical nationalism for a better understanding of the Christian conversion of North Korean migrants and their healing.

This chapter consists of two parts. The first is a brief account of Protestantism in modern Korean history, both pre- and post-division. The second part examines the basic components of Korean evangelicalism through its ritual practices and discourses about suffering in the context of national division and the late-Cold War era.

National sorrow and Protestant healing

> As we mark this centenary day of the outbreak of the 1907 Pyongyang Great Revival, we desire to see love, freedom, and peace restored in Korea.
>
> . . .
>
> We are aware, however, that today North Korea is in a time of deep suffering; that her people face great hardship and that many have died as a result. We mourn with those who mourn and are deeply concerned for the welfare of the North Korean people.
>
> (Excerpt from the proclamation of "2007 Year of Prayer for North Korea" by the Christian Council of Korea (CCK))

From the start, the rise of Christianity in Korea has been closely related to the desire of unprivileged people and national elites who sought escape from present suffering (Blair 1977; Yi 1981; Wells 1990; Park 2009; Ryu 2009). This suffering was not only that of individuals, but also of Korea at large under the control of imperial forces. Since these earliest days, Korean Christianity has come to be closely intertwined with ideas of national suffering. In each historical predicament, there were conflicting views regarding the path to salvation: in the pre-division era, there was a tension between the local Protestant leadership's interest in national liberation and the foreign (American) missionary body's convictions about church–state separation. In the division era, a tension emerged between progressive and conservative Protestants, a conflict that continues today.

The pre-division era

When William Newton Blair first arrived in Korea as a missionary in 1901, he was surprised at the "remarkable state of things in Korea, a people by nature intensely religious without any entrenched religion with priests able to hinder the progress of Christianity." He went on to explain:

> the remarkable progress of the gospel in Korea in the 20th century is [accounted for by] her preparation of suffering and humiliation. The location of Korea creates difficulties. Lying midway between China and Japan she has been for thousands of years a bone of contention between these two nations, both claiming suzerainty over her.
>
> (1977: 23)

What Blair celebrated at the dawn of Korean modernity was that the country was somehow a predestined ground for the Christianization of a people who had experienced tremendous social and political tumult. This statement suggests that the notion of fertile religious ground was based not only on a multi-religious cultural condition, but also on the suffering and humiliation of local peoples. Thus Blair suggested that the Korean people suffered not only from sins intrinsic to all human beings, but also particular agonies due to the country's physical and geopolitical condition.

When American Protestant missionaries began to arrive in Korea in the 1890s, Confucianism was losing its foothold as was the polity, the Chosŏn dynasty (1392–1910). Buddhism had been isolated for some time, while Catholicism was subject to severe and continuous persecutions for a century; and the Tonghak religion (Eastern Learning), later Ch'ŏndogyo (the religion of the Heavenly Way), was an indigenous religious and revolutionary movement against the dynasty and foreign powers that was ultimately defeated. As a result, ordinary Koreans became familiar with monotheistic doctrines thanks to Catholicism and Tonghak, although there was no one hegemonic religious institution that the people relied on (Wells 1990: 8). Meanwhile, shamanism as a folk religion had never really disappeared (see Buswell and Lee 2006 for more details).

Such chaotic spiritual and ethical conditions were caused largely by increasing foreign interventions, in particular Japanese imperial forces, that intensified underprivileged people's everyday hardships and poverty. As the 500-year-old neo-Confucian Chosŏn dynasty was being annexed by Japanese colonial rule, Protestantism, introduced in 1884, took only 25 years to gather 200,000 followers in Korea. The rapid rise of Christianity between 1895 and 1910, Kenneth Wells explains, "can be accounted for by the weakening of the traditional neo-Confucian, *yangban* [noble class]-dominated social and political structure caused by the Sino- and Russo-Japanese wars and the imposition of the Japanese Protectorate in 1905" (1990: 44). The notable turning point of that period is the 1907 Great Revival, which began in Changdaehyŏn Church, Pyongyang (the present-day North Korean capital) in January and then rapidly spread throughout the nation (Lee 2010).[3] It is significant that the Great Revival occurred when the Korean nation was being humiliated and thus it "was pursued against a background of hopelessness concerning the future of Korean society" (Wells 1990: 35). Spencer Palmer also sheds light on two local issues that effected "astounding religious movement: (1) long-standing social cleavages between north and south Korea, abetted by the discontent of the *Sangmin* [unprivileged class], and (2) the political-military struggles which centered in north Korea at the time" (1986: 82–83).

The people in the northern area of Korea were marginalized and alienated from the central government for centuries. Only a handful of northern-origin *yangban* (noble class) was hired, and yet they were not able to move up to high-ranking official positions in Seoul because of their regional origin. The famous Hong Kyŏng-nae rebellion of 1812, which underprivileged people (*Sangmin*) vigorously participated in, exemplifies how the Pyongyang area was ruled in a hostile way, by Seoul-appointed rulers, through a form of structured discrimination perpetrated by the bureaucratic government (see Kim S. 2009 for more about the Hong rebellion). As introduced in Wells' points above, the local people had undergone consecutive wars followed by epidemics and famine that caused many deaths and widespread hunger.

The series of sufferings imposed by objective conditions (neo-Confucian class hierarchy, chronic alienation in politics, peasant suppression, failures of rebellions, foreign powers' wars, etc.) led people to seek individual salvation by repenting for their sins and wrongdoings before God. Thus, the revival's leading minister, Kil Sŏn-ju (1869–1935), would shape the form and character of Korean Protestantism in which "hopeless" people sought a spiritual, ethical awakening. Although it was not directly seen as a political movement against emerging Japanese rule, Christian conversion for these people meant a search for salvation from this-worldly sufferings and a belief in the Second Coming, an idea that was familiar to Koreans because of Korean folk ideas of religious millennialism. As Chong Bum Kim asserts, "Belief in the prophecies of the *Chŏnggam nok* (Record of Chŏng Kam), which predicted the fall of the Chosŏn dynasty and the establishment of subsequent dynasties, was widespread in late Chosŏn, especially during periods of social and political turbulence" (2006: 151; see also Hwang Sŏk-yŏng's novel series, *Chang Kil-san*, for more popular writing about *Chŏnggam nok*). On the other hand, according to Wells, some more educated Christians like An Ch'angho regarded the revival as "irrelevant to Korea's burning problems" (Wells 1990: 34).

The revival and the nationwide independence movements led by Protestant leaders in its aftermath stand for two competing discourses and practices regarding state–church relations in the Christian community. On the one hand, the Korean Protestant leader of the Independence Club, and even the assembly of hit-squads aimed at Japanese officials tended to prioritize liberating Korea from Japanese colonial rule, thus believing that all Christian activities should serve this goal.[4] On the other hand, foreign Protestant missionaries perpetuated the doctrine of church–state separation, which Yi Man-yol has interpreted as a strategy to protect church development from the interference of political power (Yi 1981: 64). In the aftermath of the Presbyterian mission's letter to the churches in 1901 that advocated for the separation of church and state, ordinary Christians' interest in politics decreased. Nonetheless, it is undeniable that Korean Protestants played a leading role in the national independence movements (Yi 1981; Wells 1990; Kim J. 2006).

In my view, the two different stances about the state–church relationship played an important role in the reconfiguring of Korean-ness in the frame of a Christian worldview. Since the dawn of Korea's modernity, its history had been dominated by a series of wars and brutal colonialism that structured individuals' daily sufferings. As a way to overcome this suffering, the Protestant Church served as both a refuge for hopeless people in search of safety, and a social institution in which nationalist sentiments as well as advanced knowledge and morality were taught and shared as a way to achieve national independence. As mentioned in the first chapter, in the Korean context the concept of nation did not conflict with the universality of the Christian world.

The suffering of the Korean people, however, did not cease. While a nationalist narrative proudly proclaims that the Korean people (*han minjok*) have preserved their own culture (i.e., language, customs, foods) relatively well even during the Japanese occupation,[5] the Korean peninsula was tragically divided into two states at the 38th parallel as soon as it was liberated from the Japanese colonial rule by the Allied Forces in 1945. The Soviet military stayed in the North and the US military in the South. It was never imagined that this physical division would last so long and lead to the Korean War (1950–1953), which killed about two million civilians and one and a half million soldiers, with over seven million people separated from their families along its ceasefire line. The border is called the demilitarized zone, a four-kilometer-wide space that is a technically neutral buffer zone between the two states, and yet is the most heavily armed area in the world. The peninsula remains technically at war to this very day. There has been virtually no contact between the people of these two countries in which Cold War ideologies have undergirded modern nation-building according to the hegemonic interests of each Korea.

Division wounds (*puntan sangch'ŏ*)

Described using the terms *puntan sangch'ŏ* or *kot'ong* (division wounds or suffering), national division is a deep-seated structure of feeling of sorrow in people's post-war lives and imaginations. The division, as national trauma, is directly linked to the tragic histories experienced by most Korean families, affecting even their personalities (i.e., family separation, loss of lovers, hidden past, depression, anger, and hostility). Nancy Abelmann (2003) discovered that when her South Korean friend, nicknamed the Education Mother, talked about her sister's lost purse story, she attributed her sister's ill fate to her personality—which is not separated from their family history and national histories, including national division. Such personalized national sorrows, however, have been filtered and sanctioned by successive anticommunist regimes (1950s–1990s). These sufferings have been both institutionalized and co-opted by state regimes through national memorial ceremonies (such as the June 25 War Memorial Day), and often reduced and silenced as individual problems (as in the case of *wŏlpukcha* family, see Lee 2006).

In other words, South Korean society has had little chance to mourn adequately for their sorrows and for the dead souls of victims regardless of which side they belonged to at the beginning of national partition. Seong-nae Kim (1989), studying shamanism on Cheju Island, noted that local shamans treated individual clients who suffered chronic illnesses, in particular those who were troubled by the spirits of family members who were killed during the April Third Incident, a massacre of pro-communists on Cheju Island in 1948. Likewise, even "division minorities" such as separated families, former spies who went or were about to be sent to the North, North Korean political prisoners imprisoned for decades in the South and so forth, are still haunted by past memories and agonies.

For the Korean Protestant community, national division shaped its political identities, which are not homogeneous but largely divided into two factions: progressive (ecumenical) and conservative (evangelical). The two sides have different views on the division and North Korea. Also, when it comes to the emotional and moral project of "healing" national wounds/divisions, progressive Protestants tend to politicize grassroots suffering, while evangelicals have reduced social sufferings to individual problems so that a person requires God's blessing to be saved. As such, the ideological and theological struggles of the two sides have increased in recent years in South Korea. But the participation of theologians from each side in the debates must be encouraged because the scholarly works tend to transcend the "just say I believe" type of Pentecostal sermons most evangelical pastors have persisted in delivering.

In considering the largest differences between the two sides, it is noteworthy that it was not until 1989 that the conservative Protestants

Evangelical Nationalism in Divided Korea 31

launched the organization of the CCK as a reaction to the National Council of Churches in Korea (KNCC)'s *Declaration of the Churches of Korea on National Reunification and Peace* published in 1988. By that time, KNCC represented Korean Christians and actively led South Korean democratization and social justice. It also initiated unification movements. The KNCC, in cooperation with the World Christian Council, persisted in claiming the division as the main cause of all social injustices (labor exploitation, human rights violations, social inequality, etc.) and the United States and the then-authoritarian South Korean regime as main forces in perpetuating the division system for their own interests. In the 1988 declaration, the main points that KNCC put forward, which were later disputed by the conservatives, were as follows: first, the division of the Korean people has been the result of the east–west confrontation of the world's superpowers in their Cold War system; second, anticommunism is a sin, "We confess that the Christians of the south, especially, have sinned by making a virtual religious idol out of anticommunist ideology and have thus not been content to merely treat the communist regime in the north as the enemy"; third, "For a wider national unity of the Korean people," it claims, North and South Korean people must transcend differences in ideas, ideologies and systems; fourth, "US troops should be withdrawn and the UN Command in Korea should be dissolved" (KNCC 1988).[6]

The declaration also proposed in detail the practical actions and policies that the two Korean regimes and Christian churches should enact in order to achieve their goals. Yi Mahn-yol stresses the declaration as "a milestone in the history of the Korean national reunification movement in that it 'opened the sluice gates of reunification discussion at the civilian level' " (2006: 248).

On the contrary, when the declaration was published in 1988, the evangelicals, for their part, were upset at the KNCC's standpoints which for them were nothing but a pro-North Korean anti-American polemic against the mainstream Korean Church. Park Myung-soo (2009), a professor in church history at Seoul Theological University, summarizes the primary points of dispute the mainstream church organizations made in their announcements at the time. First, they asserted that the division was caused by the Russian-backed Kim Il-sung regime; the KNCC declaration ignored this point. Second, they could not accept the charge that anticommunism is a sin, because, they stressed, the "Korean Church" has played the role of an anticommunist bulwark for protecting the freedom of South Korea from the evil communists. Third, they pointed out that the South Korean Church has never hated North Korean people, instead they pray day and night for God to save the North Korean believers in underground churches. Fourth, they highlighted their belief that a true unification must be achieved in a way that guarantees religious freedom in a free democratic system. They accused KNCC's unification theory, in contrast, of being influenced by an outdated and proletariat-oriented South American liberation theology. Fifth, they stated that the mainstream Korean Church does not want US troops to be withdrawn from the Korean peninsula. Sixth, they argued that the Korean Church's anticommunism is a product of Christians' historical experiences. Lastly, they challenged KNCC's legitimacy as a representative of the Korean Church, as it represents only six or so denominations (*Kyodan*) (Park 2009: 124–128). The very next year, those who stood against KNCC organized CCK.

In sum, although the two sides share the belief that the division is a national tragedy shaping the Korean people's sufferings, they have somewhat irreconcilable viewpoints as to the causes and effects of national division. Thus, the two churches have suggested different solutions. These differences will be discussed later in this chapter; as background, it is necessary to understand that KNCC considered the South Korean unprivileged people's sufferings under dictatorship as a critical chapter in national suffering, while the evangelicals tended to focus nearly exclusively on war refugees' experiences. From the perspective of the latter a certain level of sacrifice was an inevitable part of the national economic development necessary for competing with the communist North. And while the evangelicals consider that the North Korean people are exploited by their "evil" regime, KNCC maintains that the North Korean government and Chosun Christian League are legitimate partners in unification talks.

Along with KNCC's declaration, Reverend Mun Ik-hwan's visit to North Korea and meeting with Kim Il-sung in 1989 truly surprised the Korean Church. As a prominent Christian social movement leader, however, he was likely respected on both sides. And for the progressive camp, his visit to North Korea was considered a pioneering adventure that initiated a new post-division era (Kim Hyŏng-su 2004). However, for the evangelicals, his philosophy of "unification is the good" transcending all ideological and religious divides was too radical to accept (Park 2009). Since then, the division between the progressive and conservative Christians became more acute. At the same time, the social influence and reputation of KNCC waned. In contrast, CCK, claiming to be the representative Christian alliance of South Korea, today made up of 61 denominations and 21 Christian agencies, began increasing

its reach as the leader of Christian movements including on unification matters (e.g., North Korean famine relief aid, activities for North
Korean refugees, missionary training for national unification), world
mission, education, environmental issues, national security, and so
forth.

For the CCK participant evangelicals, KNCC's declaration and
Reverend Mun's North Korea visit provided an opportunity for mainstream churches to unify and clarify what they said were the Korean
Church's identities—anticommunism and the North Korean mission—
as opposed to progressive theology. And in terms of the size of congregations, finances, manpower, and thus congregational influence, CCK
began leading the Korean Christianity hegemony. Therefore, some evangelicals conclude that, since the late 1980s, the conflict between the
progressives and the conservatives has not deepened, but deconstructed.
That is, by organizing CCK, the conservatives emerged as a more
empowered group in the Korean Christian landscape (Kang 2005; Park
2009). With South Korean political democratization in the aftermath of
the 1987 June Uprising, the emergence of CCK as the largest evangelical
alliance in Korean history can be thought of as the beginning of a new
era in the South Korean political and social climate.

The late-Cold War era

In March 2007, it seemed unbelievable that I was on a plane, just taking
off, flying for only about an hour, and would land in Pyongyang, the
capital of North Korea. It was real, however, and not a dream. I was flying directly from Seoul to Pyongyang over the Yellow Sea. The situation
was due to a group visit organized by a South Korean foundation working for cultural and economic exchanges with North Korea. There were
about 170 people in our group, which consisted of scholars, government officials, artists, and business owners. Although it could be seen as
a special occasion, in actuality, it was no longer that extraordinary. The
Korean peninsula seemed to have finally entered a late-Cold War era in
which the reunification of two Koreas seemed possible.[7]

In a discussion of Korean Christianity in general and evangelicalism
in particular, it is inevitable to consider national division as a specific
geopolitical condition that affected the formation of religious characteristics and subjectivity. By stating that this era is the late-Cold
War era, I mean that it is a hybrid, heterogeneous, and shifting historical juncture in which the established values, norms, ethics, and
subjectivities that were produced and reproduced in the Cold War
context have come to struggle, contest, and negotiate with each other

in envisioning a reunified nation (see Cho & Yi 2000; Lee 2006; Paik 2009). In other words, while for five decades almost all discourses and practices regarding reunification were dominated by the state government in accordance with political and military interests, ever since the Kim Dae-jung presidency (1998–2002) civil society and individuals in different positions have been able to join in discussions as to what the reunified nation should look like. Further, the competing debates have come to consider not only structural aspects (i.e., economic aid or reforms) but also cultural and metaphysical concerns (i.e., cultural integration/harmony, education, pan-Korean or beyond-Korean sense of belonging).

Indeed, at the heart of the debates are ideas about a late-Cold War subjectivity and a form of nation-state between progressives (*chinbo*) and conservatives (*posu*),[8] notions that include larger issues. I examined the difference between the two camps in the Christian community. In South Korean society, the distinctive criteria of the two categories are different from western conventional understandings. Although this understanding becomes more complicated and/or flexible depending on the issue, the local sense of the term *chinbo* largely means a mode of political and moral sentiments for those who are nationalist (though not pro-US, it is by no means anti-American), and supportive of human rights at the local grassroots level, social minorities (gay/lesbian, migrant workers, female workers, the disabled), and environmental causes. On the other hand, *posu* is the term referring to those who support pro-US and anticommunist regimes and political parties with an economic-development-first policy; they tend to identify themselves as rightists (*up'a*) in opposition to leftists (*chwap'a*).

Few people may disagree with the statement that it is the evangelical church leaders who play a leading role in *posu* camps by organizing New Right movements, anti-North Korea campaigns in terms of human rights and North Korean refugee issues, and pro-US campaigns. What these conservative movements reveal is a modality of division subjectivity that has governed dimensions of South Korean ideology, morality, and spirituality over the last few decades. The nationalism that emerged under Cold War conditions was once conceived to be atheistic. But as a matter of fact, in light of the recent late-Cold War atmosphere, what becomes visible is the fact that the Korean form of evangelicalism has been deeply intertwined in the formation of division subjectivity. This echoes Aihwa Ong's statement, "Concepts of political identity from the earliest times have almost all been based on religious continuums of greater or less moral privilege or worthiness" (2003: 7). The recent activities of South Korean evangelicals are seen as a series of alarmed reactions to the consecutive winnings of the *chinbo* camp in presidential elections, what they call a "lost decade" under the Kim Dae-jung and Roh Moo-hyun regimes.

In the meantime, there is a pan-Korean nationalist sentiment that has long been circulated within the *chinbo* camp, what Sheila Jager once termed "romantic reunification" (2003). As a reaction and resistance to western consumerism, South Korean *minjung* (people) have reinvented national cultural forms and practices.[9] Amid questions of what philosophical and spiritual ground would help to mediate national reconciliation, the role of religion has been central. Some local elites in recent years have begun reinterpreting Korean shamanism not as a pre-modern, less-developed folk religion, but as an alternative spirituality that is able to encompass other religious beliefs and ideologies including Christianity in the South and socialism in the North.

Hwang Sŏk-yŏng is one of the leading figures in this line of thought. Hwang recently published two novels, *Sonnim* in 2001 and *Baridegi* in 2007, that suggest an alternative approach to the issue of national division, one more religious than social-structural. What Hwang brings out through his novels is an awakening of the idea that the local religious metaphysics of Korea can meet the universal values of peace, not as a reinvention of a national folk religion and not as a return to a pre-modern Korea.

Translated to English, *sonnim* means "guest," but in the novel the term refers to the uninvited "guest" of smallpox, a devastating epidemic in Korea's history. By referring to this visitor with respect, in accordance with the shamanistic tradition, Korean people treated the virus quite seriously. Thus, *sonnim* is both a religious term and a performance to send smallpox away from a person, home, or village. Hwang's *Sonnim* is a fictional story based on his own experience after visiting North Korea in violation of the South Korean National Security Law in 1989 (he was consequently imprisoned for five years).

Sonnim centers its story on a historical event known as the Sinch'ŏn Massacre, which took place in Sinch'ŏn, Hwanghae Province in North Korea during the Korean War. Local residents still have memories of the tragic event and the North Korean state repeatedly brings it up to support its anti-imperialist stance against the United States. The male protagonist in the novel is a Korean American pastor in the United States who visits Sinch'ŏn, his hometown, and knows that villagers were killed not by South Korean or US troops, but rather by one another, as if possessed by ghosts. As the story progresses, Hwang seeks to comfort the dead souls who were victims of what Hwang believes to be two imported belief systems from foreign countries that "infected" Korea—Protestantism and Marxism.

By defining these two ideologies as forced modernity, *Sonnim*, in this sense, refers to the twin foreign influences of Protestantism and Marxism; these forces brought about an "epidemic" in terms of western medicine and "ghosts" in the rhetoric of Korean shamanism. Thus, they are viewed as outsiders, temporary "guests" destroying the local people. By expelling the two virus-like ideologies through a Korean *gut* or shamanistic ritual, the people seek to reconcile their past memories.

In 2007, Hwang published another novel, *Baridegi*, which tells the story of Bari, a young North Korean female refugee who loses her entire family and ends up living in London. The title itself is taken from the Korean folktale of the same name, an epic narrative ritual performed by shamans for relieving a dead soul. The novel is based on the actual life experiences of real North Korean refugees, and touches upon a range of issues: transnational migrant laborers, human trafficking, the post-9/11 US war against terrorism, and the multiple sufferings of Bari, who has the shaman-like ability to communicate with ghosts, souls, and even animals. What is fascinating in this novel is that Hwang has tried to demonstrate how the individual misfortune of a marginalized person like Bari, who experiences dislocation and instability in life, is not the fault of the individual, but rather the workings of global processes.

Like *Sonnim*, Hwang seems to be suggesting that Koreans can look to the metaphysically more universal (yet very local) cosmology to relieve and eventually overcome the sorrows of Korea's traumatic past—rather than only conventional materialist approaches (capitalism or Marxism). In the case of the two Koreas, Hwang recognizes local shamanistic elements that remain grounded in both Korean cultures as a potential mediator that can reconcile this-worldly individual and national sufferings with the souls of the dead.

However, one can ask whether there is a kind of shamanism that is legitimate or seemingly "pure" enough to be comprehensible in both Koreas. Of course, the response would be negative, because Korean shamanism itself has never been homogenous, but instead has exhibited much diversity over time and across regions. A second question might then be in what sense would shamanistic performances and cosmology motivate a broader sense of belonging between the two Korean peoples? Shamanism has been targeted for expulsion in the name of modernization in both Koreas (see Kendall 1985), while at the same time being integrated into Christianity in the South and surviving under socialism in the North. Perhaps Hwang did not intend to reinvent this indigenous form of religion as a contact zone, but rather wished to encourage readers to find a way on their own. I leave further inquiries behind but instead wish to point out that Hwang's recent works are seen as an example of competing discourses and practices regarding Korean reunification in contemporary South Korea. Keeping this nationalist trend in mind, I turn now to evangelical approaches to both social suffering and healing for salvation with a focus on the organization and theological character of the Korean evangelical church's recent campaigns.

The evangelical church and globalization

Having reviewed the Koreans keen sense of their own national suffering as developed over the long course of the 20th century, I now turn to the ways in which evangelical churches have promoted individual salvation as the salve for these wounds.

Despite stagnant growth since the 1990s (Lee T. 2006),[10] the Korean evangelical church is one of the largest social forces. Referring to local Protestant language, Korean evangelicalism tends to particularly emphasize religious spirituality (*yŏngsŏng*) and salvation (*kuwŏn*) on the level of the individual, and revival experiences as a form of ritual on the level of the collective church. Above all, there is a short, well-known idiomatic phrase that best represents the nature of Korean evangelicalism, that is, *Yesu ch'ŏn'guk, pulsin chiok*, which means "Jesus is heaven, unbelief is hell." This slogan asserts that one's salvation is granted as soon as one believes in Jesus Christ regardless of any and all past transgressions. Salvation here is not merely interpreted as the gateway to another world, but also realized in this world.

What is fascinating in the Korean evangelical tradition is that it is always longing for and trying to reproduce the 1907 Pyongyang Great Revival that I discussed earlier in this chapter. Timothy Lee also points out that "revival meetings have thrived and come to characterize Korean Protestantism," and that "the Korean church ... has become a leader of international revivalism in its own right, holding some of the largest revival gatherings ever held in Christian history—including the mammoth World Evangelization Crusade of 1980, which reportedly recorded more than seventeen million in attendance" (2006: 332).[11] As I will elaborate in Chapter 5, this longing for a miraculous revival tends to be demonstrated in intensive group retreat programs and frequent short-term missionary trips in which participants seek to strengthen their spirituality through a personal relationship with Jesus Christ.

The size of the Protestant population in South Korea is remarkable. South Korean churches claim that 25 percent of the entire population is Protestant, whereas in Asia (where 60 percent of the world's population resides), Protestants account for only around 5 percent of the population, far behind other traditional religions like Buddhism, Hinduism, and Islam. According to a 2006 report by the South Korean National Statistics Office, Buddhists constituted 22.8 percent followed by Protestants at 18.3 percent and Catholics at 10.9 percent. Combining Protestants and Catholics, Christians surpassed Buddhists—29.2 percent to 22.8 percent.

In addition, the Korea World Mission Association (KWMA) recently reported that the number of Korean missionaries serving overseas numbered 19,413 in 168 countries as of January 2009. This makes South Korea the second largest missionary-sending country after the United States; and this figure represents a huge jump since 2000, when the number was 8,103 (see Moon 2003). It has become well known that Korean missionaries target some of the most difficult-to-evangelize countries such as Iraq, North Korea, and China. As the *New York Times* reported, "[They] are eager to do God's work and glorify God. They want to die for God."[12]

Despite a number of missionary deaths in Iraq (e.g., Kim Sŏn-il in 2004) and Afghanistan (two missionaries out of twenty hostages in 2007) that led to the rise of fierce criticism against evangelical churches, it is remarkable to see that the number of missionaries overseas keeps increasing. Furthermore, evangelicals played a major role in making Lee Myung-bak a "presbyter president" (*changlo taet'onglyŏng*) in the 2008 election. Lee Myung-bak is an elder at Somang Presbyterian Church, a megachurch located in Gangnam, one of the richest neighborhoods in Korea. Despite concern over stagnant growth, the recent series of activities and incidents by the Korean church seem to reveal that they have taken the lead in Christianization at home and abroad. In addition to the scholarly works on Korean Christianity mentioned earlier, I wish to highlight some other characteristics of Korean evangelicals in the light of three major issues: pro-Americanism, anticommunist evangelical subjectivity, personalized/individualized social sufferings, and the Christianization of the nation.

The church and anticommunism

Korean evangelical messages and practices are "God's calling" as claimed by evangelical leaders who hold both secular and sacred powers in the church hierarchy.[13] Within the Korean church, a cultural space where there are both profane and sacred powers among the members, the leadership tends to monopolize the voices and activities concerning national and social concerns. Their authority theoretically comes from and is legitimized by God, and is a particular "capital" attained and accumulated according to the logic of competition in the church market. As South Korea and its churches grew at an excessively rapid pace by promoting this-world oriented theology, they have been successful in mobilizing believers to conceive of their sufferings as personal, while church authorities play a representative role by displaying that their church is also doing "good" for society.

Evangelical leaders' sermons are often irrational and emotional, and yet they are very clear when it comes to the logic of binary opposition— good versus evil. Their speeches and prayers are accepted, by and large, as divine. In their language, Marxist ideology and Christianity, more specifically North Korean *Juche* ideology and South Korean evangelicalism, are intrinsically unable to be joined, integrated, or negotiated between—or even to coexist in the same time or space. Thus, the North is imagined or portrayed as a place devoid of religion, a land of darkness and Satan where the communist regimes of Kim Il-sung and his son Kim Jong-il oppressed the northern brethren. The North is represented "as consisting of two separate realms: the repressive 'communist party' and the oppressed 'North Korean compatriots'" (Lee 2006: 37). According to this view, the communist party exerts its "evil" influence on the South; the subsequent South Korean student movements, teachers and workers unions, as well as the recent pro-North Korean regimes, are also all the result of propaganda managed and promoted by the *ppalgaengi* (literally, "Reds" but akin to "Commies," a pejorative term referring to pro-communists) that seeks to brainwash the South Korean populace. Thus, reunification of the two Koreas must be accomplished by eliminating dark spiritual forces in the name of God. Referring back to Kim Sang-chŏl's principle that I introduced at the beginning of this chapter, reunification will be accomplished by implanting Christianity and capitalism in North Korea to replace *Juche* (self-reliance).

Evangelical anticommunism is closely tied to pro-Americanism. This pro-Americanism, however, is not so much an ideological inclination, but a position that supports the continued presence of US military troops to protect South Korea's national security from the North Korean "Reds." During times of political tension or instability with the North, evangelicals proclaim a state of high alert. On October 4, 2004, for instance, the CCK organized a protest against the Roh administration's National Security Law reform. Several hundreds of thousands of evangelicals and anticommunist organizations participated in the rally, hoisting both the South Korean national flag and the American flag while burning that of North Korea. Speaking in turn, various pastors from the area's megachurches took the stand to denounce the North. The following is representative of the rhetoric from that day:

> Who can say how soon Seoul might be bombed by the North without the Law.... We should fight against the demons from the North and the demons within the South.
> (Reverend David Yonggi Cho, Yoido Full Gospel Church)

> When South Korea faced a critical emergency with demonic communism, God came to us by way of the United States.... God bless the honorable President Bush and the United States of America.
> (Excerpt from "Letter to President Bush," read by Minister Kim H. S.)

Their somewhat radical anticommunism and pro-American tendencies can be understood historically. The massive migration (around 740,000 people) from the North to the South between 1945 and 1950, and during the Korean War (approximately 650,000), anchored these sentiments. Seungsook Moon (2005) stresses that these North-to-South migrants mostly consisted of landowners and former collaborators with the Japanese colonial government. Kim Kwi-ok (1999) and Soo-Jung Lee (2006) also add that a large number of these migrants were Christian. One rationalization for their virulent anticommunism, then, is that these migrants were "natural" dissidents because of the Communist Party's persecution during this violent and traumatic period. According to this view, Reverend Han Kyŏng-jik of Youngnak Presbyterian Church founded his church with northerners and came to pioneer the bulwark against communism due to this ingrained hatred against the North Korean communist regime. The megachurch founders, like Reverend Han, had rarely articulated anticommunism as a main topic in their sermons.[14] Anticommunism appeared rather in the distinct tones of Biblical language in which "it was God who did not allow the northern communists to conquer this land during the war," and Germany and Japan were ultimately defeated because God was not with them (Han 1987: 27).

Meanwhile, sociologist Kim Kwi-ok (1999) argues that the vast majority of North Korean refugees during the war converted to Christianity in the throes of their adjustment to South Korea where they were faced with social discrimination and extreme poverty. She argues that the church thus functioned as their community support center. But it is reasonable to speculate that while Christianity clashed with communist authorities in the North (Grayson 2006), the situation for Christians was the opposite in the South. The first president, Syngman Rhee, was a Methodist Christian who had studied in the United States and later became an honorary elder of Chŏng-tong Methodist Church, the first Methodist Church established by Henry Gerhard Appenzeller in Korea. Further, Rhee appointed Christian ministers and elites to high positions in government, and gave special benefits to the church.[15] As a result, the number of Christians increased from 600,000 to 1.6 million during his 12-year rule (1948–1960). At the heart of this historical context, as many scholars and Korean civilians agree, is the construction of anticommunism as the state ideology and identity, which has been perpetuated since the beginning of the South Korean state under Rhee and through successive militant regimes. The Korean evangelicals' anticommunist pro-Americanism must be seen as a product of collaboration between the South Korean state and the church, initiated at the beginning of the divided nation and perpetuated by both.

The vocabulary of division thus did not merely emerge and replicate itself under anticommunist secular regimes, but rather was a product of the state–church Cold War apparatus. During South Korea's successive military regimes and through the Kim Young-sam administration (1993–1998), Korean evangelicals were relatively unseen compared to their progressive counterparts in the fields of civil and political movements. Their claim at that time that the church was supposed to separate itself from government echoed American missionaries' pleas against Korean anti-Japanese movements during the Japanese colonial period (see Wells 1990; Grayson 2006). In contrast, the Roh Moo-hyun regime initiated such policies as supporting the repeal of the anticommunist National Security Law, private school legal reform, examining the national past for state injustices, and controls on press ownership. These moves seemed to challenge the powers of the church, and evangelical leaders began reviving the state ideology of the past, in the name of God, to protect their hegemonic status in the South. All the evangelical anticommunist campaigns and protests have been called *gu-guk gidohoe* or "prayer meetings for national salvation."

It is hard to conclude that the vast majority of believers attending evangelical churches fully support their ministers' anticommunist campaigns. We can assume that this series of evangelical interventions on behalf of the state has not always been led by the lay men and women in megachurch congregations. More accurately, church members in general are not concerned about their pastors' involvement (or lack thereof) in political issues. As progressive pastor Kim Jin-ho stressed to me, "This is our Korean church tradition. No one tends to care what their pastor does outside of the church, although there are always some who dislike their pastor's position on political issues."[16]

This phenomenon drives us to examine another aspect of anticommunist mechanisms in the church system: if one resists one's anticommunist pastor in church, one would immediately be labeled as being possessed by evil, and therefore in need of healing by the Holy Spirit. In other words, the Korean evangelical church system works to personalize the "evil" contamination once it is considered to have infected an individual. With this in mind, I will turn to the inner workings of church rituals, in which South Korean "personal" suffering and this-worldly salvation are predominant and the processes that are governed by charismatic leaders, which in turn act upon Korean evangelical subjectivities.

Prosperity, health, and spirituality

The main hall of Yoido Full Gospel Church was filled with the sounds of voices, songs, and prayers echoed by the orchestra, choir, and about

Figure 2.1 A megachurch revival meeting at the Seoul Olympic Stadium
Source: Courtesy of the Author.

20,000 adherents who were all inspired by Reverend David Cho, their head pastor. In his 70s, Reverend Cho delivered his sermon with a powerful voice, a quick pace, and flawless articulation. I was sitting in my seat along with the crowd, listening to his long sermon and I turned to look at those who were sitting next to me: a young girl leaning her head on her mother's shoulder, as if sick; a pale-faced woman in her late 20s; an older woman next to her with her eyes closed; and a middle-aged woman. I came to feel as if I was sitting in a doctor's waiting room. In contrast to Reverend Cho's energetic sermon, they looked tired and ill, and they looked as if they were from the countryside or perhaps poor urban neighborhoods.

As the sermon was about to come to a close, Reverend Cho suggested praying together while "placing your hands on those places in your body that ache." Everyone stood up: the mother held her sick daughter in her arms; the pale-faced woman crossed her arms on her chest as if to show that it was her soul that ached, and the woman on my left placed one hand on her shoulder and the other on her belly. Many others in the hall either held their arms out above them or held their own or other bodies. I found myself placing one of my hands on the right side of my abdomen where I had suffered from shingles shortly before my field research and the other on my chest (although as I think back I don't know why I chose my chest in particular). The hall vibrated with shouting, crying, and music. Whenever Reverend Cho recited "X, Y, Z sufferings, go away in the name of Jesus Christ!" the congregation responded with either "Hallelujah!" or "Amen!" putting emphasis on each syllable, making for a powerful repetitive response. It was as if their bodies were punctuating, celebrating the sermon.

More than ten minutes later, as Reverend Cho slowed and toned down his prayer, the "speaking in tongues"—the charismatic phenomenon of speaking in unintelligible words as a sign of the Holy Spirit that is often accompanied by weeping, shouting, and involuntary shaking of the body—faded out. Then Reverend Cho reported that "a person who has suffered from chronic back pain has recovered, a person who had epilepsy has recovered..." etc. The "miraculous" healing had been realized and I actually felt as if my shingles had slightly improved as well. I came to think that the women would continue to come to church in their desire to be healed, probably with the expectation that their pain would be released sometime in the future. Thousands of people quickly and silently exited the church as thousands of other people hurriedly entered the hall for the next service, quickly taking the seats closer to the altar, perhaps in the hopes of receiving a more effective and powerful anointing by the Holy Spirit.

This first-person experience of Pentecostal worship inspired me to reconsider evangelical subjectivity as it is shaped through a series of suffering and healing rituals. First, in theory, evangelicalism emphasizes the "personal" relationship between God and the individual. However, my ethnographic research suggests that the tropes of "individual" and "personal" work to conceal the secular role of the church as a social cultural institution and its leadership, as well as the importance of membership. Indeed, for Korean evangelical Protestants, there is perhaps no more fundamental "sign" in the performance of their religious piety than regularly showing up at church on Sunday in South Korea. Church attendance is a symbolic practice through which other "sacred" experiences such as worship, hearing the Word, and praying together can be experienced. Church is considered not only as an authentic and legitimate space through which a "personal relationship with God" and healing are ultimately manifested, but also as a discursive domain in which members are expected to perform in the way that they have been socialized in accordance with church hierarchy and tacit regulations. Thus, congregations in South Korea tend to be ideologically conservative and largely anticommunist, socially docile to patriarchic and hierarchic family and church systems, active in church-centered activities (i.e., regular attendance, dawn prayer, group bible studies, and volunteering for church events). They often behave somewhat exclusively (sometimes to the point of intolerance) in regard to other faiths and denominations, and tend to be culturally resistant to certain "worldly" customs and habits such as drinking and smoking, which are seen as taboo.

Porterfield also suggests that Christian healing calls our attention to the ways in which suffering is intrinsic to living a Christian life. She states:

> Part of Christianity's appeal as a means of coping with suffering is the idea that suffering is not meaningless but part of a cosmic vision of redemption .... Thus, many Christians have accepted the onset or persistence of suffering as part of religious life, while also celebrating relief from suffering as a sign of the power and meaning of their faith.

She continues.

> Beneath this apparent paradox, a fairly consistent tendency to experience suffering as a means of both self-understanding and communion with others have enabled many Christians to rest easier with pain and death, even as healing experiences have

energized Christians, enabling some to defeat pain and death, at least temporarily.

(2005: 4)

Similarly, sociologist Kelly Chong finds that Korean women can find meaning in their suffering in the process of their conversion to Christianity. She writes: "Another central way by which women are moved toward healing and in their ability to cope with domestic situations is through the act of self-surrender," which is considered to be a crucial turning point in evangelicalism in general, and "a major source of psychic relief" for Korean evangelical women in particular (2006: 359). In other words, although there are persistent sufferings that Christians bear in their lifetime, through the conversion process, they come to translate their sufferings in Biblical terms, namely as the work of a sovereign God. Therefore, Chong argues that although Korean Christian women converting and devoting themselves to Christianity can be seen as instrumental in their liberation from a patriarchal family system, they end up accepting and reintegrating into the domestic order from which they had once wished to escape (2006, 2008).

Chong's findings on Korean evangelical women whose narratives of sufferings are linked with issues of Korean gender and family tensions suggest that what I witnessed with the women sitting next to me at Yoido Full Gospel Church was not merely a simple desire for instantaneous healing. Rather the women may have gained strength, hope, and confidence to return to their familial and social lives where they would face the same problems again and again. But they are consoled every seventh day when Sunday comes. Within the Christian community, and by other religions and atheists as well, these evangelicals are sometimes criticized for being "Sunday Christians" or "rice Christians," and Christians themselves speak pejoratively about those with superficial and hypocritical faith. Nonetheless, we are given the sense that attending church only on Sundays means something deeper than the common perception of "warming the pews" and that these individuals may feel comfort and rejuvenation once a week by attending church.

Korean evangelical concerns tend to emphasize "this-worldly life" and "the primacy of faith-healing," two of five important themes that Andrew Kim points out as examples of the convergence of Korean religious tradition and Protestantism (Kim A. 2000). What is important to note is that this tendency, pre-dating and then converging with Protestantism in Korea, was likely to have functioned as a discursive condition by which the believers came to rely on and were bound within the church system as discussed above. Just as Cho and his followers have preached, the vast majority of South Korean Protestant churches empha-size that "a material and economic paradise [is] to be realized in this life, not in the next" (Kim 2000: 120; also see Yun 1964; Ryu 1965; Lee 1977).

In relation to the formation of Christian citizenship, Korean evangel-ical leadership perpetuates "this-worldly" blessings, as represented by Reverend Cho's service above. The emphasis on worldly well-being and healing is largely interpreted as having arisen from Korea's indigenous shaman tradition, and further as an essential element contributing to the explosive growth of Christianity in South Korea (Kim 2000; Jang 2004).[17] On the other hand, there are critical views in global Christian circles regarding Reverend Cho's theology of prosperity (the three-fold blessings of God: health, prosperity, and salvation). For instance, an American Christian organization, Biblical Discernment Ministries (BDM), introduces Cho's theology on their website. For them, Cho's ministry of healing is crucial to understanding his church growth:

> Divine healing is another method which Cho uses to generate **church growth**, claiming this is the most essential element. This is unbiblical for many reasons. First, it rests on a false premise. The Bible shows explicitly that healing or miracles do not necessarily bring a person to the saving knowledge of Christ (cf. Matt. 9: 22–25, 32–34; 11: 20–24; Acts 4: 5–22). Second, it fosters wrong motivation since it encourages the crowd to come to church with ulterior motives. Third, it obscures the true purpose of healing, which in the Bible authenticates the messiahship of Christ and the apostleship of apos-tles. Finally, Cho's concept conceals the true nature of healing since he confuses functional disorders with organic illnesses. Furthermore, contrary to the Biblical pattern, Cho fails to "heal" some (all?) who desire healing.
>
> [bold letters in original][18]

At first glance, this criticism certainly sounds reasonable and valid. Yet whether it is unbiblical or not, this strong Weberian sense of Protestantism accentuating economic prosperity as a sign of blessing is not unique to South Korea, but is widespread in Third World coun-tries influenced by Pentecostal churches. Anthropologist Jill Wightman (2007) documents the ways in which the Bolivian Pentecostal Church brings physical healing forth by "altar calls" during services. She also sheds light on how the articulation of healing intersects with neo-liberal Bolivian subjectivity. Katherine Wiegele (2005) also illuminates the ways in which El Shaddai, a form of Catholicism with Pentecostal elements, gained popularity by promoting a "prosperity movement" with an emphasis on healing, prosperity, and confession in the Philippines. Thus, the Korean evangelical tendency toward material interests is certainly not only a matter of Korea's shamanistic tradition. These features have also been significantly amplified in the context of Korea's Cold War modernity.

Furthermore, the focus on physical health and material prosperity does not necessarily mean the diminution of the importance of spirituality at all. Indeed, the term spirituality is inseparable from healing in the evangelical vocabulary. For example, almost all kinds of special healing retreats or camps have *yŏngsŏng ch'iyu*, or spirituality healing, as both the title and ultimate goal of the event, which is visualized as "miraculous" experiences of direct or indirect physical healing. Practices such as "laying on of hands" (i.e., placing one's hand on another's body) for physical or spiritual healing are thus popular at these events, and experiences such as "speaking in tongues" are one of the most significant signs of an individual's spiritual revival. In the same vein, an individual must "speak" of his or her conversion experience. Spirituality must be therefore embodied. In Reverend Cho's case, he preaches a fourth dimension spirituality that involves visualization and mediation. Rather than envisaging an ambiguous faith, Cho clearly articulates faith as a concrete reality. With respect to the relationship between spirituality and physical well-being, Korean evangelical doctrine does not appear to have deviated from Biblical teaching, at least in theory.[19] However, one should note that corporeality is the only legitimate form of spirituality in practice in the tradition of Korean evangelicalism. This aspect is very significant as a context in which North Korean migrants are situated in the process of conversion to Christianity, as I shall elaborate in the next chapters.

In addition to acknowledging the interconnection between the physical and the spiritual in Christian doctrine, it is crucial to understand the ways in which the emphasis on corporeality in spirituality evolved from within a particular local historical context—post-war South Korea. Simon, a staff member at Good People, the civil organization of the Yoido Full Gospel Church, once told me a story of how Reverend Cho integrated this-worldly happiness into his theology in the Korean post-war context:

When opening his own chapel [in the late 1950s when Korean society was still undergoing post-war turmoil], our pastor [Reverend Cho] witnessed that physical illness was one of the greatest challenges in people's quotidian lives. Instead of preaching about spiritual recovery, he prayed to God for the power of healing. One day he visited a house where a poor and severe paralytic was dying. While praying he laid his hands on the poor man's body. It was a critical moment because he had never done such a thing before and the villagers were watching him. He was actually nervous and desperate thinking that if he failed his ministry career would end, too. But God blessed him with a miracle. The poor man who was dying recovered his health, and since then, the size of his church congregation mushroomed.

A dramatic miracle that the young Reverend Cho was not convinced would occur took place in a critical moment. It was not him, but it was through him that God appeared to heal such desperate people and then made his church into the world's largest church. Simon buttressed his own belief with this miraculous event even though he had not witnessed it personally. Indeed, this story was already scripted and widely known through Reverend Cho's biography and church webpage. The circulation of this "miracle" does not only imply that Korean evangelical healing, as a religious practice (the pursuit of physical and spiritual well-being in this world and eternal salvation in the next), has been a driving force in the rise and rapid growth of Christianity. The storytelling itself also redirects the teller and the audience's gaze away from other secular and institutional factors, such as systematic support for Christianity initiated by the Syngman Rhee regime in the 1950s, that were mentioned earlier. Indeed, I argue that these factors were as significant to the church as the Holy Spirit in the context of post-war Korea.

Considering the local geopolitical specificities, individual suffering, whether Christian or not, is hardly separable from the problems of the society to which the individuals belong (cf. Kleinman, Das and Lock 1997). Doubtless, Korean evangelical leaders often practice exegesis of the Bible by applying it to current social issues, but the fundamental "solution" (or ultimate healing) for the root cause of all kinds of problems is always accomplished only through "the personal relationship between you and God." Chung Yong-sup, a Korean theologian who has analyzed the sermons of well-known Korean pastors, underscores the point implied by Reverend Cho: human salvation is accomplished not through social reform or democratization, but only by a personal relationship with God. The content of all his sermons also encourages individuals to become attached to wealth, health, and success (see Chung 2006).[20]

   Scholars in Latin American studies and medical anthropology have underlined the ways in which the individual suffering and illnesses narrated in testimonies almost always stem from structural poverty, signifying social suffering, and can be used as a "weapon of the weak" (Schepher-Hughes 1994: 233, cited from Wightman 2007: 117–131). It is noteworthy that this insight, however, does not fully explain the ways in which the individual testimonies and narratives can be confined within the domain of the church and reduced to the church authority system.

   As mentioned earlier, church leadership monopolizes the processes for both the testimony of suffering and for this-worldly salvation. Under this condition, the personal relationship between God and believer is also mediated by the leadership. Accordingly, one must be cautious not to misunderstand evangelical theology as tending to value the individual *over* society. Rather, the church serves as a social unit and heterogeneous space in which individual believers are organized, managed, and mutually governed according to the techniques of membership management that have evolved for centuries. Through this social unit and space, believers share emotions and personal stories; and the church social hierarchy and norms are reproduced in the doctrine of Korean evangelicalism (see Chong 2008). Again, central to an understanding of the doctrine and the church's mechanisms is the evangelical leadership which was formed in the intersecting nexus of state support and the needs of a deprived people during South Korea's period of rapid industrialization.

Politico-religious conversion

Evangelical leaders identify Korea and Koreans as a "chosen people and nation" who will play a leading role in evangelizing the world.[21] This thinking naturally leads Korean to assume that the Christianization of all nations is the ultimate task and calling for all Christians. I witnessed that this discourse extended to the process of reunification as well as for global missions. By emphasizing the theme of national Christianization, evangelical leaders place the believers' patriotism, which is linked to this-worldly interests, into Biblical language. For example, the North Korean famine and the country's general poverty since the 1990s have been simply translated into their discourse as evidence of God's "curse" resulting from the nation's idolization of Kim Il-sung, the founder of North Korea. And, as the number of North Korean migrants who flee the North and settle in the South increases, the leaders who preached this evangelical nationalism have become more empowered as modern-day prophets, making the Christianization of the entire peninsula seem more realistic.

Andrew Kim stresses that, "Many pastors and Christian leaders advanced the notion that the establishment and prosperity of Korean churches as well as the Christianization of the nation is a patriotic and assured means to save the country from all social ills" (2000: 122). But "all social ills" here are not the same as those that progressive Protestants have tried to heal. Rather, the evangelical concept of social ills is generally linked to a sociopolitical condition in which leftists or non-Christian groups are active. However, it is in the late-Cold War context that the evangelical North Korean mission, which is given priority before unification, brings to light the ethical and theological questions about forgiveness as opposed to Korean conventional anticommunism. In short, can or should "we" forgive the Reds too?

There is no single agreement, but a slight redirection from a conventional, irreconcilable, anticommunism to an ambiguous one seems to have taken place in recent years. That is, in the logic of evangelical conversion, the "enemy" seems no longer to be an object to "smash," but one to "convert" to Christianity. The difference is still vague and not coherently shared among evangelicals, but I will briefly examine the significance of such a shift.

As mentioned earlier, South Korean division language has distinguished between the Reds and innocent victim-subjects in the North. Likewise, "we" must find out and smash the Reds within "us." Further, both Korean societies have perpetuated a racialized view of the families of the "enemy." In the case of South Korea, as the guilt-by-association idea represents, family members of those who went to the North (*Wŏlbukja*), were suspected as potential enemies because they might be "contaminated" by their bloodline (Lee S. 2006).

In other words, communism was something contagious that could be caught by or passed down to other family members. Communism in the North and capitalism in the South have been conceived as biological elements, like genetic traits, and in terms of the family metaphor, the trait may not be escapable or remediable (Hwang sees those ideologies as viruses temporarily infecting Korean national "souls," as mentioned earlier). Referring to such racialized and emotionally bent anticommunism that the right-wing advocates have internalized, South Korea-led absorption unification may inevitably entail a process of legal and ethical punishments of those who are suspected as communist collaborators (see Wilson 1997, 2001, 2003, for studies of national reconciliation processes and human rights).

However, the emergence of recent North Korean migrants and their conversion to Christianity calls our attention to the logic of conversion. Unlike first generation North Koreans (mostly war refugees), the new migrants are those who participated in developing North Korea into a socialist country. Even some former high-ranking officials in the North have come to the South and received legal citizenship as well as benefits without being accused of being division criminals. As I will elaborate in Chapter 5, they are celebrated and expected to be the vanguard of the South's North Korean mission. This conversion process implies that the long-held anticommunism sentiment is now in the process of transforming from political to religious, but that the direction is not yet fixed. At least it is becoming clearer that the evangelical zeal for the Christianization of a nation may possibly conflict with the legal and political national reconciliation processes in the future.

Conclusion

I have examined key components of Korean Protestantism in relation to its discourse and practices regarding the concepts of suffering, salvation, and spirituality. As a main contextual background, the first part of this chapter paid particular attention to the national suffering that has been historically and collectively sensed in Korean structures of feelings throughout modern history. The second part elaborated the ways in which the Korean evangelical church appears to have restored anticommunist sentiments in order to clarify an ideal unification process.

The main arguments can be summarized as follows: first, I paid attention to the extent to which evangelical doctrines of suffering and salvation are dominated by church leadership, which indeed needs further study for the Korean evangelical church. Church leaders were agents in the rise of the Korean church, in conjunction with the successive anticommunist regimes in South Korea, and integrated various forms of religious performances and discourses into Korean evangelicalism. Moreover, they tend to monopolize, legitimize, and filter the voices of members and often God. Second, by examining evangelical practices and discourses of soteriology, I ascertained that the accentuation of this-worldly blessings is not only a reflection of its exclusiveness to other religious beliefs, but also a technique by which social sufferings are individualized and individualized sufferings are healed as a sign of God's blessing within the church system. Thus, Korean evangelicals have produced and reproduced anticommunist pro-American sentiments as both secular and sacred means to revive the speed of church growth and to accomplish what they call God's calling for the Christianization of the nation and beyond.

Recalling Kim Sang-chŏl's speech from the beginning of this chapter, let me turn to the last part of that event. The event went on and on. I was hungry, as were my North Korean friends. A large number of people had already left, but the migrants were told to remain in their seats in order to receive a small gift as a token of appreciation. The gift turned out to be an umbrella. Only the North Koreans were allowed to receive this gift, one for each person. I recognized all of the migrants who were in charge of distributing the umbrellas to their migrant colleagues. I happened to receive one as an exception. As we proceeded to exit the main gate, five or six North Koreans were standing with pickets signs that read: "XXX should save my family!" "XXX is an inhumane broker, criminal!" among other things. XXX was one of the awardees at the ceremony and a team director of the CNKR, which has managed the underground railroads through which many North Koreans have come to South Korea by way of China. I mused that perhaps their family members had been arrested and sent back to the North while planning their escape or while on the CNKR's routes. CNKR's strategy has drawn media attention, so the escapees are making a life-or-death decision by choosing to leave North Korea. The migrants standing outside in the freezing cold were of course not given the umbrellas. For me, the umbrella was a fitting metaphor of the pastoral care provided by the church—care that extended only so far, to those willing to sit through the sermons, to those relatively obedient people who participated in daily cell meetings in the North—which will be further examined in the chapters that follow.

3
North Korean Crossing and Christian Encounters

We have observed lately that, amid escalating military tensions between North Korea and the United States and South Korea, some Protestant missionaries have been detained on entering North Korean territory without documentation, with some subsequently being released. In early May 2013, the news media discovered that a Korean-American detainee in North Korea, who is currently sentenced to 15 years of hard labor, is also a missionary.[1] Christian missionary work aimed at North Korea varies in form and effects; both Catholic and Protestant churches, ecumenical and evangelical alike, operate their missions following what they believe to be "God's calling," sometimes differing vastly from and often contradicting one another. This chapter examines the evangelical missionary work that is intimately tied with humanitarian aid for North Korean refugees in the Sino–North Korean border area as an emblem of South Korean churches' North Korean mission. Based on extensive ethnographic fieldwork in regions wherein certain field sites had limited access due to local security concerns, this chapter sheds light on refugees' religious conversion as a complex cultural project and process in which ideas of and practices for religious freedom and salvation become immensely contested in the very logic of "saving" in both humanitarian and Biblical terms.

There are two primary concerns in this Chinese context. The first concern is the problems of evangelical missionary work associated with universal human rights discourses. The second is the church as an intra-ethnic contact space where the refugees' religious and social lives are pre-figured. Regarding the first concern, I argue that humanitarian missionary efforts tend to reframe North Korean refugees as "exemplary victims" (Malkki 1996: 384) who need pastoral care and protection to ultimately "save" their souls. Some non-religious human rights activists

have criticized such restricted conditions in which the refugees have
no alternative. "They must obey the dictates of South Korean pastors or missionaries while they are in China," reported Kato Hiroshi
(2008), executive director of Life Funds for North Korean Refugees.[2]
While acknowledging the criticism as relevant, I want to equally highlight that the refugees quickly learn how to reframe themselves from
merely border crossers coming in search of food or jobs to victims of
human trafficking, stateless mothers, or, for some, "future" missionaries
in accordance with the humanitarian and Biblical vocabularies that they
acquire through interactions with missionaries. Conversion, for them,
is a passage that is heavily embedded with political and cultural mechanisms (cf. Hefner 1993; Austin-Bross 2003) which constitute the brute
realities that North Korean refugees in general, and women in particular,
undergo to seek salvation, whether that salvation is inherently physical
or spiritual or both.

My second concern regards the space in which such a conversion
passage is negotiated: the church, which is conceptualized beyond its
structural form as plural intra-ethnic contact zones run by Korean-
Chinese missionaries, who in turn are supervised by South Korean
or foreign missionaries. For the border crossers, the Christian Church
(*jiàohuì* in Chinese) is crucial, "must-know" knowledge utilized when
they cross the Tumen river into China,[3] and it is experienced in varied
forms with various meanings. Along the border, the church appears in
the form of aid kits (which may contain socks, medicine, bread, etc.);
a Christian taxi driver who provides free rides to a nearby city; a safe
house or shelter where refugees can hide, recover, and work; an orphan-
age (often called an "aunt's house") where separated children stay and
wait for their parents; a registered Korean-Chinese church which provides them with temporary aid or jobs; brokers who move them out
of China; South Korean missionaries or researchers; and last but not
least, a spiritual space with a lit cross at night. The church functions
as a space through and by which the refugees come to communicate
with "God," and imagine a new sense of belonging, another homeland (South Korea), and a better life and where they try to realize these
dreams by resorting to underground railroads that are initially established and largely sponsored by money and missionaries from South
Korean churches.

These aspects of the church can be considered as a core "contact zone"
(Pratt 1992) in which the interactions among the refugees, Korean-
Chinese, and South Korean missionaries are not only intersected by
spiritual knowledge and practices, but also stratified and contested in

light of class distinctions and cultural differences. With an examination of the complex interactions of these intra-ethnic groups, this chapter highlights that such an asymmetrical relationship in which the refugees are positioned at the bottom, in turn, engenders religious and ethical dilemmas regarding potential salvation.

The material presented in this chapter is based on three intensive fieldwork trips to the Yanbian area: one in 2000, and two others in 2007. During these trips I met with South Korean NGO workers, Korean-Chinese Christians, and North Korean border crossers. The seven-year time span provided me with a stronger historical understanding of the sea changes that were taking place: increasing feelings of fear and insecurity; decreasing numbers of North Korean street beggars; decreasing numbers of the churches which once cared for the border crossers; the more systemized management skills of local secret shelters; and an increasing number of defector-brokers operating underground railroads. However, North Korean refugees' liminal conditions persist, and the meanings and limits of the Christian church, in which civic and political regimes and individual agonies and desires are intertwined, remain an imperative area for study. The following vignettes discuss empirical questions about religious conversion, intra-ethnic interactions, and gendered salvation.

Religious freedom

> I don't understand why you don't have any religious affiliation. South Korea gives freedom for people to have a religion. Why do you throw your freedom away?... It's nonsense that you don't have any religion. Please go to church as soon as you get back to South Korea. Don't lose your right to be free!
>
> (Jiny, a 21-year-old North Korean female born-again Christian, 2000)

Through Ms Choi, a well-educated Korean-Chinese missionary, I met Jiny[4] at a small restaurant in a major city in the Korean-Chinese Autonomous Prefecture in China in the summer of 2000.[5] I was puzzled when Jiny first asked me which church I was attending in South Korea. When I told her vaguely, "Well, actually I can't say that I have a religion now," she seemed embarrassed. As her response (quoted above) shows, Jiny interpreted my agnostic attitude as a misuse of freedom, and thus I could not be a completely authentic South Korean citizen. I was so uncomfortable that I decided to defend myself by responding, "I guess

I have the right to be free from having a religion." Soon after, I found myself regretting this response since Jiny's eyes seemed to say that she was now searching for a compelling response to make me abandon my present attitude and declare I would begin attending church. During a moment of silence, Ms Choi proudly said (while rubbing Jiny's head and back, an act of admiration on behalf of a senior to a close younger counterpart), "Jiny is now an *almost perfect* born-again Christian."

This anecdote recounts my first ethnographic encounter; religious freedom appeared to be a core virtue for exercising true South Korean citizenship, and Christianity seemed to be reviving among ethnic Koreans in the border area where Christianity was politicized by both international human rights discourses and state powers (i.e., Chinese and North Korean regimes). This section examines the multilayered conditions and discourses that constitute Christian encounters with, and conversion of, North Korean refugees in the Sino–North Korean border area.

Christian conversion as a project

When presenting the topic of North Korean refugees in China at workshops, I have often been asked whether refugees are required to convert to Christianity to receive the pastoral care and material assistance provided by missionaries and local churches. This question is indeed fundamental and yet difficult to answer as well. Conversion to Christianity, or, in Korean evangelical terms, informing "them" about God and making it possible for "them" to accept Jesus as "savior," is the ultimate goal of "helping" the refugees, as it is believed that it is the only way to save both the body and the soul.

However, conversion becomes problematic and complicated when it is tied to humanitarian aid, which steers the physical transition toward the matter of individual interiority. Some social scientists have examined this phenomenon, at either the individual or social level, with a focus on the contexts in which these events take place. Anthropologists have called our attention to larger socio-cultural and structural problems like colonialism (Comaroff & Comaroff 1991, 1997), modernity (van der Veer 1996; Meyer 1999; Robbins 2004), and socio-political climates (Harding 2000), and to the particularizing rather than universalizing forms and meanings of conversion (Asad 2003; Buckser & Glazier 2003). Despite the rise of religion as a topic of study in the social sciences, it has long been absent from the map of refugee studies. Alexander Horstmann (2011) points out that religion has only appeared as an adjunct to politico-economic structures. Horstmann and Jung argue that an understanding of the influence of religion allows for a deeper understanding of the ways in which refugees interact to negotiate their identities and aspirations within and beyond structural conditions.[6]

North Korean refugees and their encounters with Christianity in China have been largely understudied, and yet they are reported as "problematic" in terms of the "repressive" conditions of sanctuaries as mentioned above. From a practical anthropological perspective, Byung-Ho Chung (2004) pioneers a demonstration of the degree to which strict rules and disciplines in a secret shelter impact upon young North Korean refugees in surviving stateless conditions and reconfiguring identities.[7] The secret Christian shelters are thus an ambiguous or often contradictory space as the caring system tends to put absurd restrictions upon the refugees as a prerequisite to being saved from hunger and the potential danger of being arrested by law enforcement. Given the restraints in the shelter, the refugee individuals' conversion experience to Christianity has been perceived as merely instrumental, less "true" or always "almost" rather than authentic. Drawing on critical observations and reports, I posit that North Korean refugees' conversions to Christianity can be considered as a complex set of projects and processes that cannot be reduced as deviant or an ancillary event (cf. Austin-Broos 2003).

By the term "cultural projects," I want to stress the extent to which proselytization is intrinsically embedded in evangelical humanitarian activities directed toward North Korean refugees.[8] Conversion may not be required, but such structural obstacles as omnipresent police raids, limited resources and numbers of secret shelters and missionaries, and the mobility of the refugees add to the evangelical "calling" and anticommunist hues of missionary practice. Further, South Korean churches have come to view *Juche* ideology, the North Korean national ruling philosophy, as idolatry, as essentially a religious system rather than a secular political one. Some domestic theologians and ministers propose to view *Juche* ideology as the state religion of North Korea, and thus suggest that the North Korean mission take the form of inter-religious dialogue, whereas most evangelical churches and missionaries dominant in the Sino–North Korean border area tend to insist on a "total" transformation of the refugees to born-again Christians. Their conversion is regarded as an example, enabling churches to imagine and prepare future mission strategies aimed at North Korea. Accordingly, it is the processes that engender a particular meaning of Christianity that motivate such displaced people as North Korean refugees to seek an alternative sense of belonging, an identity that is unfixed but destined to continue being negotiated either under repressive conditions or their own free will. This chapter argues that the conversion to Christianity by North Koreans in the border area is the product of a *"dialectical encounter"* (Comaroffs 1997: 5, italics in the original) with macro- and micro-powers in a particular geopolitical circumstance and is a constant perilous journey that is nearly always incomplete and envisioned both physically and spiritually.

Crossing life-death river

On the basis of some human rights reports[9] and my ethnographic fieldwork, it is clear that the main reason North Koreans cross the Sino-Korean border is to seek food resources and a better life, which can be described as being equivalent to notions of "freedom" and "hope" (Table 3.1).

In contrast to the chronic poverty in North Korea, the area of north-east China known as the Yanbian Korean-Chinese autonomous region is much wealthier. Like a majority of the border crossers, Jiny had a typical story: her family had faced the agonies and hardships confronting many North Koreans during the famine of 1995–1998. One parent, her grand-parents, and her siblings died of starvation. While the rest of the family members scattered to find food resources, she crossed the Tumen river that forms the natural border between China and North Korea at night.

Christian churches provide food, clothes, and basic medical kits for the border crossers to either take back to North Korea or to travel with further inland (ICG 2006: 5). Some family units rely on church support while moving around to evade possible police raids. There are secret shelters in remote mountainous areas far from villages, often used by young people and families, as well as some small and inexpensive apart-ments in urban areas that are used as shelters by churches. Jiny can be considered one of the luckier women in that she was able to find a safe shelter. The majority of North Korean women have been sold or forced to work in restaurants, red light districts, at karaoke bars, or in the emerging internet sex industry whose customers are predominantly South Korean men. Others are forced to marry Han-Chinese or Korean-Chinese men in rural areas. Jiny was also fortunate because Ms Choi was willing to take care of her. During the three years previous to our meet-ing, Jiny had been staying with Ms Choi in her two-bedroom apartment, where Jiny studied the Bible, prayed, learned Chinese, and heard about South Korea. She no longer worried about food, and her health was restored. All living expenses were supported by Ms Choi's church, which had connections with South Korean and Korean Protestant churches overseas.[10]

Table 3.1 Reasons for fleeing from North Korea

Reason / Year	Difficulties in living	Following other family members	Being worried about legal punishment	Anti-regime	Family conflicts	For settling in China	Aspiring freedom	Others	Total
1999	8	9	18	16	4	0	2	4	61
2000	52	99	63	44	11	17	0	11	297
2001	292	143	41	12	21	5	3	55	572
2002	462	260	87	95	55	69	4	79	1,111
2003	655	187	64	68	64	17	1	119	1,175
2004	1,098	301	94	135	77	56	7	167	1,935
2005	801	237	77	49	24	43	16	69	1,316
2006	1,142	405	42	62	44	48	22	92	1,857
Total	4,510	1,641	486	481	300	255	55	596	8,324

Adapted from "The Reasons for Fleeing North Korea" (Yoon In-Jin, 2009: 83, my translation). Note that the numbers in the columns indicate the number of North Korean refugees who provided the selected answer.

In this regard, Christianity played a significant role in her exit from physical suffering, facilitated her "sense of belonging," and provided a feeling of cultural security through the Protestant Christian network that was seen to be a universal community, a putative world existing beyond her physical limits. Studies on diaspora and migration have discussed "cultural citizenship" as a claim to live in ways different from the dominant norms of the host society (Gupta & Ferguson 1992; Clifford 1994; Rosaldo 1994; Ong 1996; Cohen 1997; Fortier 2000; Hall 2003). As a displaced person, Jiny needed to re-territorialize her identity in response to daily confrontations with the politically and culturally uncertain border zone. By entrusting herself to God and Ms Choi's care, she soothed her basic biological and cultural anxieties about survival in a desperate situation. Analytically, it is thus helpful to understand that she claimed "religious citizenship," which is not synonymous with having the legal rights that one might claim as citizen of a nation-state, but provides a feeling of satisfaction available to refugees who float along the borders of nation-states. In other words, her conversion to Christianity was both a practice of her "free will" and a strategy emerging from the negotiation of biological and cultural rights to survive in an insecure social environment.

Christianity and human rights

Individual levels of Christian conversion among North Korean refugees in China, such as observed in Jiny's case, are unlikely to be "free" from, and are rather entangled in, both political and ideological tensions. Indeed, Christianity is invested with complex and even contradictory meanings for North Korean refugees and international societies as well as South Korean Christian organizations working on the underground railroads. North Korean refugees were exposed to Christianity, in the words of North Korean founder Kim Il-sung, as a symbolic "means of western imperialism." It is reported in some international human rights media that the North Korean government considers the spread of Christianity among the refugees a special security threat, and thus when undocumented North Korean refugees are arrested in China and sent back to the North, they are allegedly interrogated in a harsh manner as to whether they went to church, encountered Christianity, or met with a missionary.[11]

It is significant that major international reports on the human rights of North Korean refugees and residents of North Korea alike hold that Christianity—acceptance of which is likely to represent "freedom of religion" in western conventional consciousness—is a central matter in the human rights debates in which international NGOs and the South

Korean right-wing are engaged.[12] Even though the North Korean constitution guarantees religious freedom, in North Korea any repatriated
border crosser who is found to have had contact with Christian missionaries or churches in China or elsewhere is accused of treason and
with threatening national purity and unity and could be sentenced to
a lifetime of hard labor or even execution with property confiscation.
Simultaneously, the Chinese government prohibits foreign missionary
activities and has increased both the penalties on local Chinese churches
helping the refugees and the rewards to those who report such cases
to the police. Meanwhile, it is these sanctuaries and local churches in
China that North Korean refugees rely on most to survive their plight
while enduring minimal freedom of mobility in the name of safety.
Additionally, it is in these same venues that the tensions between state
powers (i.e., North Korea and China) and international human rights
discourses are circulated as narratives that engender omnipresent fears.
It is important to stress that the consequences and impacts of the
politicization of Christian encounters and involvements gravely affect
and complicate individual refugees' everyday lives and, in particular,
what conversion to Christianity means to them in aspiring to this- and
other-worldly salvation.

Conversion and intra-ethnic asymmetry

Overseas Christian missions are inherently cross-cultural encounters
and yet the contribution of anthropological studies of missionary activity is relatively little appreciated among Korean missionaries. Darrell
L. Whiteman, founder of the Network of Christian Anthropologists,
states that, "because Korea is one of the most homogeneous societies
in the world, Korean missionaries easily confuse Christianity with their
Korean cultural patterns of worship, so their converts are lead [sic] to
believe that to become a Christian one must also adopt Korean culture"
(Whiteman 2004: 82). He points out that non-western missionaries,
such as Koreans, tend to make the same mistakes that their western predecessors made in the era of colonialism. Here, "Korean" should mean
South Korean. I emphasize that Korean cultures can be considered in the
plural in light of mission activity in the Korean-Chinese Autonomous
Prefecture where North Korean refugees concentrate. This section investigates the church and secret shelter system, the logic of gender, and
thus the complex and contradictory meanings of intra-ethnic interactions among North Korean refugees, South Korean missionaries, and
Korean-Chinese Christians. The term "asymmetry" is used in order to
illuminate the ways in which refugees are positioned in a category of

"rescue-subject" in the evangelical humanitarian mission. "Rescue" theory and practice stem from the images of exemplary victims who are supposed to behave in helpless, obedient, sorrowful, weak, and poor ways. They should be skinny, appear older or younger than their years, and be short and dirty. Their cultural identity is little appreciated, and their soul is considered to be in need of purifying.

North Korean refugees' conversion and their belief in the Bible are always suspected by South Korean missionaries who perceive that the conversion from *Kimilsung-ism* to "modern," or more precisely, South Korean, Christianity is nearly impossible. Further, North Korean masculinity is always a subject to be controlled, while females are portrayed as passive victims. As will be demonstrated, the underlying mechanism of asymmetrical intra-ethnic relations in the mission process is a misrecognition and stratification of cultural differences among ethnic Koreans.

Renegotiation of "Korean" Christianity

Since the early 1980s, South Korean missionaries have put forth tremendous effort in supporting the rise of Korean-Chinese Christianity in the Yanbian Korean-Chinese Autonomous Prefecture, home to some 48 percent (850,000) of China's ethnic Korean population of two million.[13] It has been reported that over the last 20 years almost all ethnic Korean villages have come to have their own churches, whether that church be a house church or a registered Three-Self Patriotic Movement church.[14] Roughly 8 percent (approximately 120,000) of China's ethnic Koreans identify themselves as Christian, compared to just over 5 percent of Han-Chinese and 3 percent of other ethnic minorities in China.[15] Since the mid-1990s, in Korean-Chinese society the church has emerged as a contact zone in which South Korean missionaries, Korean-Chinese, and North Korean border crossers have come to interact with each other.

It is still the case however, that China is a socialist country and perpetuates its control over the "religious market."[16] In particular, South Korean missionary activities in the Yanbian area are highly monitored and restricted for reasons of "national security." Foreign missionaries are neither allowed to lead regular church worship, nor to perform religious activities (e.g., singing, praying, and distributing literature) in public spaces, such as on the street or in squares. The majority of South Korean missionaries tend to conceal their identities and act as businessmen/women, educators, or tourists.

Despite the structural obstacles of state surveillance, however, the church has served as a stage for the reunion of ethnic Koreans in the Sino–North Korean border area.[17] Operating a secret shelter or safe house for North Korean border crossers demands special techniques and strategies. One of the preferred methods has been for Korean-Chinese Christians to take care of North Korean border crossers directly, while South Korean missionaries supervise the shelters or churches and provide finances and supplies. This type of mission strategy was used to ensure safety. With the exception of some bolder missionaries, including Pastor Chun from Durihana Inc. (Missionary Foundation), who was imprisoned for eight months in China,[18] few South Korean missionaries have directly worked at either secret shelters or in the underground railroads.

The shelter operation system, in which the primary caregiver is Korean-Chinese, has been associated with an assumption that the degree of cultural difference (language, ways of thinking, behaving, human relationship building, etc.) between Korean-Chinese and North Koreans may be smaller than that between South and North Koreans, because the two former groups have both gone through life in socialist societies. Korean-Chinese missionaries have played the role of local agents supervised by South Korean missionaries. In essence, the way that secret shelters are operated reflects the hierarchical relationship established in missionary fields, just as Andrew Orta (2004) observed in Andean society.

What is significant in this field of evangelical humanitarian endeavor aimed at North Korean refugees is that North Korean conversion to Christianity is "measured" by South Korean missionaries or Korean-Chinese Christians. In stark contrast to my impression of some refugees, who spoke to me about how they "believe in God, Jesus Christ as my savior" and want to be trained in South Korea to become missionaries, most missionaries from both South Korea and North America distrusted the refugees' "performance" of faith. A South Korean-born Korean-American missionary, Mr Song, who was in his late 50s, told me about conversion: "First and foremost, they need to change their brain (*kol*)." His account began with the biological term, *kol*, which North Koreans use to indicate the head, as in "I have a headache" (*kol ap'ŭda*), or mentality, "That guy looks insane" (*kol i isanghan kŏt katda*). He described the refugees' body and mentality as "completely contaminated by *Kimilsung-ism*. Until the *kol* is replaced, nothing is possible" (author's personal conversation with Mr Song (pseudonym), April 20, 2007). For years he operated his "own" shelters about an hour away from Yanji, China. In the middle of a mountain, men and women, whom he called "my children" (who were all in fact adults) resided in separate houses about 30 minutes by foot from each other. As his metaphor of "my children" indicated, the relationship between him and his North Korean care receivers was that of a family patriarch and off-spring. Nonetheless, he highly doubted whether his "children" would be able wipe *Juche* ideology or *Kimilsung-ism*, the North Korean national philosophy, from their "brain" and assimilate into a capitalist society, let alone into the Christian faith.

Similar examples of suspicions regarding religious conversion among North Korean refugees prevailed. When I first encountered the conversion dispute in the summer of 2000 in China, another South Korean missionary, also an academic, asserted to me that "based on my survey data with 500 refugees in shelters, I came to conclude that converting North Koreans to Christianity would be impossible, as far as they continue to compare Jesus in the Bible with Kim Il-sung [the founder of North Korea]" (author's interview with Reverend Kang (pseudonym), August 7, 2000). Assuming that I was a missionary, he advised me against ambitions of evangelizing North Korean border crossers, but to only serve them in a "pure" humanitarian way. Mr Song and Reverend Kang were convinced that *Juche* ideology was embodied so intrinsically in North Korean subjects that their spiritual transformation would be unlikely to occur.

By contrast, for Korean-Chinese missionaries, North Koreans' comparative understanding of the Bible signified that their conversion to Christianity was feasible. A male Korean-Chinese missionary told me that, "They [North Koreans in his shelter] understand the Bible with little problem. I guess it is because Kim Il-sung is considered as the sacred father and is worshiped like God" (author's interview with Mr Jang (pseudonym), August 11, 2000). In the same vein, on several occasions, while talking to refugees at secret shelters I have been given accounts like this one:

> I was first hesitant to read the Bible which is written in very small characters. But shortly after reading line by line, it was as if I was reading our North Korean textbook. The series of unreal miracles, Jesus' love to his disciples and the poor, the way that the writers cite what Jesus said and did, and so on led me to think "wow, it's just what I have learned and practiced my entire life in our republic [*konghwaguk*]."
>
> (Author's conversation with Mr Choi and Kim at a secret shelter, August 14, 2000)

For South Korean Christians, however, it is unthinkable to compare Kim Il-sung with Jesus. While North Korean adults tended to struggle to integrate what they had learned (*Juche* ideology) with what they were learning (the Bible), South Korean missionaries were unlikely to accept such a rationalization process. For Korean-Chinese Christians playing the mediator role between the two sides, as well as serving as the primary caregiver for the northerners, North Korean conversion to Christianity, as Ms Choi expressed, seems always "almost." This "almost born-again" trope suggests that North Korean spiritual transformation is conceived of as less authentic and less complete in China and among South Koreans.

"Runaway": Ethical dilemma in pursuit of freedom

Political antagonism that views Christianity as a matter of national security, and cultural hierarchy among South Koreans, Korean-Chinese missionaries, and North Korean refugees comes into play in "defining" the conversion of North Korean refugees. In addition, the refugees' undocumented status that exposes them directly to such issues as human trafficking, violence, labor exploitation, and so on, maximizes constraints in all aspects of their everyday lives. To ensure their freedom from such extreme conditions it is sometimes considered better to bring them individually or as part of a small group through the underground railroads to safer places such as South Korea, European countries, and North America, where they can claim refugee status; this is what some individual missionaries or organizations, like Pastor Chun's Durihana, Inc., do. However, this has become more complicated as a large number of North Korean refugees are women who, in addition to having been sold as brides to Chinese men, are also either pregnant or have borne children in such relationships.[19] According to the *White Paper on Human Rights in North Korea 2013* (Korea Institute for National Unification 2013), the number of children borne of North Korean refugees in northeast China is about 20,000.

I witnessed how Biblical teachings, such as the admonitions for "young women to love their husbands and children" and to work in the home, being "kind, and submissive to their own husbands" (Titus 2: 4–5), are used to legitimize the restricted lives of North Korean refugee women vis-à-vis their child(ren) in China. Even a US-based NGO was encouraging North Korean women, once they had married a Chinese man, to stay in China instead of helping them to escape to South Korea or other places where they might go, if illegally. The "mother" subjectivity often obscures their victim identities (individual undocumented refugees and victims of human rights violations), although they have no legal protection (marriage with a Chinese man cannot grant any legal status to undocumented North Korean women). Maternal instincts and sense of duty are added to the already extreme conditions in which these women are nevertheless struggling to negotiate a better position in appropriating the trope of "runaway." The following vignettes document the case of North Korean Christian women who were trapped in such situations.[20]

While giving me a ride from a city bus terminal to a village about 200 miles from the North Korean border, Pastor Chang, a Korean-Chinese in his 50s, requested that I not say anything positive about the lives of North Korean refugees living in South Korea to the villagers I would meet. Chang serves as a minister in the Korean-Chinese church, which is separate from the village's Han-Chinese church. In this Han-Chinese dominated village, 0.8 percent of inhabitants are Korean-Chinese, while 0.2 percent are other ethnic minorities. Originally, the number of North Korean brides was 25 or so, all of whom were married to relatively poorer Han- or Korean-Chinese peasants in the village. Each of them was a member of Pastor Chang's church. In the past few years, however, five women had "run away," enticed by a South Korean missionary to move to South Korea. With anger Pastor Chang said, "That man may be celebrated as a hero among South Korean Christian activists, but here in my village, he is a bastard who betrayed me and destroyed families." By his account, the missionary's "human rights rescue" activity and the North Korean women's "journey" toward freedom were really a crime that destroyed families in the name of heartless, selfish escape. Since then, he added that the villagers no longer welcomed but had become hostile to South Korean visitors. In the meantime, the remaining North Korean women in the village wanted to know how their "runaway" friends lived in South Korea. Interestingly, the Korean term "runaway" (*tomang kanda*) became a tool that the North Korean women could use for leverage in improving their positions in both the domestic sphere and within the village.

For instance, previously violent husbands and family members began treating the North Korean brides better in order to keep them in the family and within the village boundary. Sook, in her mid-30s, had fled from her first husband and family, who had treated her "worse than an animal" and by whom she was "frequently beaten, threatened with death." She was rescued by her current church network and remarried to a Korean-Chinese man who was much nicer, though with a minor mental handicap. When Sook became a leading lay member of the church, her husband also converted. Like a shadow, he followed her from home to church for dawn and evening prayers every day, partly in fear of her possibly running away.

The term runaway was also used by the women themselves as a grave threat or warning aimed at their husbands, in particular to obtain something they deemed necessary, such as better treatment or the right to attend church. Another North Korean woman, Myung-sun, told me that she could attend church regularly after she threatened her Han-Chinese husband by saying, "If you won't allow me to go [to church], I'll run away." In the same vein, adults in the village were known to say, "Your mother may run away" as a way to control children's behavior. As it is a woeful concern for a child to imagine a mother's potential flight at night, the choice to use the metaphor of "runaway" engendered an ethical dilemma for the North Korean women as well.

Within the course of my conversation with Myung-sun at her house, her nine-year-old daughter kept coming into the yard and peeking through the open windows. Myung-sun explained, "She is really afraid that I might run away all of a sudden, leaving her behind." "Have you ever tried before?" I asked. "My daughter has never let me stay alone. At night, when sleeping she wakes up from time to time and checks that I am with her, sometimes she even ties her leg to mine." Although she did not answer whether she had attempted to flee, her account implied that she had at least spoken of the possibility. Indeed, given her living conditions, I would not have been surprised. Although many North Korean women crossed the Sino–North Korean border to survive famine, most of them had high school educations and had high self-esteem and dignity as "children of the Supreme Leader Father Kim Il-sung." Myung-sun grew up in a decent family just as average North Koreans had in the past, but now she lived in a thatched-roof house with two small bedrooms, a tiny kitchen, and an attached dirt stable. Except for the flat screen TV set, which was the newest household item, all the surfaces of the house were uneven; the thatched-roof looked as if it would collapse with the first heavy rain of the coming summer season; the home's interior mud walls were patched with magazines and school texts, and had numerous cracks from top to bottom. Even the floor we were sitting on, and where she would sleep with her daughter at night, was bumpy.

Based on her gray hair, wrinkles, and missing molars, I guessed she was about ten years older than me; but in reality she and I were the same age. She stated that her husband, his father, and two younger brothers had spent all their money and borrowed from relatives some ten years prior in order to procure her marriage, making her the most costly possession of the family. As such, she was expected to reproduce the family and had a daughter. Thanks to her management, the family debts had been paid and she had saved enough money to renovate the house. However, just several months before renovations would have started, she was able to contact her family in North Korea for the first time in years and sent them nearly all the cash she had. "I didn't come to China only for myself," she said, "but for my family members left in North Korea. For the first time, I finally reached my family and knew that they were in a desperate situation so I sent some, actually a lot, of money that I had. I didn't tell my family [in China] that. If they knew, maybe I . . . ." She was unable finish this last sentence. Omitting, evading, and silencing are common among North Korean refugees when being interviewed, particularly on the subject of future plans or expectations that are always uncertain and insecure. She was the mother of a daughter who needed her and the daughter of a mother who was unwell, starving, and fragile. Now her life burdens were multiplied by her intention to take care of her North Korean family who desperately needed her financial support.[21] As a powerless and stateless migrant,[22] her mundane position was extremely marginalized when coupled with transnational family obligations.

This situation is different from the model used by Kelly Chong (2006), which sheds light on South Korean women's reintegration into the South Korean patriarchic family structure through conversion to Christianity and devotion to church activities. Outside of church-going, few or no alternatives are available for married women to resist Chinese male dominance, except for actually running away. For the North Korean women in this poor rural Chinese village, gaining a little more power within the structure of male-dominated family relations through church serves as a means to "agentively submit" (Mahmood 2001) themselves in the asymmetrical intra-ethnic relationship with South Korean missionaries and Korean-Chinese caregivers (e.g., pastors and missionaries) in China. This is due in part to the fact that the actual practice of "running away" is sometimes made possible through the church (as shown in the previous cases of five women runaways assisted by the South Korean missionary Mr Kim). It is also the asymmetrical nature of a relationship that tends to stimulate the refugees to long for that better life in South Korea that they had felt was inevitable after leaving North Korea.

Conclusion

Illegal or limited status, chronic poverty, hard labor, domestic violence, trafficking, deportation, imprisonment, sexual/physical abuse, family obligations to both a current Chinese family and those in North Korea, and much more were the circumstances in which most North Korean women found themselves for years in China. Such structural conditions and moral burdens aggravated their marginal position, while at the same time pushing them to seek alternatives. One highly viable option was provided by and through churches, which are plural as aforementioned.

Thus far, this chapter has attempted to contextualize the processes of North Korean refugees' Christian conversion and its contested meanings in the Sino–North Korean border area. By bringing religion and the claim to religious membership into the human rights discourses in which states and international regimes are involved, this research has highlighted the politicization and criminalization of Christian contact and conversion by human rights discourses and state forces. The second part of the chapter approached churches as intra-ethnic contact zones in which North Korean religiosity was likely to be "measured" and rarely granted "full" status according to such asymmetrical structures of intra-ethnic relations. The last part reconsidered theories of North Korean women's victimization in light of the structural and moral burdens that such marginalized married women were dealing with. For married North Korean women, church-going had multiple meanings, with the church serving as a means and end for some married women to empower themselves in the Chinese male-dominated family structure while allowing them to endure spiritual-moral burdens and ever growing economic-political obstacles.

The intention behind using an emic approach to the terms of religious freedom, "almost" born-again, and runaway that appeared in different vignettes is not to categorize or define, but rather to elaborate the complexity and dynamics of the matter of conversion among North Korean refugees who interact with their South Korean and Korean-Chinese counterparts. What might these documented vignettes drive us to consider about the nature of North Korean missionizing? Note that South Korean churches tend to appreciate North Korean refugees as potential first unifiers who serve as a "litmus test" in the experiment of face-to-face missionizing and the expectation of further spiritual revival in the North. On the ground, however, the projected identification of refugees is contested and compelled through actual human interactions. As both individual and social events and, in my view, passages and processes, it is necessary to reflect that the conversion of North Koreans to Christianity is a complex series of negotiations with such obstacles as South Korean-centric nationalism, lack of cross-cultural recognition, and historical antagonisms.

4
Heroes and Citizens: Becoming North Koreans in the South

"Why do they keep coming to our country? There are people dying of hunger here. They just receive our taxes," said a man who was sitting right next to our table at the restaurant to his friend. The TV was broadcasting that a group of North Koreans was arriving at Inchon international airport. I found myself shaking with anger and wanting to yell at him. But I felt too terrible to do so.

(*Kŭmhee ŭi yŏhaeng: Aojiesŏ Sŏulkkaji 7,000km* (Kŭm-hee's Journey: From Aoji to Seoul 7,000km), 2007: 213–214 (my translation))

The previous chapter shed light on the multilayers of plight and coping strategies of undocumented North Korean migrants in the Sino–North Korean border area, where they seek to reconstruct familial, social, and divine ties. Their networks are fragile, or in Mark Granovetter's term (1973, 1983) weak, and they are often desperate under the insecure local conditions in which there is no legal protection granted to them. However, these weak ties work strongly for some migrant individuals and families who take the underground railroads for better and safer lives via Mongolia, Vietnam, Cambodia, Laos, Thailand, and Beijing, to name a few routes toward South Korea and some western countries. This chapter is devoted to investigating their initial period of resettlement and transition in South Korea, with particular focus on North Korean identity politics and resettlement programs promoted by the South Korean state in a broader historical perspective. It aims to provide a retrospective look at the characteristics of ethnic nationalism and identity politics as lived experiences of increasing number of North Korean migrants in South

Korea where multiculturalism discourses have emerged as a new norm. The fact that the nation is depicted as and believed to be predominantly homogenous must be taken into account with respect to the geopolitical specificity of North–South Korean relations (Choe 2007; Park 2009). I argue that Korean ethnicity should not be taken for granted as a self-evident unit with a homogenous culture and identity, but rather as a product of the complex social processes of boundary making (Wimmer 2009). It is right to stress that North Korean subjectivities have been shaped through performances of individual and national imaginations and negotiations that are quintessential to modern nation-building in Korean history.

The transition of newcomers from the North into South Korean capitalist society has been evaluated as unsuccessful in the mass media and scholarly studies. For instance, between 2006 and 2013, about 10 percent, approximately 2,000, of the total number of North Koreans in South Korea re-migrated to western countries such as the United Kingdom, the United States, Canada, Germany, Belgium, and Norway (Chung 2014). In addition, there are a handful of North Koreans returning to the North and participating in anti-South Korean propaganda.[1] It is worth stressing that North Korean migrants' issues have always been considered part of a long-term reunification policy intimately associated with an assumption of what a post-division citizenship should and would look like in South Korea. Accordingly, a sizable number of sociological studies and survey reports investigate problems that hinder the migrants from safely adjusting in their new home nation, that is, South Korea.

Some have pointed out that one of the main causes of their maladjustment is not rooted in their lack of will to adjust to the capitalist system, but in South Korean society where social discrimination against them is prevalent (Jeon 2000; Chung et al. 2006; Jung, Son & Lee 2013). Other intellectuals have addressed the potential problems of Korean ethnic nationalism, which is by no means singular, in terms of how it ignores not only internal cultural differences (e.g., Grinker 1998; Kwon 2000), but also multicultural values that encourage appreciating other ethnicities and customs. Following Bhikhu Parekh (2000), sociologist Myoung-Kyu Park (2009) asserts the necessity for a "spirit of multiculturalism" in the reunification process.[2] This self-reflexive and critical view proposes that the South Korean public be more rational and tolerant to the presence of "others," including the recent flow of North Koreans, and also reflect on the enduring state-led developmentalist nationalism on the other.

The South Korean government's support system for North Korean migrants reflects the state policy direction. There is little doubt that it also works as a crucial motive for the majority of the migrants deciding to migrate to South Korea, and intimately determines the conditions of their initial period of resettlement (Jin, Lee & Kim 2009). Considering North Korean migrants' subject-making processes, I highlight the ways in which they become depoliticized in the state domain and discourses. After they arrive in South Korea, the government's settlement program mobilizes North Korean migrants as "regular citizens," who are productive, creative, self-sufficient, and shaped to survive the neo-liberal market economy. Concurrently, they are positioned in an imagined reunified nation. In other words, the newcomers are projected as citizens of such an imaginary world, expected to be model first-generation unifiers.

In light of the migrants' identity in an imagined nation, I take inspiration from the concept of "figured worlds" found in *Identity and Agency in Cultural Worlds* by Dorothy Holland et al. (1998),[3] which "rest[s] upon people's abilities to form and be formed in collectively realized 'as if' realms.... People's identities and agency are formed dialectically and dialogically in these 'as if' worlds" (Holland et al. 1998: 49). While still being positioned in an increasingly competitive capitalist society in which they are expected to assimilate, it is a culturally and historically figured unified nation for which they are either silenced or narrating. I argue that within these "webs of power linked to nation-state and civil society" (Ong 1996: 738), however, they tend to remain as "Other" situated in a virtual world (Table 4.1).

Heroes to burdens

On February 25, 1983, Lee Ung-pyŏng defected from North Korea by flying a MIG-19 fighter jet to the South, leaving his entire family behind. The South Korean Chun Doo-hwan regime, which had taken office by coup d'état, took this opportunity to display its political and moral legitimacy over North Korea.[4] A few months later, on a rainy day in April, Lee cried "Long Live South Korea!" (*Taehanmin'guk manse!*) at Yoido Square where there was a welcoming ceremony combined with an anticommunist convention, with around two million people holding umbrellas and pickets proclaiming "Let's smash communists!"

Over 20 years later, North Korean newcomers in the airport were reluctant to show their faces, and wore masks instead. While Lee Ung-pyŏng held public press interviews, few of the later newcomers allowed

73

Table 4.1 Statistics for North Koreans in South Korea

Numbers of North Korean migrants in South Korea by year (up to December 2014)

	~1998	~2001	2002	2003	2004	2005	2006	2007	2008	2009	2010	2011	2012	2013	2014 (estimate)	Total
Male	831	565	510	474	626	424	515	573	608	662	591	795	404	369	304	8,251
Female	116	478	632	811	1,272	960	1,513	1,981	2,195	2,252	1,811	1,911	1,098	1,145	1,092	19,267
Total	947	1,043	1,142	1,285	1,898	1,384	2,028	2,554	2,803	2,914	2,402	2,706	1,502	1,514	1,396	27,518
Proportion of female migrants	12%	46%	55%	63%	67%	69%	75%	78%	78%	77%	75%	70%	72%	76%	78%	70%

Numbers of North Korean migrants in South Korea by age (August 2014)

	0–9 yr	10–19 yr	20–29 yr	30–39 yr	40–49 yr	50–59 yr	Over 60 yr	Total
Male	587	1,503	2,224	1,918	1,161	433	308	8,314
Female	590	1,781	5,378	6,105	3,242	983	867	18,946
Total	1,177	3,284	7,602	8,023	4,403	1,416	1,175	27,080

Table 4.1 (Continued)

Former occupations in North Korea of North Korean migrants (August 2014)

	Managerial	Military	Laborer	Unemployed	Service	Art & Sports	Professional	N/A (youth, etc.)	Other	Total
Male	335	613	3,503	2,981	69	69	198	299	67	8,134
Female	104	95	6,825	10,027	981	159	374	266	115	18,946
Total	439	708	10,328	13,008	1,050	228	572	565	182	27,080

Education received in North Korea of North Korean migrants (August 2014)

	Preschool	Kindergarten (2 years)	Elementary (4 years)	Middle (6 years)	College (3 years)	University and post-graduate (4 years +)	Unschooled	Other	Total
Male	387	116	712	4,962	690	896	347	24	8,134
Female	366	157	1,102	13,981	1,833	971	455	81	18,946
Total	753	273	1,814	18,943	2,523	1,867	802	105	27,080

Home provinces in North Korea of North Korean migrants (August 2014)

	Kangwon	Namp'o	Yanggang	Chakang	Pyŏngnam	Pyŏngbuk	Pyungyang	Hamnam	Hambuk	Hwangnam	Hwangbuk	Kaesung	Other	Total
Male	206	59	977	62	402	342	318	723	4,513	251	158	44	79	8,134
Female	309	66	2,302	116	535	387	219	1,717	12,791	161	221	26	96	18,946
Total	515	125	3,279	178	937	729	537	2,440	17,304	412	379	70	175	27,080

Source: Ministry of Unification, ROK, http://www.unikorea.go.kr/content.do?cmsid=1518.

researchers or reporters to take their pictures or write down their real names or even their ages. They worried about their family left in China or North Korea who might be arrested or even punished with death. In order to avoid this, they usually hoped to bring the rest of their family members to South Korea.

While Lee brought an MIG-19 fighter jet and classified secrets that the South Korean regime valued at the time, these newcomers bring nothing but their own bodies and stories of how they have undergone famine, atrocities, sexual abuse, labor imprisonment, and family separation in North Korea and/or China. These are not valuable and are unwelcomed by the state. While Lee was awarded about 1.3 billion Korean Won (1.4 million USD) in compensation, which was about 480 times the average annual income of South Koreans in 1983,[5] and continued his profession with the South Korean Air Force, most newcomers today end up having temporary or part-time jobs. More significantly, these new-comers seldom or never tell their southern counterparts that they are from North Korea, due to the fear of being seen as strange (*pyŏlnage bonda*) and being discriminated against in the job market (for adults) or at school (for young people). Subtle differences in speaking and behaving often become remarkably significant markers that occasion real fear and discrimination.

For early "heroes" like Lee, however, there is an irony. For example, Lee was celebrated as a national hero and his life was guaranteed by the state, but the rest of his family, left behind in North Korea, were allegedly persecuted.[6] This led to South Korean civilians perceiving these defectors as inhumane, selfish, and spiteful: "How cruel are they to leave their wives and children, parents and siblings behind for only themselves?," "Do not trust them because they once betrayed and would betray again," and "They just keep demanding without working hard," are a few examples of major discriminative prejudices levied against northerners by southerners (Yang & Chung 2008). This distrustful cultural bias has been conjoined with a reproach from the leftist and progressive forces that accused North Koreans of collaborating with the authoritarian regimes (Chung 2008). These kinds of negative cultural biases persist and newcomers are likely encounter them in South Korea, adding to other stresses felt by the migrants, such as being psychologically depressed, having feelings of alienation, and/or finding it difficult to have a sense of belonging in South Korea (Yang & Chung 2008). Meanwhile, the political meanings of "anticommunist national heroes" have gradually faded away, as has the cash compensation awarded by the state.

Andrei Lankov (2006) argues that the difficulties North Korean migrants face in the adjustment process in South Korea are mainly caused by two factors. First, he points out that the South Korean government "has moved to the policy of quietly discouraging" (2006: 107) the migration of northerners from high-ranking backgrounds by decreasing cash rewards in favor of normalizing the relationship with the North Korean regime; and second, the recent "defectors" are mostly from working class backgrounds and are not in a position to pursue "normal" careers, and thus must rely on the low level of family welfare provided by the government support system in South Korea. While partly agreeing with his points about demographic change—increasing populations of people from working class backgrounds from mostly northern cities far from central power—and the "outdated" knowledge and skills that recent newcomers bring, I doubt his underlying principle that presumes that the North Korean regime collapse would be triggered by the mass exile of the middle and upper ruling classes. This scale of exile was partly effective in the case of German unification, but what is missing in this structural approach to understanding the former "heroes" and newcomers alike are cultural and emotional dimensions; for instance, the bitterness of life and feelings of alienation despite the economic prosperity of former "heroes."

Compared to former defectors, it is true that those who have arrived since the 1990s receive a smaller cash award and no guarantee of employment. They are mostly expected to assimilate into a neo-liberal social welfare state. Yet, unlike post-socialist Eastern Europe and post-wall Germany, the transition of former socialist North Koreans into capitalist citizens is not merely about economic life (cf. Berdahl 2005). Rather, my ethnographic data suggests that it becomes more complex and ambiguous as the newcomers encounter South Korean society, which has been conceived as their other homeland, where the state does not provide economic stability and a political meaning for life (i.e., heroes or heroines). They find themselves situated in a new order of racial boundary making, together with foreign migrants and other Korean returnees (e.g., Korean-Chinese).

In other words, as the state begins depoliticizing their presence, what the newcomers encounter on a daily basis are negative cultural biases that characterize them as being lazy, dependent, violent, and ignorant burdens; at the same time, South Koreans feel sympathetic towards them. Their being is still symbolically valued in envisioning a possible reunification of two Koreas. Korean scholars and critics nearly always stress the importance of understanding the migrants first as unifiers who would or should work for the reunification of two Koreas on the one hand, while acknowledging the cultural differences of the two Koreas on the other (Chung B. 2006; Jeon 2007; Chung 2008; Yoon 2009).

What follows is a brief analytical summary of the changing meanings given by the state to North Korean migrants in South Korea.[7] In his seminal article, Byung-Ho Chung (2009) divides the northerners into six groups according to their social definitions.[8] With reference to his categorization of the changing definitions, I divide them into three categories: anticommunist heroes, defecting compatriots, and new settlers. The first period of "heroes" was much longer than the latter ones; the number of the migrants has explosively increased since the mid-1990s when the North suffered from a great famine, and reached 25,000 as of 2012. South Korean civil societies organized campaigns for North Korean famine relief, followed by peace campaigns for understanding North Korea beyond the Cold War; the 1997 Asian crisis, commonly called the IMF crisis by South Koreans, also occurred in this period. It is worth bearing in mind that both South and North Korea sought to normalize their relationship while undergoing severe crisis as a consequence of the changing global climate—the collapse of the socialist bloc and the world economic crisis.

Anticommunist warriors (1945–1993)

The North and South Korean states governed their subjects and determined what type of access the individuals and families had to the rights, benefits, and resources the state grants to full citizens. Countless dissidents in both states were persecuted and the rights and opportunities of their family members and relatives were restricted through the guilt-by-association system in the Cold War era. This guilt-by-association system was allegedly officially abolished in the 1980s, but effectively existed in security screening until recently in South Korea.

South Korean modern nation-building was equivalent to a project of constructing "proper" politico-cultural citizens who were ready to serve and protect "our nation" from communism and communists ("Reds"), and by devoting themselves to national economic development. Such masculine, militant, and anticommunist norms of good citizenship have been perpetuated as the modality of modern South Korea through division politics, which Soo-Jung Lee refers to as "South Korea's competition with and negation of the legitimacy of North Korea based on the ideology of anticommunism" (2006: 2).

The northerners who emerged at the birth of national division[9] have been shaped by this doctrine of anticommunist citizen-subject making.

Their physical appearance and the anticommunist propaganda lecturing tours they carried out for the state constructed North Korean stereotypes among South Koreans. In addition, their socio-cultural status in South Korea has depended heavily on the government's legal and administrative support system. The state played the role of "a strong cultural and political actor" (Kelleher 2004: 19) in the making of northerner subjectivities in South Korea.

Referring again to Byung-Ho Chung's (2008) social classification of northerners, I consider the first three of his six groups as being made into and becoming anticommunist warriors.

System selective migrants are people who fled from the socialist North to the South at the dawn of national division between 1945 and 1950. They were called "Crossers to the South" (*wolnamin*), and the village they settled in, in Seoul, was called "Liberation village" (*Haebangch'on*). War refugees (*p'inanmin*) consisted of approximately 650,000 northerners who moved down to the South during the Korean War (1950–1953). They became "synonymous with 'Christians' and 'Anti-communists'" (Chung 2008: 9). These two groups comprised the first generation of northerners and together are known as *Silhyangmin*, or displaced people. Soo-Jung Lee articulates that "*Silhyangmin* have been publicly produced as 'enunciating subjects' 'who speak for the anticommunist state'" (2006: 4).[10]

In the decades between 1962 and 1993, a small number of defectors fled the North. Called "heroes who returned to the state" (*Kwisun yongsa*), they began receiving special treatment and financial rewards, as the then-militant Park Jung-hee regime set up the Special Relief Act for Patriots and Heroes Who Returned to the State. They were treated similarly to the patriots of independence movements, and taken care of by the Ministry of Patriots and Veterans Affairs. The amount of the award, *borogeum*, increased if one brought weapons and valuable information. Before 1993, however, the number of "heroic defectors" was no larger than ten per year, and the financial burden on the government for compensating them was not that heavy.

The images of "heroic defectors" published in the mass media during this period had a great influence on South Koreans' apprehension of the stereotype of the "poor, starved, and oppressed" North Korean; namely, they thought that North Korean defectors should wear a shabby military uniform or outdated clothes (Kang 2006). When they reappeared in public for press conferences or special anticommunist lectures sometime after arriving, their physical appearance demonstrated a clear "before and after," since they were now dressed in suits. Their bodies were a marker of "poor" communist North Korea where they were oppressed and starved, and a converted emblem of "modern and superior" South Korea.

Also, the anticommunist propaganda lecturing tours most defectors had to carry out, aimed at South Korean audiences, contributed in part to reproducing the "Red complex" and anticommunism. Lee Sang-soo (1992) discovered that some of the "heroes" coming to the South in the 1960s–1970s had lectured, on average, 4,000–8,000 times by the early 1990s. The content of the lectures reflected how the South Korean militant regime wanted to portray the North Korean socialist regime: namely as warmongers, and brutal "Reds," and citizens who were "living on thin gruel" (*Kangnaengijuk*), deprived of all agency and basic freedoms[11] (Lee 1992). They performed in the vocabulary and grammar of the "division language" (Chŏn 2000).

The format and content of their lectures were largely managed by national security agents. However there were times when they happened to tell or show a "truth" that gave a positive impression about the North while answering questions from audience members. For example, Lee Sang-soo (1992) introduces an episode that Mr M experienced. Mr M had some of his family members' color photos. A national security agent took them from him, asking, "How are there color photos in the North?" But Mr M was able to keep secret one of his sister's photos. One day he went to lecture before college students and there was a female student who asked many questions about everyday North Korean life in detail. To aid in answering the questions, he showed his sister's color photo to the audience. As a result, after the lecture, the agent investigated his house once more and confiscated his last photo.

Many of these speakers developed a "fluency" in delivering these scripted speeches thousands of times. The false and misleading information that they relayed slowly transformed into a kind of truth, and in this way they became agents of creating a false reality which was eventually discovered to be wrong. For example, Mr Kim, who came to the South in 1999, once told me,

> I realized that there were some imposters among famous North Korean lecturers. For instance, one man has been saying for years that "there is no ancestral worship allowed in North Korea. No other than Kim Il-sung can be worshiped, so if one did such things, all his family would be persecuted," things like that. I was perplexed to hear that while in the audience with other South Koreans. It was because my family continued to do such traditions every year, and I lived in

Pyong-yang. He was lying before me, but I was not able to offend him, because it might hurt our [North Korean] image before South Koreans.

Nonetheless, what the "heroes" did became a conventional life trajectories that the newcomers tended to follow. Initially, the so-called anticommunism lectures were, for some heroes, their main income source and almost a mandatory national duty to compensate for the support of the South Korean state (*Yonhap News* 2007). Either scheduled by the government or other conservative civil organizations, some "famous" lecturers continued to be invited and paid for their lectures. Subsequently, the format of the testimonies became a specific genre that South Korean audiences became familiar with, and that North Korean border crossers were expected to perform before their audiences.

Brethren settlers (1993–1997)

I turn now to the changing definitions and support systems of the government since the 1990s. The fall of the Berlin Wall and the collapse of the Soviet Union led to the post-Cold War era in world history. Such a historical transformation awakened the South Korean people to the fact that the Korean peninsula remained the last divided nation. Although some Marxist activists leading social movements for democracy and unification were perplexed by losing a socialist model nation-state, the popular desire for peace in the peninsula transcended previous concerns about ideological competition with socialism.

The first civilian president after consecutive militant regimes in South Korean history, Kim Young-sam, promoted a unification policy of "peaceful cooperation and reconciliation" with the North Korean regime, and emphasized human rights and quality of life improvements, humanitarian food aid, and economic cooperation. The North Korean migrant issue was situated within this unification policy, and this administration did not want the migrant issue to disturb the inter-Korean relationship. In a sense, the Kim Young-sam administration's policy toward the migrants was unstable. In the case of North Korean wood-cutters in Russia who wanted to be exiled to South Korea, Kim Young-sam denied their request, reflecting his "selective" acceptance policy.

However, as the North Korean economic situation worsened and the country faced a devastating famine, the number of North Koreans crossing into China in search of food increased at a rapid pace. The number of those who continued on to South Korea also increased.

While most defectors in the previous decades were from relatively elite groups like government officials, party members, or military officials, the new migrants were from less privileged social groups including factory workers, farmers, women, and even young adults, which demonstrated how the North Korean food distribution system had collapsed (Chung 2003). The following illustrates how policies for migrants have changed since the Kim Young-sam administration.

"North Korean brethren who returned to the state" (*Kwisun tongp'o*) became the term used to refer to North Koreans who came to South Korea between 1993 and 1997. The Kim Young-sam administration enacted the Act to Protect North Korean Brethren Who Returned to the State in 1993, after which the newcomers became treated as economic refugees, and the government division in charge changed from the Ministry of Patriots and Veterans Affairs to the then-named Ministry of Health and Society. During this time, the government subsidy for housing and settlement was reduced so that each individual received about 7,000 USD for resettlement and about 8,400 USD for housing.

The change in supplements implied that the previous act was established to lure potential defectors as a way of competing with the North. Kim Sang-gyun underscores this aspect of the previous act that "promoted regime and other political propaganda, and its main targets are spies, soldiers from the North and etc. And the services including excessive reward and so on given to them are too much" (1994: 47–48, cited in Yoon 2001: 291, 11n).

Combined with the change in political climate, the principle of equity in this issue arose. That is, the newcomers were now supported by the welfare system in which they were given parity to South Korean low-income citizens (*Yŏngsemin*). However, the term "returned to the state" (*Kwisun*) implied political defection, while the term "brethren" (*tongp'o*) reflected a symbolic victory appealing to South Koreans—as if "we" South Koreans should welcome with affection our "brethren" who went through difficulties under the "outdated" socialist North. However the reality of this change was harsh for the new "brethren."

Ambivalence arose as a result of the new definitions (*Kwisun*) and the little support that northerners were given by the government. The new arrivals during this period underwent serious adjustment problems—unemployment, poverty, and social discrimination. Contrary to their expectations, the "brethren" were no longer "protected" by the state and half of them were unemployed (Song 1996). In addition to material poverty, culture shock, and psychological loneliness, feelings of guilt impeded their social adjustment process. Moreover, the North

Korean famine caused an increase in border crossers in the Sino–North Korean border area and the South Korean government needed to consider a better support system for the newcomers (Yoon 2001; Chung 2008).

Struggling for definition (1997–2007)

Over the past ten years, the North Korean population in the South has changed tremendously. Above all, the state has come to see the issue of North Korean migrants in the context of long-term plans for national reunification. The Ministry of Unification took over the matter from the Ministry of Health and Society. The Kim Dae-jung administration (1998–2002) tried to maintain a balance between the normalization of inter-Korean relations and support systems/programs for the newcomers. Since this book is primarily concerned with the migrants who have emerged since the mid-to-late 1990s, I will first discuss some definitions and then examine the meanings of the state contact zone.

The first definition is for "residents who escaped from North Korea" (*pukhanit'alchumin*) (in use between 1997 and 2004). In 1997 the Act for the Protection and Resettlement Support for the Residents Who Escaped from North Korea was passed. Based on this Act, the Hanawon (House of Unity) was established in January 1999 as a government settlement center, operated by the Ministry of Unification. As such, the South Korean government support system for the newcomers became part of long-term plans for national unification. The Kim Dae-jung administration provided about 36,000 USD per adult for settlement. While the government officially and legally defined them as *pukhanit'alchumin*, *t'alpukcha* began to be used more often in civil society and mass media. *T'alpukcha*, or North Korean defector, tends to refer to both those who came via another country, like China or Russia, and those who arrived directly in the South.

The appellation *Saet'ŏmin* (2005–present) emerged when the Roh Moo-hyun administration tried to neutralize the terminology used for newcomers from the North. *Saet'ŏmin*, which was chosen through a popular contest, means "new settlers." The government decided on the name change because *t'alpukcha*, which has been the term most widely used, implied two negative nuances. *T'alpuk* implies political escape from the North; *cha* is a suffix from a classical Chinese noun (zhě, 者) that is translated as "nom" in Korean. "Nom" meant ordinary people in the pre-modern period, but it became a derisive moniker. For the same reason, *changaecha*, "the disabled," was changed to *changaein* since *in* is from *saram*, meaning "people."

South Korean conservatives and some North Korean activists working to change the North Korean regime rejected the new term. Instead they preferred *t'alpukcha* (North Korean defector) or *chayuichumin* (free migrant). In the meantime, shortly after beginning their new life, considerable numbers of newcomers spent large amounts of their resettlement money to pay off brokers and to bring the rest of their family members from North Korea or China to South Korea. Many lost their money to swindlers. As a result, the government decided to distribute the settlement money over longer periods of time.

Wolnamin, P'inanmin, Silhyangmin, Kwisun yongsa, Kwisun tongp'o, Pukhanit'alchumin, T'alpukcha, and *Saetŏmin* are the terms that the South Korean state has used to officially conceptualize North Korean border crossers who have settled or want to settle in South Korea. Not merely legal terminologies, these terms reflect the politics of Korean state nationalisms.

This genealogy of conceptualizations about the northerners shows us the ways in which political meanings have been potently bound in the making of the northerners' subjectivity by the state. For decades, they were "enunciating subjects" (Lee (2006)'s *Silhyangmin* case) serving the anticommunist state. They were "performing" as anticommunist lecturers, performing what the state wanted to tell and show about North Korea.

Accordingly, the different appellations changed over time and reflected the differences in the state compensation that was essential to the social adjustment of North Koreans. Andrei Lankov asserts that the previous "heroes" could adjust to South Korean society more easily than current defectors because they came from the North Korean elite (he stresses that this was "inevitable" because of the North Korean Stalinist border control system which allowed no illegal penetration, and only high-ranking officers had access to the border area) (Lankov 2006). Immigrant individuals' adaptability, based on former social experiences and education, is considered to be an important asset but more significant should be a host country's willingness to accommodate it. In this respect, it is the state that has exerted an enormous impact on the newcomers' success in their initial period of social adjustment in the South (Figure 4.1).

IMF crisis, sunshine policy, and "new settlers"

The purpose of this Act is to provide such matters relating to protection and support as are necessary to help North Korean residents

escaping from the area North of the Military Demarcation Line (here-
inafter referred to as 'North Korea') and desiring protection from
the Republic of Korea, as quickly as possible to adapt themselves
to, and settle down in, all spheres of their lives, including political,
economic, social and cultural spheres.

(Article 1 (Purpose), Act on the Protection and Settlement Support
of Residents escaping from North Korea)

As aforementioned, the South Korean government settlement support
system has shifted its main purpose from "protection" to "focusing on
capacity building for independence rather than on material support"
(Suh 2002: 71). The notions of self-support (*chahwal*) and self-reliance
(*charip*) emerged as the main goal of the system, which is designed
as part of long-term plans for nation unification. The Ministry of
Unification has begun to deal with North Korean migrant issues as
humanitarian concerns (*indojŏk munje*). The newcomers from the North
are distinctive as the only group receiving a special package of benefits,
including legal and social support from the state, that access to which
is somewhat restricted for other Korean diasporas, such as Korean-
Chinese, Koreans from the former Soviet Union, and Korean-Japanese.[12]
This is a result of policy, which deals with the issue of migration strictly
within the frame of national unification. I will now examine the ways in
which the government humanitarian project "silences" the migrants for
the purpose of normalizing an inter-Korean relationship in a changing
politico-economic context.

While natural disasters devastated the North with a great famine in
the mid-to-late 1990s, in 1997 South Korea was facing the so-called IMF
crisis. Survey data shows that over 80 percent of the South Korean population expected the newly elected President Kim Dae-jung, a former
dissident against the past authoritarian regimes, to give priority to overcoming the crisis while only 2 percent of the people were concerned
with national reunification (Paik 2009: 283, f.14).

But Kim Dae-jung blended the two tasks as a means to break through
the crisis. Following the IMF standard, the Kim Dae-jung regime began
promoting neo-liberal reforms in the financial and business sectors in
Korea, and simultaneously promoted the normalization of an inter-
Korean relationship. This was the "Sunshine Policy,"[13] aimed at achieving peace on the Korean peninsula, in favor of overcoming the debt
crisis at a rapid pace. It also opened up an era of neo-liberal post-division
South Korea. While putting enormous efforts into the normalization
of the inter-Korean relationship, the Kim Dae-jung administration

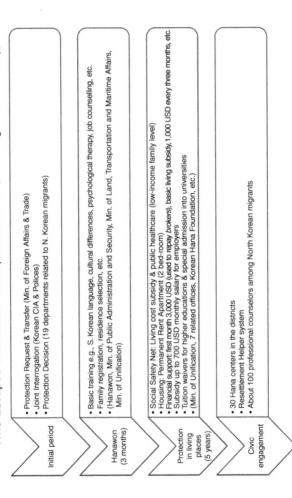

S. Korean Government's Support System

- The Act for the Protection and Resettlement Support for the Residents Who Escaped from North Korea (Initiated in 1997, Kim Yŏng-sam Presidency)

Initial period
- Protection Request & Transfer (Min. of Foreign Affairs & Trade)
- Joint Interrogation (Korean CIA & Polices)
- Protection Decision (19 departments related to N. Korean migrants)

Hanawon (3 months)
- Basic training e.g., S. Korean language, cultural differences, psychological therapy, job counselling, etc.
- Family registration, residence selection, etc.
- (Hanawon, Min. of Public Administration and Security, Min. of Land, Transportation and Maritime Affairs, Min. of Unification)

Protection in living places (5 years)
- Social Safety Net: Living cost subsidy & public healthcare (low-income family level)
- Housing: Permanent Rent Apartment (2 bed-room)
- Financial support: first month 3,000 USD (used to repay brokers), basic living subsidy 1,000 USD every three months, etc.
- Subsidy up to 700 USD monthly salary for employers
- Tuition waivers for higher educations & special admission into universities (Min. of Unification, 7 related offices, Korean Hana Foundation, etc.)

Civic engagement
- 30 Hana centers in the districts
- Resettlement Helper system
- About 100 professional counselors among North Korean migrants

Figure 4.1 The South Korean government's support system for North Korean migrants

Source: Ministry of Unification, Republic of Korea, http://www.unikorea.go.kr/content.do?cmsid=1442. Modified by the Author.

launched a new support system for the growing number of North Korean newcomers. Stated simply, the Kim Dae-jung regime accepted all North Koreans who wanted to come to the South via a third country, but depoliticized the issue. That was a great improvement over the previous Kim Young-sam regime that selectively received migrants. Beginning with an examination of the government-controlled initial settlement process for the migrants upon their arrival in the South, I will elaborate the ways in which North Korean migrants become a homogeneous entity of new settlers who are expected to live in a particular way "now" and in the "future"—a government-figured world which is, however, less concrete owing to the mixture of new welfare standards and some remnants of the Cold War legacy in the operation procedure.

Recoding the settlement process

The state controlled settlement process for the newcomers is comprised of an interrogation system that evolved over decades in the context of the Cold War, and a neo-liberal administrative system that is designed to increase policy efficiency in practice. As a social field, nonetheless, the process is a series of human interactions that is embodied through narratives and bodily and facial expressions.

North and South Korean interactions reveal unexpected cultural differences caused by a half-century long national division. Thus the feelings towards and understandings of one another are accompanied by broader discourses of human dignity, humanitarianism, and pan-Korean nationalism. However, those metaphysical languages are simply translated into the everyday vocabularies that in turn are explicitly "unspoken." Rather they are circulated as a form of gossip and sensed through gestures, which are often misinterpreted due to cultural differences.

The newcomer's initial period of settlement from arrival and through their stay in the state-run facilities looks somewhat different from the scenario the official government language describes. Most North Korean migrants are likely to be seized with half-fear and half-anticipation when they arrive at the South Korean international airport.[14] The feeling of fear is mixed with guilt about family members who were left behind in either North Korea or a third country, and they are faced with the uncertainty of their future in the South (Kim K. 2004). Meanwhile, they arrive expecting a new life as legal South Korean citizens, and that they no longer need to worry about raids and hunger. After passing through such dangerous obstacles, some adults may anticipate that the state would literally take care of everything.[15]

With no time to organize their feelings, they are immediately sent to the *Taesŏngkongsa*, where they are subjected to a joint interrogation. This is a border inspection station where national intelligence agents interrogate each person in order to distinguish fake or unqualified migrants (e.g., spies, criminals, or Korean-Chinese) from "real" migrants, and then classify the migrants according to the value of the information they can provide about North Korean national secrets. Thus, all migrants are encouraged to "tell the truth" and engage in the practice of confessing to the investigator in this center.

In recent years, the investigation course in the *Taesŏngkongsa* has become shorter than before. But even in the early 2000s, a large number of the migrants, no matter what their ages and genders, were likely to be treated as criminals. By 1999, some migrants were reportedly beaten, humiliated, and tortured during interrogation and stayed in the center for months.[16]

Those who pass the interrogation are sent to Hanawon where they experience more freedom than in the *Taesŏngkongsa*. When I first visited Hanawon in early 2001, there was no education program for young adults, whose numbers were multiplying at the time. All the classes were copied from the ones that had been taught in the *Taesŏngkongsa*, where they were taught only to adult defectors before Hanawon was built. As the director at the time was looking for civilian support to set up a schooling program for children and young adults, I participated in establishing the Hanadool (one two) school, which was the first civilian-run weekday program in such a highly classified government facility.[17]

Hanawon was, for me, a strange space. The area was fenced with barbed wire and guarded around the clock by two riot police companies. No civilian was allowed to come inside without an authorized appointment. The uniformed trainees were informed that the heavily armed condition was necessary to protect them from a possible North Korean terrorist attack. The rules and schedules were orderly and divided, and the trainees were managed and disciplined to be docile and obedient.

Hanawon is a space where interactions between South and North Koreans is characterized by inequality. South Korean officials who had once been proud of themselves and excited to work with the "brethren" found, after a month of working, that they had lost confidence in and were disappointed with the northerners. To them, the northerners looked opportunistic, materialistic, selfish, violent, sexually spoiled, hypocritical, and moreover—not like "us."[18]

In the same vein, the northerners were confronted with something unlike what they had imagined. When they were taken to tour Seoul, they bought tailor-made luxury suits and went up to the Hwanhwa 63

City (a.k.a. 63 Building, a skyscraper on Yeouido island) to see the prosperity of capitalist South Korea. This contributed to their feeling that
they were being treated as national heroes and heroines just as the earlier defectors had been. It seemed as if middle-class life was guaranteed
and would be realized for them (Chung 2000).

In reality, however, the majority of them were no longer politically
valued defectors, and were treated as an uncivilized "Other" in need
of being "trained" with little freedom to move. They were supposed to
follow the rules because they had yet to receive their own Korean ID.
Without holding legal citizenship, their identity, life security, present,
and future, were all uncertain and fragile.

Nonetheless, they were allowed to do many things during breaks
between lectures and on weekends at Hanawon. Frequent phone calls
to reach friends, family members, or relatives in China or even in North
Korea are common. Few care that an unauthorized attempt to contact
anyone in the North from the South is a serious violation of the National
Security Law.

Becoming familiar with the practice of consuming may be the first
exercise leading to assimilation into the market economy, though most
migrants are not totally unfamiliar with the practice of purchasing.
Even before receiving their personal Korean ID, many can hold the
most expensive cellular phone in their hands. However, most have
difficulty imagining that the first month's bill may well exceed several hundred dollars to cover all the international calls made while at
Hanawon.

In sum, the beginning of their settlement process is accompanied by a
complex mix of culture shock and depression, as well as involving their
first interactions with and emulation of South Korean people and capitalism. The process is mainly guided by and coupled with South Korean
state expectations and diagnoses that are accompanied by barbed wire
fencing and strict regulations—the state is "omnipresent." Considering
Hanawon as a contact zone in the initial period of the newcomers'
identity configuration, there is much ambiguity and complexity that
should be investigated further. The following sections discuss two competing discourses influencing their identity transition in this "liminal"
condition.

The neo-liberal modality of citizenship

Although the new state settlement support system tends to depoliticize
and mobilize the newcomers in their assimilation into the South Korean
value system, the ways that each different government agency treats

them are not coherent (Chung 2008). At *Taesŏngkongsa* they are interrogated as if spies; at Hanawon they are welcomed/protected like national assets and trained as new citizens; the Ministry of Labor treats them as low-income citizens, regarding them as unqualified laborers; while local police officers, who often excuse minor crimes, watch out for them as potential criminals; and so on.

A significant factor operating at the state level may be the principle that they are expected to assimilate as "regular citizens" into the South Korean value system as soon as possible. While there are moral campaigns appealing to South Koreans to show tolerance and consideration for their "brethren," the task of social adjustment is put on the newcomer's own shoulders. Support programs designed to aid the migrants' transition to life in the South, however, tend to give less consideration to the cross-cultural dimension of the process than to underlining the importance of "erasing" North Korean ways of thinking and behaving, and refashioning newcomers according to advanced South Korean norms for faster and more successful resettlement.

Biases among South Koreans that construe northerners as lazy, violent, ungrateful toward their southern helpers, selfish, good at lying, opportunistic, and so on, are often attributed to the embodiments of souls brainwashed by *Juche* (self-reliance) ideology or *Kimilsung-ism* (the North Korean official ruling philosophy that accentuates collective national self-independence from foreign influences (see the first section of Chapter 1 for more discussion about *Juche*)). For example, some researchers have asserted that the main obstacles to the migrants' initial settlement process are their fixed "North Korean" ideas and ways of interpreting South Korean society (see Kim K. 2004: 123–127). And thus it is surmised among South Koreans that their cultural habits should be reformed.

> North Korean defectors are products of their environment, who bring to the South a complex set of North Korean attitudes and values. Since that value system can interfere with their adjustment, it needs to change. For example, their emphasis on saving face stems from having lived in a conformist society. It is not only an obstacle to rational thinking but can even be the cause of failure in South Korea's market economy.
>
> (Suh 2002: 75)

These reductionist arguments imply that North Korean cultures and cultural behaviors are useless. Instead, what the newcomers are expected to learn and accept as soon as possible are the norms of good citizenship. Shaped along the line of neo-liberal reforms developed since the IMF crisis, the norms of good citizenship stress self-reliance, self-support, creativity, and above all the creation of an "employable" individual as a model citizen (see Song 2006: 202–203). The concepts of independence and free will are highly valued and thus for the migrants "individual freedom" is perceived as the essence of South Korean capitalist society. Shortly after beginning the "free" life in the South, however, they realize that this "freedom" is different from their previous understandings (Kim K. 2004).[19] They realize that freedom in a capitalist society requires capital. And they encounter, beneath the surface, the reality of South Korean society, where individuals rely on established social networks of family (*hyŏryŏn*), school (*hakyŏn*), and region (*chiyŏn*), which they do not have.

In recent years, researchers and Hanawon officers have asserted the need to diversify training methods to meet individual differences, with the aim of providing better training, resulting in a higher employment rate. However, this does not mean that the support system would appreciate or allow individual or collective cultural diversities, but rather those diversities would be suppressed throughout the training courses. With reductionist rather than cultural relativist points of view, the state settlement system as a social force tends to keep "Otherizing" the migrants, while depoliticizing them. In other words, South Korean state regime that has pursued the normalization of inter-Korean relations based on ethnic nationalism is likely to incur an identity crisis by marginalizing the migrants, and thus they find themselves expected to become nothing other than productive laborers.

The lingering Cold War

The state aside, Korean conservative media and organizations tend to describe the migrants as both "anticommunist heroes and heroines" and victims of the North Korean regime. This political conceptualization of the migrants was a strategy of the South Korean anticommunist regimes. Continuing the legacy of a still powerful hegemonic group, Korean conservatives as well as international conservatives link the issue of North Korean border crossers to human rights issues with the aim of encouraging North Korean regime change. Within this anticommunist political scheme, newcomers, as deserving national subjects, are likely to feel the need for symbolic compensation. That is, their political citizenship seems to be constructed in a concrete manner. Supported by the conservatives, they also make complaints about the government support system.

However, some also soon realize that the conservatives utilize them as an instrument to achieve and maintain their own hegemony. Conservatives are more interested in defectors who can testify about the brutality of the North Korean regime and who can cooperate with them by criticizing the progressives as pro-North Korean. Just as with the former anticommunist regimes, those who came from elite backgrounds are more valued than the majority of underprivileged migrants to the South.

Nonetheless, as far as the conservatives organize campaigns intended to generate a symbolic meaning of life, some migrants continue to rely on and contribute to the conservative anticommunist movements by providing the required testimony. Given the tradition of the North Korean "story telling market" that has been in place for decades, some migrants become professional anticommunist lecturers as the former "heroes" did.

In a sense, for conservatives, solving North Korean human rights issues is not a goal in itself but a means to reproduce and enhance their anticommunist identity (Chung 2004). Under the authoritarian regimes they ignored South Korean human rights. Further, the notion of human rights is controversial in South Korean conservative dialogue, because they have hardly meditated on its philosophical and historical backgrounds but have appropriated it as a new political apparatus of anticommunism.

Up to the 1980s, South Korean authoritarian regimes had ignored the cultural dimensions that were part of the "heroes'" social adjustment processes in the South. The number of defectors by then were so few that the probation system to which each defector was subject was relatively well managed by the state. The migrants' daily struggles and negotiations with cultural differences, in terms of ways of thinking and behaving in the realms of gender, class, and religion, have hardly been examined but instead have been long silenced until recently.[20]

In this regard, my opinion differs from Andrei Lankov's; he stresses that these early migrants had little problem in adjusting to South Korean society because they were from elite social backgrounds (2006). I propose, instead, that the politicization of the northerners, lacking cross-cultural perspective, functioned and functions as a discursive condition by which the defectors were and are presupposed to perform ideologically anticommunist culturally capitalist norms and values with little question.

By making the political central to the migrants' identity, cultural diversities and gaps among North Korean migrants have simultaneously been ignored. This view tends to see North Korean society and its people as a homogeneous body seamlessly controlled and molded by *Juche* ideology. The migrants' testimony before South Korean audiences, using division language, portrays North Korean realities as inhumane, brutal, devastating, and horrible. The format is similar to the lectures that the former "heroes" delivered in the 1980s, but the contents have changed: while the past anticommunist lectures were more focused on warning about the military threat from the North, recent migrants are supposed to elaborate on human rights abuses in the North.

When the South Korean state ceased granting migrants a concrete anticommunist identity, some migrants (in particular those who are ex-military officers, ex-agents, ex-party members, etc.) started to organize their own groups and actively participate in anti-North Korean movements led by South Korean conservative evangelicals.

Conclusion

The 1997 Act established state support programs for the migrants as part of long-term plans for national unification. By examining recent support programs, especially those run by the government, I have demonstrated how the state training system tends to assimilate the migrants within the norms of neo-liberal good citizenship in South Korea. This reflects the state's lack of cross-cultural tolerance. Within this frame of acculturation, the migrants are prone to suffering an identity crisis.

On the other hand, despite the state's apolitical definition of the migrants, the Cold War legacy has persisted. While the state has moved away from utilizing the migrants as agents of anticommunist propaganda, conservatives continue to define the migrants using a new language of human rights aimed at North Korea and South Korean "leftists." As this discourse and practice seem to translate their "North Korean identity" into symbolic capital that can be exchanged as a substantial asset, it becomes an attractive social field in which the migrants participate.

In his recent volume *Ethnic Nationalism in Korea*, Gi-Wook Shin calls the South Korean unification proposal an "ethnic homogeneity-national unification thesis," and as "a position that declares that a divided Korea must and will be reunified because Koreans are ethnically homogeneous and have been so for thousands of years" (2006: 186). He also points out that the North also stresses "the value of ethnic/racial nationalism in the 'theory of the Korean nation as number one'" (2006: 187).

My analyses of the state's apolitical approach to the migrants suggest that the state-run diagnostic training process attempts to erase

North Korean ways of thinking and behaving, while the conservatives' language disallows *Juche* ideology whether in its cultural form or as a temporarily "brainwashed" mindset.

In this light, the South Korean version of reunified nation-building would also become what Pierre van den Berghe (2006) stresses as "nation killing," because the newcomers' settlement process reflects suppression of all cultural diversities. On the one hand, I thus partly agree with Roy Richard Grinker, who argues that unification "can be a euphemism for conquest, a gloss for winning the war...and [based on a belief] that North Korea must be totally absorbed into the South, its state destroyed, and its people assimilated" (1998: 23, 49, quoted from Shin 2006: 187). On the other hand, I am hesitant to confirm that this South Korean ethnic homogeneity-national unification thesis works without conflict on the ground. More significant problems seem to be outside the scope of this thesis. Rather, as a figured world, it is formed and forming "as [a] social process and in historical time" (Holland et al. 1998: 55) in which North Korean migrants are situated. Indeed, their settlement processes show that the myth of ethnic homogeneity that has been the hegemonic discourse in both North and South Korea is problematized. Thus an alternative sense of belonging is negotiated in the interaction between the migrants and their southern counterparts. My story moves on to the sites where my various discussions will culminate.

5
The Freedom School

"I am the future of the nation!" This is the motto of the Freedom School (FS), which sounds decisive, heroic, and definitely nationalistic. The school's name suggests that "freedom" is what the refugees didn't have in North Korea. The dean of the school, Mr Song, a 46-year-old gentle Christian and former college instructor of North Korean politics, stresses with great conviction that the motto is given by God to empower these "brethren" to be born-again national leaders. The motto is a sacred message hung on the wall, interestingly printed in a "cute" font on a square cloth on which there is also a map of the Korean peninsula. The motto is attached to a pink heart with wings, and smaller pink hearts are embroidered here and there (see Figure 5.1). It was made several years earlier, to represent that the future of a unified Korea must be carried out not by masculine warriors of God, but by love, big and small. On the wall on the other side, "Love and bless you!" (*sarang-hago ch'ukbok-hapnida*) is written in various colors on another cloth, and is attached to the wall right above a bulletin board panel. The appearance of the wall and ceiling decorations make the FS look like a Sunday school classroom for children. In a sense, it is. "What we are doing for them is simple. That is, just like *fixing a necktie* if it is not put on in the right way, we assist them to make up for some minor shortcomings," stated a deacon of the FS advisory board.

Fixing a necktie sounds much more pragmatic and softer than imagining a national future. The FS is actually carrying out both tasks at the same time. "We" and "they" are all Koreans, sons and daughters of Our Father. But "they" have been living far away for a while, and have recently "returned" to the bosom of Our Father. They need to be refashioned to become "normal" in the South. Unlike foreign missionaries, who often immediately find major apparent cultural differences in their mission subjects, South Koreans at the FS assume that they need to fix only the very "minor errors" of their northern counterparts.

"We" and "they" are ethnically homogeneous, and the presumption is that Korean culture is inherently embodied in all Koreans. Such ethnic nationalism in which race, ethnicity, and nation are conflated throughout Korean modern history (Palais 1998; Shin 2006) is at the heart of the Christian mission for North Korean migrants and North Korea (Figures 5.1 and 5.2).

In examining the FS as a contact zone between South Korean Christians and their northern counterparts, I highlight the ways in which North Korean migrants are trained to refashion their "outdated" ways of thinking and to conform to those of South Korean Protestant capitalist norms. At the same time, I want to stress that the process of "fixing" also touches on complicated and dynamic reactions and negotiations between southerners and northerners: co-ethnic relations are mediated by Christianity/God; emotional struggles are often silenced in the name of Jesus Christ and through the metaphor of family; the apparent disparity in socio-economic and class status between South Korean hosts and the migrants is likely to be obscured by the principle of ethnic homogeneity; rational misunderstandings are skipped over or simply negated by the belief that God will speak to "your hearts" (Harding 2000); and present individual sufferings are shared or ignored

Figure 5.1   "I am the future of the nation!" motto
Source: Courtesy of the Author.

Figure 5.2   "Love and bless you!" motto
Source: Courtesy of the Author.

for "the future of the nation" that God has already prepared for "us." As such, the tensions and tacit harmonies coexist and are mediated by Biblical idioms (love, mercy, blessing, chosen, provision, etc.) and by the shared sense of ethnic homogeneity. That is, the Bible and Korean ethnic consciousness manage co-ethnic relations in the FS, an emblem of the Korean Church.

I consider the FS to be a heterogeneous space, or "heterotopia" to borrow from Foucault (1986), implying the dual (real and imagined) meanings of late-Cold War Korea. Like the metaphor of a garden, as suggested by Foucault, FS programs contain almost all the core subjects necessary for learning about Protestant ethics and capitalist etiquette, and the key information for employment and small entrepreneurship in South Korea. This "modern" microcosm is "a space that is other, another real space, as perfect, as meticulous, as well arranged as ours is messy, ill constructed, and jumbled" (Foucault 1986: 27). I do not, however, want to give the impression that the FS is a fixed site, one in which all social reality is tightly scripted or controlled. In concert with the concept of a figured world from previous chapters, the FS as a cul-turally constructed space is constituted "as if" it transcends "Cold War identity" (Kim S. S. 2007) and experiences with cultural differences in the school allow South Korean Christians to imagine their interactions as a simulation of a unified condition.

In light of the FS as a social space of asymmetrical yet dynamic co-ethnic relationships, following the discussion in Chapter 3, it is

useful to build on previous anthropological works on Christian mis-
sionization in colonial and post-colonial contexts. Attending to the
relationship between foreign missionaries and local indigenous people,
anthropologists have in part underscored the role missionaries played
as a crucial imperial force in the local transformations from the "prim-
itive" to the "civilized" (e.g., see Burdick 1993; Hefner 1993; van der
Veer 1996). Equally, the studies have not overlooked the "dialectical
relations" between missionaries and local people. Missionary work thus
inherently contains a tension between two different subjects and even
tensions between the missionaries themselves and the Lord as well as the
Christianity they practice. Andrew Orta (2004: ix) stresses, "As an effort
to convert diverse peoples of the world to what is taken to be a universal truth, and as an effort that at the same time inevitably gives rise to
a range of regionally 'flavored' religious identities, global Catholicism
well reflects a tension often attributed to globalization." Elisa Sampson
Vera Tudela (2000), in analyzing a new form of hagiographic writing
in the 16th–18th centuries, illuminates how the authors created that
kind of religious writing in the process of "cultural interchange" and
"negotiation" in the colonial New World environment.

   While keeping in mind this point of undetermined inter-group relations with respect to the Korean church's global project of a North
Korean mission, I maintain that the way the church provides services
for the migrants makes them a distinctive social institution that "seek[s]
to produce a new man through a process of 'deculturation' and 'recultur-
ation'" (Bourdieu 1977: 94, cited in Comaroff 1992: 70) in the late-Cold
War northeast Asia context. Increasing flows of people and cultural
products under the shadow of significant remaining Cold War tensions
in the region bring our attention to the matter of "dismembering and re-
membering" (Comaroff 1992: 70) of the people on the move, physically
and metaphorically, that constitute such global flows. Drawing on Pierre
Bourdieu's concept of habitus—though they do not explicitly use this
word but refer to bodily habit—John and Jean Comaroff instead draw
our attention to the individual human body that "mediates between
self and society" (1992: 70).

   I am inspired by the way that the ultimate goal of the Korean church's
provision of service for the new arrivals from the North is achieved by
converting them into the bearers of a modern and new South Korean
value system through envisioning Christianized unification. As crystal-
lized in the deacon's metaphorical phrase "fixing a necktie," Korean
Christians who work on the migrants' behalf tend to measure their
degree of social adjustment, personality, and more importantly their
religiosity, by their bodily appearance and behaviors. Speaking Seoulite

language, whitening the skin, and bodily manners that convey obedi-
ence are a few among many examples of things that are taught with the
aim of making "successful" North Korean subjects in the job and religious "markets." It is ironic, however, that the FS staff always stresses
the "interior" mind over the "exterior" body.[1] This does not mean to
say that it is a conventional Cartesian body–mind binary opposition.
Instead, it indicates the dualistic, incoherent, often contradictory, and
more importantly somewhat hypocritical (as some migrants told me in
secret) characteristics of Korean Christians' language and practice.

Why then do the migrants willingly or unwillingly submit themselves to the church system? By providing ethnographic vignettes
of the FS, rather than directly answering this query, this chapter
seeks to capture the cultural processes of "transcending" and "enduring" the socio-ideological chasm between North Korean migrants and
South Korean Christians—seemingly similar but historically different—
through a medium and in the name of Jesus Christ. With the notion
of "transcendence," I intend to avoid an understanding of Christianity
as "a kind of secondary phenomenon or top coat that has been applied
by external forces [the state or colonial missionaries]" (Cannell 2006:
12, see also 39–45 for the term "transcendence"). Rather, I consider
Korean Christianity as a primary force and vehicle for the North and
South Korean participants acting in a heterogeneous figured world—an
imaginary condition that simulates the future of a unified Korea. The
rest of this chapter will crystallize classroom metaphors and explore
the healing camp ritual during which two different national subjects
encounter cultural differences, interpret and misunderstand them in
their own terms, and yet simultaneously express love and affection in
both a sacred and secular sense.

Religious and secular spaces

In this section, I examine the FS, which aspires to be an imaginary
national ethnic enclave where South Korean Christians and North
Korean migrants cluster and struggle to seek co-ethnic assimilation and
"true" Christianity. These are not equal, but are asymmetrical co-ethnic
relations premised on and continued from the Chinese context in
Chapter 3. Thus, it is the migrants who are expected to "listen" to and
"follow" what South Korean Christians teach and guide. Indeed, I maintain that within the basic logic of their conversion to Christianity, which
is the ultimate goal of the mission (yet can, in theory, be "chosen" by
an individual's "free will"), the migrants are mobilized for salvation in

order to take decisive action, to make "an absolute break between a pre-Christian past and the present," just as Olivia Harris observed of the 16th-century missionaries in the Andes (2006: 53). In order to stand and "perform" conversion narratives before South Korean believers, that is, to speak in Korean evangelical language, it takes time. And it is not merely the language per se; rather it is the "discipline of body" (Cannell 2006: 29)—or the reforming of bodily habits, as the necktie metaphor implies.

From the standpoint of Korean evangelicalism, as I have mentioned throughout this thesis, *Juche* is considered to be an evil spirit which not only brainwashes "innocent" people, but also lives in their bodily habits. In order to reset their mind and body, the South Korean Church, which is by no means singular, tends to consider that the Bible alone may not work the transformation, but may do so in combination with proper "education." Korean Christian history has, from the beginning, had its roots in controlling personal behaviors. The first generation of foreign missionaries not only led campaigns but also institutionalized regulations against habitual drinking, smoking, and gambling, as they viewed these as the main causes of the poverty and poor health conditions in 19th-century Korea.

The FS program is, however, run in an evolved and tolerant manner. Most FS class hours are occupied by lectures as part of the whole-person education (*chŏnin kyokyuk*), on the basis of Christian spirit, in order for the migrants (*kyoyuksaeng*) to successfully settle down in South Korea (taken from an FS pamphlet). At the beginning of my fieldwork in the FS, I sat on a chair in the middle or relatively rear rows with the migrants, "as if" I was one of them, paying full attention to the lectures hoping to catch what the FS was teaching. The contents of the lectures were fascinating for me, and I tried to memorize or write down almost everything that was taught about the economics of daily life: for example, not only how to succeed in running an online shopping mall and how to prepare for a job interview, but also about manners and etiquette, including how to bow, talk, dress, and so forth, for building new human relationships necessary to be "[t]he liberal, free-market subject as the model of citizenship" (Ong 2003: 8). I even found myself moved by the lectures about the importance of positive thinking and a purposeful life, and the realization of the true love of Jesus.

It did not take too long to realize that most trainees were not interested as I was in the "contents" of the lectures and the meanings delivered through language. It was not only because of the language gap, namely the South Korean language that had become "much too westernized" in contrast with the nationalized North Korean tongue, but because the training process as a ritual—a rite of passage—seemed more important. Indeed, the FS itself serves as a lived ritual space, transforming secular meanings, and sacred moments. In other words, it is neither the Bible, nor the core knowledge, but the integration of the two into one in their hearts and body that is mediated by the FS. Although some migrants memorized thousands of verses of the Bible in China, they are aware that they cannot fully know the "truth." Instead, they come to agree that at stake is a holistic corporeal feeling, one that can best be sensed in the sort of mood that is created in the FS itself.

Ritual of love and performing sincerity

Noting that Susan Harding (1987) takes the significance of "rhetoric" and "nonsensuous, linguistic means" over ritual, Simon Coleman (2006: 167–169) argues that "language cannot simply be divorced from sensual forms," and that for the adherents of the Word of Life, a Christian organization, the orality (uttering) of words is equally or more significant for the speakers than the "fixity of the written word" (reading). I support Coleman's view and at the same time want to add that equally important are the various forms in which words are performed: singing gospel songs, decorating a space where a group of people gather, and even participating in a ritual process are not secondary, but equally serve to "witness" and "catechize" the words. From this standpoint, I intend to juxtapose two different depictions of the FS. The first is an outsider's point of view—fact-centered, objective, and informative. The second may sound nostalgic and metaphorical. The purpose of this comparison is to illuminate the FS as both a real and an imagined space in which the migrants and their southern counterparts are situated and refashioned to become other selves—ideal citizens. More significantly, as the FS space serves as a ritual stage, norms such as sincerity (*sŏngsil*), self-reliance, and independent subject-making with which the migrants are to be "re-membered" in the South are also empowered in a sacred frame.

The so-called objective, outsider's view, is as follows: the FS operates every Saturday and Sunday for male and female North Korean adults aged from 20 to 60. The number of trainees selected each semester (eight months long) is around 50, with 80 percent being female and 20 percent male. This reflects the current trend in the North Korean migrant population in South Korea and abroad. In order to enter this program, the candidates submit a personal career paper with a recommendation letter. They then take written exams, and, finally, undergo individual oral interviews. Once admitted, they are required to attend class from 9 a.m. to 4 p.m. every Saturday and Sunday, and not to miss more than two days in order to receive the so-called monthly scholarship, which is about 230 USD. Although the scholarship has been criticized by both outside and inside observers who point out that the money can be seen as "bait" to attract North Korean migrants, staff members consider it to be an important component. As for program content, classes are largely divided into two broad categories. Put simply, the first category concerns how North Koreans, as individuals, achieve economic and social success in life either by opening a business or gaining employment at a work-place; and the second category concerns raising North Koreans' level of religiosity. The former classes are mainly taught by Christian CEOs or professors from a particular field and the latter by FS staff members, as they are all well-trained Christians. Overall, the program aims to give its North Korean trainees lessons for successful living in a South Korean capitalist system that depends on individual efforts.

The FS is not merely a black box in which migrants are "disciplined." It is, rather, vitalized and becomes a metaphysical space where the peo-ple are beloved and blessed with each other. This is the other meaning of the FS, which is transformed by people who like to sing the song "You were born to be loved":

> You were born to receive His love
> Within your life, you've been receiving this love
> You were born to receive His love
> Within your life, you've been receiving this love
> From the creation of the world, the love of God has begun
> And bears its fruit through our fellowship
> Because of your existence in this world
> We share this great joy among us
> You were born to receive His love
> Within your life, you've been receiving this love
> You were born to receive His love
> Within your life, you've been receiving this love

With outspread arms, "we" look each other in the eye and exchange smiles on "you" and "love." The FS classroom turns into a "figured kingdom" in which South Korean evangelical ideas and finances are invested and to which some 50 "chosen" North Korean migrants are believed to be "led" or "invited" by God's hands every year. It is a space of love and blessing, which should be key values for both the present and future lives of the migrants, who in turn will become leaders of a future Korea, a unified and Christianized nation. Referring to the words beautified on the walls, it seems as if there is no Weber's "iron cage," no Marx's "alienation," no Nietzsche's "nihilism"—and more importantly—no "South and North" allowed in either imagination or practice, but only "pink"-colored optimism based on the life and teachings of Jesus of Nazareth. Every Saturday and Sunday from nine in the morning, the FS space is filled by the 50 or so North Korean newcomers "listening to" the words, the lectures, and messages, and also "practicing" what they have learned and rehearsing for what they are supposed to do in the near future. They are FS trainees, potential "disciples" prepared to serve themselves as individuals and serve the nation, entities which are theoretically seamlessly integrated.

Outside of the FS, South Korean reality is harsh. Popular perceptions about North Korean migrants have shifted to consider them a new minority group, that of the Other within. Although it is believed that South and North Koreans are ethnically the same and that they share a language and basic customs, this myth of ethnic homogeneity often turns out to be a burden, and is easily recognized as being a falsehood. In the meantime, statistics show that about 70 percent of the migrants "regularly" participate in religious activities and that more than 85 percent of them appreciate the various types of assistance that they receive from their religious affiliations while settling in South Korea (Jeon 2003, 2005; Choi et al. 2005). In this light, South Korean authorities and Christian leaders as well as the migrants themselves agree that the role of the church is crucial for the migrants' effective settlement in the South (Suh 2002; Kim Y. 2004; Jeon 2007). Here the term "effective settlement" refers not only to the church's substantial role as a welfare agency for the migrants, but also to the awakening of the church's apostolic role in guiding/converting the migrants to capitalist Protestantism in evangelical terms. That is, the church's mission for the migrants encompasses two tasks—the secular and the sacred, as has been shown elsewhere in missionary history.

The FS is an emblem of Korean church activities that emphasize recovering the human dignity of North Korean migrants by establishing a "personal relationship with God." The FS is a ritual stage mediating and mobilizing this relationship. However the relationship becomes a tri-cornered one: migrants–South Koreans–God. These tri-cornered relations mediate with one another: God leads the migrants to the South, South Korean Christians lead the migrants to God, and the migrants serve to strengthen their southern counterparts, whether voluntarily or involuntarily. It is as if South Koreans play the role of the preacher, who, Susan Harding says, "'stand[s] in the gap' between the language of the Christian Bible and the language of everyday life" (2000: 12).

"Mediated" by South Korean Christians in the aura of Jesus' love, the migrant adults are expected to be born again as "ideal citizens." Norms like sincerity, hard work, self-reliance, and independence, also emphasized by the government, are likely to be understood as the "truth" in this and other worlds in the FS setting in which North Korean trainees are treated as potential employees or business owners. The lectures are offered by Christian, self-made business owners and professional employment agents, and are typically useful, impressive, and lively. Among the new values listed above, it is the concept of sincerity (*sŏngsil*) that emerged as the most important attitude the migrants should have in order to be successful in South Korea. *Sŏngsil*, in the FS lecture series, means a complex set of mindful and bodily manners that include being modest, obedient, gentle, enduring, hardworking, and unselfish. *Sŏngsil* becomes more meaningful in a social system. That is, in a company setting, the migrant is supposed to be obedient to his/her South Korean boss, and work hard with few complaints. In the case of a self-owned small business, one must serve one's South Korean clients. One day after an impressive lecture delivered by Mr Ko, a self-made business owner who once failed but was able to recover, Director Kang of the FS added his own comments:

> There may be two reactions in your mind. First, "Wow, what a huge sum of money, is it possible?" Second, "I don't want to have to work so hard again even in South Korea". Remember those whose passage has been so hard among *Uri sik-gu-dŭl* (our family, the graduate migrants between 2001 and 2005)—they are all successful in their business. For example, there is a plasterer. Although you can think "hard work again?" he now has two South Korean employees. He does not tell them he is from North Korea though. You can be rich like Mr Ko. His business is one we can emulate. Of course, there is also the case of the man who graduated in 2002 and failed since the company system was unstable. It seems really a great occupation. Further, Mr Ko is willing to give you preferential treatment. The only thing you need is *sŏngsil* (sincerity). Above all, you must be sincere, if not, we will all lose face.

In his account, it is clear that Director Kang projects his assumptions onto the migrants. His premise is that the migrants "don't want to do such hard work again in the South," implying that they are somewhat lazy, lack will, and are dependent. Such negative attitudes are simply interpreted as a by-product of *Juche*, and thus what they need is to be "sincere" not only for themselves but also for the FS "family." The family metaphor in relation to the migrants in a church setting is also considerable. The migrants are perceived as "returning sons and daughters" and are situated as younger siblings in the Korean family system. Resembling to Sheila Jager's (2003) analysis of the Korean War memorial—a carving of a South Korean big (literally) brother soldier embracing a younger and smaller North Korean soldier—North Korean migrants are automatically subordinated in the Korean ethnic hierarchy. In this light, *sŏngsil* represents familial, social, and religious obligations that the newcomers are expected to adopt in place of the outdated *Juche* custom. Further, *sŏngsil* is not merely emphasized in verbal language. The FS also provides lectures for North Korean migrants as to how to behave properly in front of their bosses, co-workers, and clients. The lectures include how to bow, smile, dress, walk, shake hands, and talk.

How and to what degree then do the migrants interpret and willingly accept the new values and attitude reforms? Do they agree that *Juche* ideology ruined their soul and body? Do they believe that if they work hard following the instructions they learn in the FS that they can then succeed in this-worldly life, and ultimately return to the North in glory? What difference do they perceive between the FS programs and the ones that they received in Hanawon, the government settlement facility, and what they learn in a job training center? Through observation I was able to ascertain their reactions and some answers. However, I soon realized that their reactions and responses to South Korean services such as the FS program are not explicitly expressed in spoken language at the time that they receive support. Another aspect of the FS is the space and time appropriated by the migrants in silence. I will show that the FS classroom can be appreciated for its multiple meanings and dimensions when examined beyond the official programs (Figure 5.3).

Heterogeneous classroom

I would like to propose that the FS classroom is a symbolic and metaphoric contact zone mediating the relationship and interaction between North and South Koreans. The FS classroom, as a metaphor, extends to a place and time during the ten-minute-long break time every hour.[2] While joking with each other in the classroom, sipping a cup of coffee in the hallway, and smoking cigarettes outside the building, the behavior and small talk the migrants share are crucial to understanding the construction of their identity. Restrooms, classrooms, hallways—wherever they are during their breaks—are spaces in which the migrants make their own cultural time and space, thus in

Figure 5.3   Business practice: Weekend street restaurant selling North Korean foods
Source: Courtesy by the Author.

many ways appropriating the FS to their own ends (see Clifford 1994; Cohen 1997 for a concept of ethnic space and time). They gather as small groups or couples and enjoy sharing information about jobs, or discussing vulgar North Korean topics in their northern dialect for fun, news from North Korea, or chit-chat about South Korean soap operas, newly purchased cell phones, clothes and accessories, and about skin care and health treatments, and on and on. I was often told that one of main reasons for coming to the FS was for hanging out with *uri saramdŭl*, or "us," in that they could resolve the stress they accumulated throughout the daily labor of working under South Koreans by communing with other North Koreans.

In the same vein, it is necessary to move my angle of vision from the lecture platform where South Korean Christian elites deliver good words, to where North Korean trainees are sitting in the chairs. While sitting with them in the classroom, it was interesting to perceive how they created strategies in their own ways, while diluting, reinterpreting, ignoring, and filtering the discourses and lessons that the South Korean lecturers offered.

Just like other school classrooms, a dominant power is created from the positioning of the lecture platform up front and power descends down to the back rows. Also like other classrooms, not all of the audience pays full attention to every single word and lesson delivered from the lectern. While South Korean Christian lecturers enthusiastically teach how to fill out resumes, how to build good human relationships at the workplace, how to succeed in life, and other such useful things, among the North Korean trainees sitting in the chairs, there were various "other" deeds that I could catch glimpses of: falling asleep, sending messages by cell phone, scribbling on paper, chit-chatting with the person next to them, and so on. These behaviors suggest that not all the intentions and efforts of the FS program can be absorbed—even by those who seem to listen carefully in the classroom.

By extension, the FS weekly group Bible study that the trainees are supposed to participate in (although not all can do so) is also a window through which we can get a sense of the micro-interactions between the trainees and their southern counterparts. There are four groups and each meets at around dinnertime once a week. A group Bible study is normally organized with opening prayer, reading of verses, and comments, which are all led by a South Korean who is an elder, a deacon, or a staff member. Soon after the formal study, they have an evening meal together that is prepared by a host or hostess. The meal is a "hybrid"—a combination of Yanbian, North Korean, and South Korean styles. There is a formal regulation against drinking, but if a South Korean leader does not come to the study, they enjoy drinking and chatting instead of reading the Bible. Each member in a group hosts the weekly meeting by turns, and they come to visit each other's apartment complexes (most North Korean adults live in small, leased apartments assigned by the government after the Hanawon training) and comment on the host/hostess's sense of decoration, family relations, and so forth. All these aspects are likely to be seen as multi-functions of the group in which North Korean participants not only learn a Christian way of thinking and manners and share personal wishes through its formal event, but also experience their own cultural and ethnic belonging.

By describing the heterogeneous FS classroom, I wanted to uncover a hidden dimension that exists in a lively manner in between and betwixt public performances—lectures, regular cell meetings for Bible study, and Sunday worship—which are not undermined by this hidden "break" in which they can "breathe," but are rather integrated in ordinary practices. In this light, the notion of transcendence that I discussed earlier in this chapter may be understood as a state that allows the various and even competing desires and powers to coexist. Interestingly, however,

FS staff members, as coordinating agents wishing to manage the regular and public programs without secular interventions (the other deeds, drinking at the cell meeting, etc.), tend to devalue the "break" dimension, but instead insist on fixing, erasing, or concealing. Thus, tensions arise and accelerate in the case of an intensive ritual which demands its participants to firmly follow the regulations.

Healing camp

Broadly, it can be said that the FS calendar from beginning to end is organized as a rite of passage aimed at the migrants. At a micro-level of observation, the healing camp I participated in can also be seen as a rite with the phases that Victor Turner (1979) elaborates.[3] Instead of illustrating each phase in detail, however, I want to shed light on the way in which the ritual as a process and as a series of symbols ended up having multiple meanings and provoking contradictory and ambiguous feelings among the participants. In particular, I argue that misunderstandings of signs and symbolic performances accentuated the unprecedented and very delicate cultural borderline between South Koreans and their northern counterparts.

Yet, with this point I do not mean to make a teleological criticism of the FS and the wider Christian mission. What seems to be a failure may crystallize as a different form of flexibility and transcendence in Christianity. Webb Keane stresses, "Christianity in whatever form it takes is embedded in ordinary practices, it creates recurrent practical means by which these concepts [i.e., iconoclasm, spirituality, conscience, agency, worldliness, and transcendence] can be lived in concrete terms (Asad 1993), even when the result contradicts official ideology" (2006: 310). As a form and means of Korean evangelical Christianity, the FS bears those concepts and invites further discussions.

This section will thus lead us to review the limits and potentials of Korean evangelical nationalism in bringing to fruition its vision of "the future of the nation." The following consists of two subsections. Instead of going through all the details of the ritual process, I focus on the underlying intentions of the healing ritual and its outcomes.

Wounded souls

In mid-September 2006, the FS designed a two-day outdoor activity for North Korean trainees. The purposes of the camp were: to heal wounded souls through an experience of God's advent; to help them discover the true dignity of their existence within God; and to cut off their past life and rebuild a new life with Jesus Christ. It was apparent that the ultimate goal of the camp was to convert the North Korean migrants. Historically, this goal is not that new, as throughout the history of Christianity ultimate healing is completed when people convert to Christianity (Porterfield 2005; Wightman 2007). This list of purposes, which is short and concise, also represents the more or less negative image most South Korean adults have of North Korean migrants—their soul and heart are wounded, their self-esteem is low, and their past is ruined and contaminated.

Based on her three-year-long missionary work for North Korean migrants in the South, Chu Sŏn-ae, an emeritus professor in a theological university, argues that the church is the only agency that can save North Korean migrants and it is God's special and precious calling for the Korean Church in this era (2008: 26–27). She warns that North Koreans are different from other foreign migrants because their whole life has been full of a series of unimaginable sufferings. They must be seen as physically and mentally disabled patients; their victim mentality, grudges, anger, hostility, frustration, and wounded hearts prevent them from receiving any sermons and words. She proclaims that, without deep understanding and love, ordinary people would be easily discouraged from serving them. It is only those who experience God's love who can overcome the frustrations of serving the migrants and give them true help.

As with the various training systems, "true" help has normally been designed to assimilate migrants into the Korean capitalist system in as short a time as possible. Similar to the US homeless sheltering industry, as Vincent Lyon-Callo (2004) problematizes, it has been considered an urgent and taken-for-granted task for South Korean agencies (government and civil organizations) to transform the northerners into productive citizens not only for themselves but also for national unification.[4]

The healing camp was not only meant as an intensive turning point for the FS trainees to convert to new Christian citizens. It was also a contact zone in which South Korean Christians, North Korean migrants, and God and Jesus Christ were expected to interact with each other. From a South Korean standpoint, North Korean trainees were supposed to play the role of novices, "temporarily undefined, [and] alive to the asocial world" (Turner 1979: 19). Following the FS 2006 calendar, the healing camp took place in the middle of the term—North Korean participants had passed half way through the FS course while getting familiar with most Christian ways. By this point, around ten North Korean migrants who were not willing or able to follow the rules and

ways required of them had already left the FS. The rest of the participants had come to know what they were supposed to do in a certain
time and space. In the same vein, FS staff members seemed to believe
that it was time for the migrants to feel God at a sacred place.

"Go away in the name of Jesus!"

As I talked with participants at the camp, it became clear to me that they
interpreted and understood the symbolic practices in different ways.
This was illustrated in a conversation I had with some women at the
camp. Eun-sil, in her mid-40s, was rather annoyed at the ritual process
in which she was "forced" to recall past memories, and by another conversation with a woman who had seemed "possessed" during prayer.
The first time I was at the camp, I was taking a walk with several female
North Korean migrants while enjoying sunshine and fresh air during a
break. I asked a casual "how are you" question, and did not expect a
serious response. The answer I received was unexpected:

> Me: How was your last night? Did you feel good?
> Eun-sil: To be honest, I didn't like last night. It was bad for me to
> be forced to repent. I have no idea why I was made to recall those
> sufferings again. I had tried to drown my sorrows by drinking, day
> after day, upon arrival in the South, and just recently I resolved
> to change my life. But I almost go crazy whenever I am forced to
> remember those bad memories...

Eun-sil's reaction to the healing ritual the previous night was the
exact opposite of what the FS was hoping to elicit. Not all North
Korean migrants have gone through the same difficulties, but most
of the bad and tragic memories of what they have experienced could
be seen as relating to strategies they had to inevitably choose, or
kinds of misfortunes they happened to face while undergoing desperate
social-economic-political situations. Memories of family separation by
death, being chased by Chinese policemen, human trafficking and
sexual abuse, their children who have been left behind, and so on,
reflect what most North Korean individuals have experienced repeatedly. It may be a personal survival strategy for these individuals to bury
such memories in the past.

For some North Korean migrants, religious sins and past wrongdoings are not different, as seen in the history of the Christian mission
throughout the world. While recognizing one's voluntary disconnec-
tion from God is significant in the former category, the latter entails

mistakes, faults, intentional legal and moral violations in general, and idol worship—what Mr Kang calls Kim Il-sung ideology, particularly within the North Korean migrant population. In the end, even personal wrongdoings and past traumas are politicized and totalized in evangelical nationalist terms. In addition, there are quite a few migrants who feel guilty, as if they are traitors. They had a strong sense of nationalism based on *Juche* ideology, but, in escaping their "motherland," they see themselves as having become "selfish traitors" who, in betraying their country and even the rest of their family members, have sought only to live for themselves.

In other words, their identities have been transformed from a communist national being who once was willing to die for "our motherland" against US imperialism (as promoted by the North Korean regime) to individual refugees seeking food resources for themselves and family— selfish traitors in North Korean terms (see chapters 1 & 4), and to division minorities who need to assimilate into the South Korean capitalist system. In the healing ritual process, they were urged to be born again as Christians who were required to repent their past and be reborn to Christianize a reunified nation in the future. In this regard, South Korean evangelical discourse works to politicize North Korean sufferings and re-nationalize their identity configuration. As such, individual efforts to overcome past traumas are replaced by something national through various rites for recovering spirituality. Rather than as an individual and family group economic migration, South Korean Christians who lead the various religious programs tend to interpret their northern counterparts' passage as one signifying a political, national, and evangelical pilgrimage where they were predestined to escape from the "dark northern part," and be led by the "light of gospel" toward the "southern land of freedom." The slight differences between North Korean migrants and their southern counterparts in interpreting the meanings of migration in turn happen to produce another conflict between them regarding attitudes and perceptions toward religious rites for spiritual restoration.

Moreover, the methods of the Pentecostal healing ritual, including loudly praying together, speaking in tongues, crying, and so on, are not familiar to most North Korean migrants. This set of rituals is in fact a particular form of culture and language in South Korean Christianity, and is particular to the Pentecostal Christian tradition to which the FS belongs. While South Korean staff members of the FS often reproach the northern trainees for their hesitance and passiveness in the rituals, I propose that the North Korean trainees' conversion would not be complete until they became used to this specific form of cultural performance (see Harding 1987, 2000; Stromberg 1993; Lester 2005; Wiegele 2005).

Nonetheless, one may propose that North Koreans in general are good at "performing," by crying with joy or deep emotion. A common scene on North Korean TV was North Korean citizens in their best clothing—men in western suits or a national uniform called *Inminbok*, people's clothing,[5] while women wore traditional Korean dress—jumping up and down, holding and shaking fake flowers, shouting "*Manse, manse!*" (cheers, cheers) and tearfully crying before their great leader Kim Jong-il. Some interpret this scene as an exemplary sign of Kim's idol cult, so they assume that all North Koreans are good at "performing" a similar form of religious practice. Yet my ethnographic notes suggest that for some migrants the meaning of crying was something neither understandable nor acceptable as a sign of "openness" before God, but rather a "strange" or "what the hell are they doing?" type of action.

These contradictory understandings between South Koreans and the migrants bring to light the notion of "sincerity" in religious terms. Previously I pinpointed *sŏngsil*, or sincerity, as a key value that the newcomers must acquire if they are to accomplish living a successful life in the South. In the Protestant understanding, Keane defines sincerity as that which "characterizes a relationship between words and interior states. To be sincere is to utter words that can be taken to be isomorphic with beliefs or intentions" (2006: 316–317). While Keane maintains the relationship between language and heart, for the North Korean migrants' the key element is integrity: an integrated mind and body, an integrated condition between one's speaking and behaving. While "language" or "uttering language" is always important in the western and evangelical tradition, North Korean as well as South Korean criticisms aimed at evangelical leadership often rest on the importance of consistency in speaking and action. The degree of spirituality in Korea is not solely attached to "speaking" but "behaving."

A sincere believer in the Christian domain can be translated into Korean as a "true believer" (*ch'amdoen sinangin*), one who practices his/her belief, and "true" believing is practicing, not speaking. Thus, as I mentioned above, a North Korean migrant woman's reaction of "what the hell are they doing?" to the Pentecostal healing ritual can be seen simply as a matter of "learning particular linguistic and ritual grammar." That is, it was just her unfamiliarity with the specific ritual practice. South Koreans must know that the scenes of North Korean masses' shouting *manse!* is rarely experienced by people in provincial areas outside of Pyongyang, the capital of North Korea. Indeed, over

80 percent of the migrants are from the cities close to the Sino–North Korean border, far away from the capital.

On the other hand, her reaction can shed light on the increasing number of North Korean Christians who stop attending church, largely due to the fact that they witness hypocritical behavior in their church pastors or members. Sincerity in Christianity is also related to *sŏngsil,* which I translate into English as sincerity. A *sŏngsil-han saram,* or sincere person in one's social life, is equivalent to *ch'amdoen sinangin,* or a sincere believer in church. At this point, we can acknowledge that sincerity emerges as a contested and competing discourse and practice among the co-ethnic interactions between the migrants and their southern counterparts. Due to the asymmetrical power relations in South Korean hegemonic discourse, it is the migrants who are expected to acquire "sincerity" which South Koreans claim is missing in North Koreans. The following vignette reveals the tension or miscommunication between the two actors in interpreting the healing outcome.

At one point during the healing camp, a young woman, So-yong, looked possessed by the spirit. Her face was wet with tears, her arms and legs were shaking, and the symptoms were not medically related. Nonetheless, she did not accept that it was a spirit possession. After this, I happened to have a conversation with her and Chae-eun, who at the time were both attending a theological school.

Me and Chae-un: Good morning!!
So-yong: I am fine today, but I think I still have a headache.
Chae-eun: Did you take a pain killer?
So-yong: Yes, I did, but I think it'll get better soon.
Me: I guess you were possessed by Holy Spirit, weren't you?
So-yong: Well, I don't know what it was. I just could not move. Maybe because I was too tired, since I haven't taken a rest in recent days.
Chae-eun: Did you work hard lately?
So-yong: Yes, I have taken exams. You know it's hard to read books and there are lots of things to memorize....So I haven't slept for three days...

Interestingly, the conversation ended up becoming a friendly exchange between two ladies who were interested in talking about their hometown and finding a social connection instead of discussing So-yong's possession state from the previous night. But for me it was striking that they concluded that the reason So-yong fell to the floor was not thanks to a spirit possession, but because of bad health. Although they were sincere Protestants attending a theology college, they seemed not as interested in legitimizing their religiosity among themselves. The night before, Mr Kang and Pastor Choi had led the healing ritual for four hours. The two ministers practiced the "laying on of hands" on So-yong for over half an hour. The laying on of hands is a symbolic method to invoke the Holy Spirit in occasions of healing service, blessing, baptism, and so forth, and is practiced by various denominations. Kang and Choi were allegedly good at practicing it for healing. The previous night, in fact, Kang and Choi were shouting "Go away! I command you in the name of Jesus, go away!" It meant that they were practicing the laying on of hands to "cure" So-yong's soul that was presumably possessed by a demon, not by the Holy Spirit.

Before I had the conversation with So-yong, I happened talk briefly with Mr Kang and Pastor Choi. Kang whispered in a low voice, "Well, it was almost done, but eventually they didn't fully open their minds." And then he seriously stated,

> You know we are all the same nation (*han minjok*). I said to myself "one step more one step more"...Last night, I felt that I was almost there. But they didn't fully open...I don't know, but there is something like a *glass* between us and them. I can't break it. The more I want to break it, the more they seem to make the glass thicker. I don't know what the *glass* is and why I always feel that way...I think it may be due to the fact that they were drowned in Kim Il-sung ideology for too long...

His last account manifests that what both Kang and Choi were attempting to do to So-yong was to remove the demon of Kim Il-sung from her soul. However, that night I had witnessed them fail and they had let another female volunteer take her to a room to rest. In that moment Kang lamented that he was not able to open their minds and exorcise *Kimilsung-ism*, and the experience reaffirmed the metaphorical glass between "us" and "them." From Kang's perspective, So-yong's state was precisely a spirit possession but by an inner demon, the deeply embodied "evil" *Juche*. So-yong claimed it was caused by a burnt-out condition, fatigue that in turn was caused by carrying out heavy duties as a mother and a student in her early 40s. Recalling the purposes of this camp—healing wounded souls, finding true dignity, and cutting off the past and rebuilding a new life—there might have been someone who experienced a conventional "blessing," such as establishing a personal relationship with God, from this experience. If so, then we may need to recognize that the relationship between God and the migrants is much easier to reconnect than the relationship between the migrants and South Korean Christians.

Conclusion

I have examined the FS as a multidimensional, heterogeneous figured world in which the chasm between and negotiation of ideologies between North Korean migrants and South Korean evangelicals unfolds. The first part of this chapter explored two different dimensions of the classroom metaphor. On the one hand, the FS imagines itself as a social laboratory that provides essential programs to help selected migrants adjust to South Korea. I have demonstrated how, using the notion of *sŏngsil*, or sincerity, the migrants are expected to erase the outdated *Juche* mindset and become productive citizens. On other hand, I have paid attention to a hidden zone and "break" time that do not belong to the formal programs. I attempted to illuminate how the migrants appropriate such between and betwixt space and time to make the FS a more meaningful space for them.

The second part was devoted to illustrating the healing ritual, in particular its intentions and outcomes. It was designed to mobilize the migrants to reestablish their personal relationship with God. But such rebuilding requires an absolute break from the past. The healing, thus, means a recovery of dignity by destroying *Juche*, which is thought to remain in the migrants' souls. After the healing ritual, however, I encountered unexpected reactions and interpretations from both sides. By analyzing three main opposite and ambivalent accounts, I have opened up the ambivalent nature of Korean evangelical nationalism for further discussion. In sum, I have pictured ongoing conflicts, negotiations, and miscommunications rather than reconciliation between the newcomers and South Korean Christians.

As for the causes and contents of conflicts which are largely unspoken in the name of love and blessing, my findings suggest that in the context of supposing a unified condition, it is not only "the antagonistic identity constructs," as Roland Bleiker argues, "that emerged with the division of the peninsula that will undoubtedly survive and pose problems" (2005: 99) in the assimilation process between South Koreans and the migrants in the FS setting. But, from the migrants' standpoints, it is also the South Korean "myth of modernization" that is produced throughout the rapid industrialization in the 1960s–1980s; what most scholars in Korean studies call "compressed modernity" (Chang 1999; H. Cho 2000; Koo 2001; Abelmann 2003) and a "culturalist view" embedded in the hegemonic sense of Korean ethnic homogeneity. For South Korean Christians, it is *Juche* ideology that contaminates the migrants' minds and bodies. Such views regard *Juche* as responsible for the migrants' refugee mentality. However, Korean psychologists and neuro-psychiatrists have pointed out that 30 percent of the migrants show post-traumatic stress disorder caused by famine and their endurance of dangerous conditions in China, worsened by culture shock in the South (Jeon 1997, 2000; Hong et al. 2005; Jeon et al. 2005).

The degree of culture shock may be much greater than South Koreans assume. Lee Ung-pyŏng, who defected from the North in a MIG-19 fighter jet in 1983, passed away in May 4, 2002. He was only 48 years old. As a model "national hero" from the North, he was soon promoted from captain to major, worked as a professor at a Korean Air Force university, married the daughter of a professor in his school, and had two sons. He allegedly worked very hard, but collapsed one day due to an unexpected illness. It was reported that before his death he often said "I have lived in Seoul more than a third of my entire life, but I haven't fully assimi-lated in South Korean society yet—just like oil is floating on the water."[6] His unfortunate and untimely death appeared to enunciate the reality that new arrivals from the North, whose numbers keep growing, were undergoing many difficulties in adjusting to South Korea.[7]

South Korean scholars and civil organizations consider the German unification case as an example of multidimensional social transforma-tion that the Koreas might prepare for in the near future (Kang and Wagner eds. 1990). The comparison between Korea and Germany has worked to mitigate the state manipulation of the "fantasy" of the unifi-cation and "myth" of ethnic homogeneity, at least in South Korea. It has served as a way for the mutually antagonistic North and South regimes to ease the totalitarian control that has been held over their people for decades. But now the fantasy of the unification and myth of ethnic homogeneity seem to take on different shapes and meanings. On the one hand, people worry about the so-called unification costs. Compared with pre-unified Germany, the economic differences between the North and the South are so vast that there is concern that the unification may immediately lead to national bankruptcy. On the other hand, there is ethnic nationalism that is still pervasive in influencing the meanings of national unification.

As I maintain, Korean ethnic nationalism rests on a belief in the shared bloodline. It is a product of Korea's particular modern history—colonial experience, national division by the Great Powers, and post-Korean War Cold War identity politics have contributed to the construction of ethnic nationalism (see Shin 2006). But I do not support the idea that this ethnic consciousness is homogeneous and synony-mous with a decisive patriotism. Observers often bring out several examples illustrating the increasing ethnic nationalism in the South; the first may be the spectacular 2002 scene on Seoul's streets, which were filled with hundreds of thousands of people wearing "Red Devil" uniforms cheering their national soccer team in the Korea–Japan World Cup series. But they have overlooked the other side of the scene in which some young people, who were the most enthusiastic leaders of the parade, preferred Mild Seven (Japanese cigarettes) or Malboro (American ones) to This (a cheap Korean cigarette). That is, this recent form of ethnic nationalism is different from the earlier version that led the Encouragement of Korean Production Movement in 1920s colonial Korea. In this light, the flexibility and appropriateness of recent ethnic nationalism, which can be seen as a commodity in the highly market-oriented Korean context, must be underlined in the discussion of its relationship with other socio-cultural fields.

Gi-Wook Shin stresses that "South Koreans who have a strong belief in ethnic homogeneity understand the complexities of the unification process and realize that there are indeed real barriers between the two sides" (2006: 199). His survey data used for the chapter look relatively positive, because "Only 16.7 percent support 'hegemonic unification', saying that the current South Korean system should be the basis of a unified Korea. In contrast, 31.8 percent support a unified Korea based on elements equally from North and South, suggesting willingness to accommodate" (2006: 200). His study of the relationship between eth-nic nationalism and unification suggests a different perspective from that of Habermas (1996) and Grinker (1998) who focused on the poten-tial for the Korean belief in ethnic homogeneity to ignore and suppress real differences between the two Koreas in the unification process. Shin argues that this belief serves to motivate South Koreans to pursue uni-fication and "does not necessarily obscure the differences... or promote hegemonic unification by the South" (2006: 201). In particular, his sur-vey reveals that the younger generation tends to show more flexibility in terms of cultural tolerance than older people who view ordinary North Korean people as victims of the communist regime (see also Lee S. 2006; Kim S. S. 2007).

While Shin sheds light on the South Korean sense of ethnic homo-geneity as a motif of national unification, Kim Young-soo's study (2004) based on a survey with high school and college students, suggests that ethnic consciousness or *tongp'o ŭisik* facilitates their willingness to accept North Korean migrants in the South. For instance, young South

Koreans strongly agree with migrants settling in their own neighborhood and the idea that they should be cared for by a state welfare system.

But Kim also finds that college students are relatively more sensitive and somewhat intolerant about matters that conflict with their socioeconomic interests. That is, they tend to disagree with the idea that young North Koreans should be eligible for the Special Admission for Koreans Overseas in Korean universities and special employment which had been given to earlier "national heroes" in job markets. Kim points out that this ambivalence is part of the young South Korean generation's attitudes toward their imagined brothers and sisters from the North. It suggests that young South Koreans are likely to be sympathetic to North Korean migrants, and yet at the same time they consider some of the special advantages the state provides to the migrants as unfair, with little regard to fundamental differences between them and the migrants in terms of socio-economic capital. College entrance in South Korea is a competitive and alarming battle, in which young people and their parents invest greatly to win. Increasing dominance of the neo-liberal market philosophy, which emphasizes individual competitiveness, is intertwined with ambiguous pan-Korean ethnic nationalism in practice. This tendency leads us to inquire into what evangelical nationalism has been and is envisioning with respect to these young generations.

South Korean evangelicals leading the right wing take a tough stance on the "Sunshine policy" and North Korea; for them, national reunification is "meaningless" until North Korean society becomes one in which "religious freedom" and basic "human rights" are granted to all people on the basis of a "free market economy" (Lee J. 2006). Reverend Kim Jin-hong, who has played a leading role in political democratization since the 1980s, is now a leading figure of the right wing. Together with that of Reverend Seo Kyong-sŏk, his "conversion" to the right was shocking to the progressive and civil society groups in South Korea. Referring to his accounts, which are now conceived as hegemonic discourses in the evangelical church, national reunification is an outdated "conservative" fantasy. In his worldview, the leftists and socialists cannot find a place to reside. Over the past ten years, South Korean people have come to have plural imaginations about the next generation's future. Henceforth, Korean history may observe increasingly dynamic, complicated, and multidimensional debates about the future—that future which is supposed to be carried out in the pink-colored love with which FS migrants decorated their "I am the future of the nation!" poster.

6
Narrativization of Christian Passage

The significance and advantages of incorporating the life histories and personal narratives of individual refugees and migrants are consistently emphasized in anthropological contributions to refugee and migration studies (e.g., Malkki 1996; Black 2001; Rajaram 2002; Powles 2004). The narrative perspective is vital because it can demonstrate the lived experiences of individual refugee-migrants over the course of, to use Michel Agier's (2008) notion, the destruction of their established life (confinement in camps or life on urban margins) and the actions taken to establish a new life. Individuals express their experiences in socio-culturally shared forms; narratives are forms of expression that are "socially constructed units of meaning," according to Edward Bruner (1986: 7). In this spirit, this chapter examines the conversion narratives of North Korean migrants—narratives that construe suffering, perilous migration, and the development of a new self in the evangelical language of what I term "Christian passage."

Describing North Korean migration as a Christian passage high-lights that these migrants almost always journey from the Sino–North Korean border area under the sponsorship and aid of Korean Protestant churches and missionaries located in northeastern China, and, above all, testify to the divine efficacy of their direct interactions with their new Father God. As North Korean migrants convert to Christianity in their journey from North Korea and China to South Korea, I first argue that their narratives demonstrate their acquisition and use of evangelical language to reshape their past suffering and form their new sense of self. Following this, I argue that these Biblical vocabularies encourage the erasure of institutional or human mediation, instead allowing only for the recognition of a supernatural power as the mediator responsible for their religious conversion and passage from the "dark" North to the

"Canaan" of the South and leading, further, to a future reunified Korean nation-state.

By focusing on the narrativization of religious and refugee experiences, this chapter investigates the religious conversion of refugee migrants to a mainstream religion in a host society. Such identity transition has been studied in the context of cultural hybridity and the negotiations made by individuals and host communities in mainly western societies (cf. Winland 1994; Ong 2003).[1] Cambodian, Vietnamese, and Hmong refugees in the United States and Canada have been subjected to a new cultural citizenship: to an "American" set of norms and rules, in which Christianity, along with western individualism, consumerism, and social welfare systems, seemingly altered and/or reproduced the boundaries of their "traditional" ritual and religious values and practices. The juxtaposition between "new" western and "old" traditional religions and their syncretic or eclectic phenomena has mostly been discussed in terms of cultural citizenship or subject making. In this context, religion and its accompanying institutional involvement and intervention tend to be reduced to the realm of the private and made divergent from the political. However, the conversion of North Korean migrants and their affiliation with Protestant churches is not only seen as a process of new subject making, but also extremely politicized in the context of Korean national division and human rights discourse. Thus, the case of North Korean migrants shares some of the traits associated with other types of migrants who have undergone conversion, but differs in the ways North Korean migrant conversions are heavily inflected by the geopolitical reality of Korean national division. My work illuminates a Christian project that facilitates North Korean refugee conversions and their spiritual and political loyalty shifts in ways that enunciate evangelical anticommunist propaganda. However, the supposed teleological transformation of the converts becomes ambiguous and contested as they claim future leadership in calling for national evangelization.

With respect to the socio-political specificities of North Korean religious conversion, this chapter engages in a set of inquiries about conversion narrative. For one, refugee-migrants' narratives tend to be used on the websites of humanitarian organizations for the purpose of evoking sympathy in potential donors. Provocative visual images interspersed with stories serve to multiply a rigid stereotype of every refugee as a helpless, "speechless emissary," to use Lisa Malkki's (1996) term, highlighting the lack of recognition of each refugee's personal agency. Conversion narratives are in principle a confession of faith by a person who gives up his or her agency and submits to God. Essential to religious narratives is the teller's first-person delivery of his or her experiences with divine power, and the individual's free will and choice, as a Christian, to accept "Jesus Christ as my savior." For Korean evangelicals in general and new converts in particular, it is imperative to believe in essence that by throwing themselves before the Lord they will "dwell in the land, and enjoy security" (Psalm 37: 3). Such a seemingly agentive form of submission is only a part of the conversion process, which, as theologian Lewis R. Rambo (1993) asserts, is not universal but varies under different historical circumstances. The narrativization of conversion experiences is thus in need of interpretation with respect to the socio-political predicaments that North Korean converts come to reshape by means of learned vocabularies and Biblical terms.

As a form of ritual, there is little doubt that conversion narratives generate "the dual effect of the conversion, the strengthening of their [believers'] faith and the transformation of their [believers'] lives" (Stromberg 1993: 3). Susan Harding succinctly posits that "fundamental Baptist witnessing is not just a monologue that constitutes its speaker as a culturally specific person; it is also a dialogue that reconstitutes its listeners" (1987: 35). My intention is not to suggest that refugee and religious narratives are entirely different, but rather to highlight the ways by which refugee narratives of conversion become more complex and compelling than a refugee or religious narrative on its own.

North Korean refugee conversion narratives are showcased as evidence of God's greater works for the Korean nation as a whole among Korean evangelicals. These narratives are largely hosted by conservative churches that provide the migrants with financial and social benefits. In return, by thematizing miracles, national evangelization, and human rights, the migrants provide new spiritual inspiration for South Korean (and sometimes foreign) believers. In this genre of expression, North Korean narrators no longer appear as helpless. Instead they are the chosen ones and are seen as those who receive—not from aid agencies, but from divine power—and those who serve as the means of God's will. Additionally, past suffering is evidence of God's providence, and the present is seen as precious preparation for the future.

Such a "positive" life transformation, however, calls for interpretation in the broader contexts in which the narratives are situated. For example, North Korean converts deliver faithful testimonies before South Korean or overseas believers who are donors (or would-be donors) to either underground missionary work or North Korean human rights campaigns. Their conversion narratives and testimonials often reproduce Cold War sentiments, not in the secular political sense, but in a bipolarized religious sense. Therefore the term "refugee," as it appears in the Bible and is experienced through North Korean conversion narratives, comes to stand for those who can be considered God's warriors and who are destined to work for a Christianized reunified nation. The remainder of this chapter introduces and analyzes the main storyline of the testimonials of two North Korean refugee converts, Hasa and Grace (as they will be known in this chapter), and then concludes with a summary and further research questions.

Evangelical language and "refugee" passage

North Korean conversion narratives include details that have never been addressed in North Korean literature and reports and that are likely intended as promotional—not only for foreign readers, but also for their own people. That the authenticity of their stories is directly linked to their religiosity is arguably controversial, and does not escape the Cold War legacy that reproduces a binary opposition between North and South Korea. The evangelical language that migrants acquire and perform in the institutional Korean church setting demands special attention for its unique complexities. It is worth noting that the primary audience for North Korean refugee converts is not the North Korean people residing in their home country or even those in exile. These testimonies are mainly delivered to South Korean believers and occasionally to foreigners, as my first case shows.

The excerpts below are from the testimonials of Hasa and Grace, both female converts who deliver stories of their conversion experiences aimed at South Korean and foreign believers. For these women, giving testimony is seen as a public activity. Church is not merely a "private" spiritual space separate from the public and material world. Though this space is sometimes ambiguous and contradictory in practice, it serves as a "stage," a sacred and secular altar where these women's identity and faith are reborn, reformed, and revitalized as they "speak" again and again. Before continuing on to the main analysis, I will note two points. First, the video streams of Hasa's testimony that I cite here are all available on various church or individual websites. Also, I do not include a male testimony as there are no significant differences between the content and structure of stories told by either men or women, and because the number of male North Korean converts invited to churches is significantly lower. This reflects the gender ratio of the North Korean migrant population and the specific nature of North Korean refugee migration. As of 2014, 70 percent of the (approximately) 27,500 migrants in South Korea are female.

A born-again God's warrior

When I first viewed Hasa's testimony, I was astonished by behavior that seemed right out of a theatrical performance. She spoke very emotionally, cried, sang, played the accordion, and recited Bible verses. Her testimony was very reminiscent of a one-woman play or performance. It was given at a special concert for North Korean migrants in the spring of 2007, in the main hall of a megachurch in South Korea. Hasa was on the stage multiple times to sing and present her testimony along with professional South Korean gospel and popular singers. On our way back home by train after the concert, she gave me her autographed album single, signed "God bless you! From Hasa (Former North Korean Warrior, People's Army Sergeant), 2007." Because she always introduces herself as a runaway military soldier who has become a born-again warrior for God, I call her Hasa (Sergeant). Below is a transcribed excerpt from her religious testimony that is available online:

> Hello everybody! I am a runaway soldier who served the North Korean military for seven years before I came to South Korea. From a North Korean perspective, I may be such a bad person who deserves the death penalty. However, I am still a soldier, a re-born warrior of God. Coming to South Korea, I just changed my mission to fight for God, from within God.

Hasa, in her mid-30s at the time, was studying church music at a Presbyterian university. She praised God because she had been "doomed to be killed without knowing our God forever in desolate North Korea, where there is no Holy Spirit." Hasa describes the North as a place where she was sure she would be shot to death as she fled the army. Even though fleeing from national duty is considered a crime even in some more liberal countries, in the Biblical idiom of being "God's warrior," her "crime" is, instead, a sacred act.[2]

Many North Korean migrants arrive already aware of the social bias held by their southern counterparts. Furthermore, they know that South Koreans have little knowledge about and interest in the realities of the North. In addition to describing her conversion and border crossing, Hasa's testimony serves to educate listeners about the trajectory of changes in North Korean society. Her account includes very significant clues for understanding how North Korean society is declining and fragmenting rather than being dominated by absolute totalitarianism. Although economic decline began in the late 1980s, it was the death of Kim Il-sung on July 8, 1994, that had a resounding impact.

The people of the North felt as if this world had ended, as Hasa vividly describes:

> The North Korean people including myself believed that the Great Leader Kim Il-sung would never die and would live with us forever for generations, even after our own deaths. In retrospect, it was such a delusional thought. Even though it was hard to believe, I came to accept Kim's death, as I was seeing... the wives of officers living [near my army unit] run into our camp, bursting into tears and shouting out "how can you [Kim Il-sung] leave us? Please tell me. Is this real or just a dream?" They just rushed out of their homes, without putting their shoes on, coming out as soon as they heard the news from the army speakers. In front of our base, there was a plaque with the slogan "May the North Korean soldiers have honor" which was written by the Supreme Comrade Kim Il-sung. The wives were choking with sobs, passing their hands up and down over the plaque.

In the video, Hasa acts as if she were one of the wives, crying and speaking in a trembling voice. She reinterprets her belief in Kim Il-sung as a delusion, and the ruling system, in which she took part, as cultism. She reached this conclusion, "only after I received our Lord," meaning after she acquired a Christian worldview and vocabulary. It seems that her *Kimilsung-ism* belief system waned rapidly after Kim Il-sung passed away and in the wake of the natural disasters that worsened the great famine between 1995 and 1998. She also lost her parents, who died of starvation. In her narrative, her parents worked for the Worker's Party, but the party did not provide any food resources. Thus her parents were "killed" by starvation. Even more tragic was that "the Party and the leader made my parents be buried like animals, without any graves. On the surface of where they were buried, cars and tanks were traveling, making dust." She cries tearfully and exclaims that, "this is just what is called human dignity in the North." Human dignity, a core value in *Juche* philosophy (the North Korean official ruling philosophy), is challenged in her account in light of what liberal societies call "universal" human rights. The notion of human dignity or *In'gan Jonŏmsŏng* may echo for South Korean audiences the "individual" human person's inherent and fundamental rights, as stated in the 1948 Universal Declaration of Human Rights.[3]

As a born-again God's warrior, Hasa continues to narrate the ways in which she fled from her military base after she lost her will to serve the country and wanted only to "survive" with her younger brother, who was about to die from starvation. There were two main causes for her loss of will—the consecutive deaths of Kim Il-sung, whom she had believed in as if he were a god, and her parents who were not properly buried, after which she herself was prepared to die. She describes how she put her gun and gear down on the ground in front of officers who were scolding her to "do your guard duty correctly!" and walked away from her military unit, unhurried and fearless. She was not caught and instead made her way to Tureen (or Tomun), a border city in China across the Tumen river from North Korea, hoping to find her relatives. Her father had actually been born in Tureen and moved to North Korea in the late 1960s, migrating when the Cultural Revolution (1966–1976) was at its peak after the Chinese Great Famine (1958–1961). Her brief reunion with her father's relatives in Tureen reveals very interesting facets of contemporary history with respect to the relationships between the two Koreas and their diasporas, particularly between North Korea and Korean-Chinese people, who have been largely forgotten or ignored in South Korea.[4]

After narrating why and how she ran away, Hasa invites audience members into her moments of border crossing, which, as elsewhere, are always a life-threatening event for illegal crossers. She brought along her 16-year-old brother, too weakened by hunger to walk, but, eventually, they were able to reach the Tumen river, a natural borderline between China and North Korea. The water's current was much faster than she had expected, but there was no other way except to swim across. Instead of swimming in the strong current, she resorted to floating and bobbing for about 30 minutes. Once she reached Chinese territory on the other side, she was unable to locate her brother. She reasoned that her brother must have been too weak to swim and had drowned. After arriving at her uncle's home, she cried and mourned for ten days. Thanks to her uncle's family, she was able to mollify her grief and some months later she opened a private accordion institute through which she made her living. As time passed she came to accept that her brother had died. At this point in her testimonial, her voice changes and she shouts: "My brother appeared in front of me!"

In response, the audience begins to applaud. She couldn't believe that it was real, as one year had passed since she had lost him in the river. But he had survived and now looked very different, having grown and regained his strength. Even more surprising was that he had come to find her with a male South Korean missionary, and they began trying to convert her to Christianity.

He was talking about the Bible of God, which I had never heard about. He told me, "You should receive God right now. This is not an accident. God sent me and this missionary worker to you." The revival of Jesus, the Gospel of Mark, etc. Everything was new to me. He also told me that the land we are now standing on was designed and made by God before we were born. I responded, "Stop saying that! You sound like a fool!"

Initially she resisted her brother and the South Korean missionary, who continued to visit her almost every day and who repeatedly told her "God loves you and I love you in the name of Jesus Christ." She was disgusted to hear the same stories over and over, but she liked to listen to some gospel audiotapes given to her by the missionary. In her narrative, describing her ongoing resistance to conversion is more important than how her brother survived and converted to Christianity. Most North Korean testimonial presenters selectively present details, stating that it would take days to recount all they had experienced prior to arriving in South Korea. While omitting complex situations, Hasa brings listeners to the most critical and dramatic moment, namely her conversion moment.

One day, she was arrested by the Chinese police and imprisoned before the inevitable deportation to North Korea, where she knew she would be imprisoned, tortured, and possibly executed as a national traitor for having run away from her military duty. Unexpectedly, it was Jesus, and not her relatives, who rescued her from prison:

> Bleeding Jesus appeared to me [audience applause]. Jesus was bleeding from the side of his forehead, and from his right side, as much as his heart pumped out. With surprise I opened my eyes, yet he disappeared. Again, I closed my eyes, he appeared; opened and disappeared.... I began to beg him to save me... "My dear Hasa, you are a sinner. I am bleeding because of you!"

She articulates that she did not accept Jesus even though he sent her brother and a South Korean missionary to her. Her mind was cemented with *Juche* ideology and her heart was too hard to penetrate. It was God's will that put her in solitary confinement, cut her off from her relatives, and showed her the image of Jesus's suffering to make her realize her sins. Miraculously, she was saved at the very last moment by a Korean-Chinese prison guard official. Loaded into a military truck with other women, the official took her off the truck and outside the walls in secret and said "Run away as far as you can. I saved you because you look exactly like my daughter." In a life-threatening situation Hasa experienced Jesus in person. However, she was not "saved" until the very last critical moment when God sent her the compassionate guard.

The last part of her narrative claims that God chose and saved her for a greater purpose, the reunification of Korea:

> I believe that the Lord prepares us to be the vanguard for reunification. So if we are the cart for the evangelical reunification that the Lord plans, you [South Korean believers] should be the wheels for the cart armed with devotional prayers. I ask you to push the cart of evangelization forward together!

Explicit in this account is that Hasa claims a leadership role in the process of an evangelical reunification and mobilizes South Korean believers—the wheels of the cart—as the crucial foundational support.

God led me to Canaan[5]

Grace, a North Korean migrant in her late 40s, was serving as a *chŏndosa*, or catechist, a church position given to those who graduate from a theological school or program before ordination as a pastor. As evidenced in her narrative below, she first experienced God's miracles while in China. The Lord "responded" to her prayers even though, according to her, she did not know how to pray. As a stateless migrant at the time, prayer was the only method and power she felt could be relied upon. In the Sino–North Korean border area, North Korean border crossers like Grace are threatened with human trafficking, labor exploitation, physical violence, or the possibility of being arrested and forcibly deported to the North where various levels of punishment await the "selfish reactionaries." Successful crossing and navigation through these various dangers is often attributed, by the border crossers, to their being saved and led to South Korea by "God." North Korean refugee converts' testimonies thus begin with worship and speaking of their submission to God. From the beginning, they clarify how Protestant conversion has changed them. In her short conversion narrative, Grace states:

> Now I will live only for Jesus. Because I know now that He has listened to my prayers and that He is the way and the life for me.

Referring to John 14:6 (New King James Version), "I am the way, the truth, and the life. No one comes to the Father except through Me," she declares Jesus to be her savior and Lord. Her second line "Because ... He has listened to my prayers" implies her theological inclination, which follows a dominant trait of Korean evangelical Protestantism: an "answer-theology" that focuses on "religious experience" rather than "doctrine," its "this-worldly" oriented theology emphasizes health, wealth, and spirituality as God's blessing. This seeing/experiencing-is-believing religious focus is more prevalent in Korean mainline churches than relationship-theology, which emphasizes doctrine and the necessity of belief without directly seeing/experiencing (see Kim S.G. 2007). Grace's emphasis on her experience of a God who listens inspires audience members to be ready to experience another "conversion" by listening themselves to what God has done for her (Harding 2000). She gives evidence to prove that her prayers were heard:

I had to leave North Korea because of my family's extreme poverty, which began with the waning economy in North Korea after Kim Il-sung died in 1994. So in September 1998, I told my family I would go to China to make money and left. But it wasn't easy to make money.

In four months, I was homesick for my children, so I re-crossed the Tumen river. But I was arrested and sent to a labor camp (*rodong tallyŏndae*), where people who committed minor offenses and repatriated defectors are imprisoned. There, I was diagnosed with typhoid fever. In a month and a half, another person was diagnosed with it. That other patient died on the day of her release and I was sent home to treat the disease, but my husband caught it and died while I recovered in forty days. Only those who lived in North Korea can truly understand the situation we were in.

Dead bodies were scattered about on the streets. If an animal died, it was taken to be eaten, but when a man died, no one bothered with the body. So I tried China once again. In October 1998, ten days before the election for Kim Jung Il, I escaped North Korea (leaving my three children behind), and this became the reason I would not be able to return to North Korea.

When Grace first went to China, the number of North Korean border crossers was estimated at around 100,000–300,000.[6] The majority came from border towns in heavily industrialized and urbanized areas with little land available for farming (Demick 2009). The Tumen river marks the border and some spots are shallow enough to walk over within minutes. Many border crossers went back and forth between China and their homes bringing food resources, money, medicine, and more to support their family members who were starving or ill. Grace's accounts of the labor camp and the dead bodies are key elements that describe both individual and collective experiences of the famine to a non-North Korean audience. The moment when she was about to die of typhoid fever highlights both the extremely poor conditions of the labor camp and the possibility of God's hand in saving her, in contrast to the deaths of the other patient and her husband.[7] That Grace recalls her recovery as taking exactly 40 days is particularly auspicious. It cannot be known whether or not her recovery took 40 days, but the specificity of the number resonates with more than one Biblical reference: Jesus fasting for 40 days, Moses wandering in the desert for 40 years, Moses spending 40 days and 40 nights on Mount Sinai to receive the Ten Commandments, and so on. Grace's 40 days could easily be seen as referencing any or all of these events. Even though the veracity of her statement cannot be verified, when delivering her testimony to certain audiences it is likely that the mention of 40 days serves to authenticate her experience with God, her conversion, her status as someone who was called to do God's work and, consequently, how God has chosen (some) North Koreans to be leaders in the Korean (Christianized) reunification.

One day Grace heard that the children she left behind in North Korea had also made their way to China. She began to search for them, looking everywhere. It was at this time that she first heard about God from a friend who told her that if she prayed hard, she would find her children:

> I even consulted shamans, but they only talked nonsense. I first got to hear about God through a friend, and when I heard that if I prayed hard, I would find my children, I began to pray in words that I didn't even understand at the time. I said in my prayers that God is the one who really created the world, and since God made people that the Korean Unification is also in His hands. If He were really God who is almighty, then since it had been almost two years since I last saw my children, if He could help me find them again, I would do anything for Him. Within two months of prayer I was reunited with all three of my children, and I began to work in a restaurant at a retreat facility that belonged to a church.

Prayer is a key component in Korean evangelicalism, providing a channel between Christians and God in the name of Jesus Christ. It is not uncommon for people to turn to prayer when faced with dire circumstances. Although they claim not to know how to pray, they beg for help by saying "Please grant my wish, and then I will do anything for you." In Grace's prayer, God replaced Kim Il-sung, whom she had once believed was the "One" who was leading her and the Korean nation to carve out their own destinies. But similar to the majority of North Korean border crossers, Grace was not able to do anything but "pray" to find her children. That she found her children proved to her that God had answered her urgent prayer.

Coincidently, when I went to China in 2000, I made several visits to the church where she had once worked. The church was well known because many North Korean migrants came there for aid. When I visited, I was told that the retreat center where she had worked was under construction through financial sponsorship from a South Korean church. The construction was an alternative way to employ and help migrants. However, I witnessed struggles and conflicts among South Korean missionaries, Korean-Chinese Christians, and the migrants. Moreover, the church minister, a South Korean, had frequently been imprisoned by the Chinese for helping migrants. Considering the local geopolitical situation, the fact that Grace was able to work there could be taken as a sign of very good luck. However, the church was not able to maintain her employment:

> One day the church told me they couldn't pay me anymore and I must find a way to support my family. Then I began to pray again and received His answer. His answer was for me to go to South Korea—to Canaan—after traveling through China, Vietnam, and Cambodia. God helped me reflect on non-believing, poor nations and God-loving South Korea, and He let me realize why North Korea is in such a poor state and also what I must do.

This form of Protestantism that accentuates economic prosperity as evidence of blessings is not unique to South Korea, but exists widely in Third World countries influenced by Pentecostal churches. Even Catholic churches, for example El Shaddai in the Philippines, gain popularity by stressing this-worldly successfulness (Wiegele 2005). Similarly, the natural disasters, wars, and large-scale deaths from starvation that have recently occurred globally are also interpreted as a consequence of those populations not accepting Jesus Christ as their savior. For instance, Reverend Kim H. of K megachurch (pseudonym) gave a sermon on the colossal tsunami that killed tens of thousands of people in Indonesian and other south and southeast Asian coastal communities in December 2004. He attributed the cause of the disaster to the fact that the majority of Indonesians were Muslim (Chosun Ilbo 2005). Reverend Cho delivered a sermon during a Sunday service in his Yoido Full Gospel Church regarding his visit to Pakistan:

> One day, I went to Pakistan to lead a revival service. It is normal that there are about 10 to 12 children in one household. It is because the country is so poor that children frequently starve to death. So it is said that only half of the children survive. They undergo devastating poverty. Is that poverty God's blessing? No one considers poverty as a joy or blessing. It is a curse (*kŭkŏtŭn chŏju ipnida*).
> (Cho 2005: 56 cited in Chung 2006: 296–297, my translation)

In line with such evangelical views on the relationship between economy and religion, Grace attributes the main cause of North Korea's poverty to its religion. She also interprets being led to South Korea as evidence that God wants to show her "the reality" and have her acknowledge what she is destined to do. Her escape journey mimicked a pilgrimage. Her narrative continues:

> Accepting God as my savior and meeting [reuniting with] my children did not end my suffering. A farewell occurred after this reunion, as my daughter was sent back to North Korea. But God stayed with me all the way to South Korea and even now it is such a treasured memory for me. My daughter came to South Korea two months after I arrived. As God said in Psalms 34:18 "The Lord is close to the brokenhearted and saves those who are crushed in spirit" and John 15:7 "If you remain in me and my words remain in you, ask whatever you wish, and it will be given you." I indeed experienced that when I asked him on my knees, He granted my wishes; even when I was as a dead person, I found there is nothing God, the creator of life, cannot do; and I can love and help not only the souls of North Koreans but also those who are suffering just like me here in South Korea.

> My vision is to build a church to serve as a mediator not only for those who are going through family problems but also to help the ten thousand North Korean defectors in South Korea to accept God as their savior so they can send the Gospel to their families who are left behind in North Korea rather than just crying for them.

In her testimony, God relieved some of her suffering when he eventually brought her and her daughters to South Korea. This short conversion narrative reflects key characteristics that religion, Christianity in particular, holds for displaced people like Grace. They move through a religious network: first, God is the only substantial agent to whom institutional intervention and support is attributed; second, ardent prayers born out of the desperate and extreme conditions experienced by North Korean migrants like Grace mediate the relationship between person and God— prayer is the core element of the networking; third, conversion and religiosity are personal and territorial. While the aforementioned network convinced Grace of God's presence and works, her before-and-after transformation was spiritual and territorial. Even though her first experiences with God and reliance on the church initially occurred in China, her religiosity remained incomplete until she and her family arrived in South Korea. Considering Thomas Tweed's definition of religion as "the kinetics of itinerancy" (2006: 123), Grace's religious and territorial journey would continue in her service toward fellow North Korean migrants.

Conclusion

Both Hasa and Grace describe their life transformation as moving from being lost to being chosen. This transformation shifted them from "ordinary" North Koreans to famine survivors bearing witness to mass starvation; from surviving inhumane treatment and "a living hell" in North Korea to becoming undocumented border crossers and eventually to being saved by a divine power that allowed them to become South Korean citizens and to work as missionaries in the conviction that God's plans are particularly assigned to them. The significance of their conversion narratives is threefold. First, in relation to identity politics, North Korean converts reconfigure their past and present state of being and becoming in Biblical language while implicitly affirming their leadership role in evangelical and humanitarian missions within and beyond the established church hierarchy. Attributing the result of missionary works to God is customary in reformed Christianity in general and Korean evangelical churches in particular. In the learned practice of confessing faith, North Korean converts firmly evoke the authenticity of their religiosity and commitment before former and potential donors. In this light, North Korean converts present themselves not as passive recipients but as actors in benefitting from both God's provision and the organized transnational missionary networks.

Second, seeing North Korean conversion narratives as a ritual performance reminds us of the continuing Cold War legacy as a result of which a certain group of people has been subjectified as an emblem for state propaganda. Borrowing Ann Anagnost's (1997) concept of "enunciating subjects," Soo-Jung Lee (2006) provocatively stresses that the majority of North Korean war refugees (*Silhyanmin*, or displaced people from the North) who migrated to the South across the 38th parallel before and during the Korean War (1950–1953) have been mobilized to speak for the legitimacy of the anticommunist state regime in postwar South Korea. The rapid growth of Protestant churches up to the late 1980s is indispensably bound with their ardent role in supporting and leading the state's anticommunist propaganda efforts. State agencies such as the National Security Agency, the Ministry of Defense, and the National Police Agency functioned to make anticommunist sentiments routine by organizing public lectures in which some former North Korean "defectors" were obliged, if not entirely forced, to demonize the North Korean communist regime and society as a whole. While they maintain historical continuity, there are also unique distinctions in contemporary North Korean conversion narratives that show converts as more than state-sanctioned enunciating subjects speaking for the state regime. Their position is differentiated by their claim to be chosen by God and by their dedication to mission work. The perceived sacredness of their calling is partly intermingled with a revival of anticommunism and partly an evocation of spiritual inspiration.

These seemingly reciprocal and dialogical aspects of North Korean narrativity thus cannot be fully understood without reference to interactive or contact perspectives, and this is the last point this chapter takes into account. With her seminal concept of mythico-history, Liisa Malkki (1995) draws our attention to the salient effects of narrativization and the multitude of ways Hutu refugees continue to contour their past and present events and the world in the context of refugee camps. One must not regard the telling and retelling of mythico-history as only a collective practice of homogenization, but instead recognize it as a form of identity politics with the aspiration of recognizing and being recognized in the contemporary socio-political landscape from which they were forcibly displaced and confined. Religion and religious discourses are instrumental in the search for a future-oriented meaning of life.

7
Conclusion: Free to Be

Toward the end of the FS program, North Korean trainees take part in what the South Korean church calls *P'asongsik*, a ceremony that churches or missionary organizations hold for commissioning short- or long-term missionaries. *P'asongsik* signals the end of their ten-month-long training at the FS, and consequently the beginning of a new life journey as a model citizen. This much was expressed by the manager of the FS, and I consider this commissioning ceremony literally and metaphorically sufficient to allow for an open-ended discussion with which to conclude this book. The ceremony was, for the FS, the final stage of a rite of passage (van Gennep 1960), proclaiming a quality shift in the trainees' status and identity into future missionaries and first unifiers. This is believed to be the ultimate condition of freedom in faith. The idea relates to the primary concerns of this book, namely, the transcendence and reconciliation that are aspired to through human–divine interactions in contact zones. In this vein, Webb Keane stresses that "transcendence haunts modernity in three unrealizable desires: for a self freed of its body, for meanings freed of semiotic mediation, and for agency freed of the press of other people" (2006: 310). As a key characteristic of Christianity, this mode of transcendence is premised on a state of separation and yet it is unrealizable. Indeed, the Christian aspiration to be free within God is deeply intertwined with political, familial, economic, and national-global concerns and contexts, as exhibited by the globalization of yoga and qigong (van der Veer 2007). In the Korean case, however, I contend that its Korean version may require a process of reconciliation of two separated subjects.

Over the past half a century, we have witnessed, as Arjun Appaduraj (1996) spotlights, our societies grow smaller and transnational flows of products which accelerate peoples' transcending activities across borders, whether in the imagination or in practice. In the case of divided Korea, however, its people have hardly attempted to cross the cease-fire line to the other side. In the same vein, in each territory, few have fully dared to transcend Cold War logic in their imagination or daily practices. Nonetheless, the flows between the two Koreas occur in divergent ways and manners. It is through underground railways by way of China, Mongolia, Vietnam, Cambodia, and Thailand, to name a few, that North Koreans migrate to South Korea and beyond; and their migration is directly and indirectly entangled with Christian missionary networks, discourses, and identity politics (chapters 1 and 3). Further, their resettlement processes can only be understood with respect to local and global political climate changes, national identity constructions, and the neo-liberal market society in which churches play a significant role in configuring urban citizenship (chapters 4 and 5). By employing Mary Louis Pratt's concept of contact zones in which the migrants experience forced, vigorous, radical, or often gradual interactions with state forces, human traffickers, missionaries, and God, I tried to demonstrate the ways that the migrants struggle to accommodate them in their own terms. In this sense, the role of the church founders who led the rapid growth of Christianity in post-Korean War South Korea (Chapter 2) could be equated to some North Korean migrant converts who claim a leadership role in national and world evangelization (Chapter 6). At the heart of these accounts is a discussion about the nexus of modernity, nationalism, and religion embedded in people's life trajectories, which continue to flow out through broader transnational currents that, my ethnographic data suggest, are constantly converging with religious ones.

In this light, I am convinced by the metaphor of crossing and dwelling that Thomas A. Tweed uses in defining contemporary religions as "confluences of organic-cultural flows that intensify joy and confront suffering by drawing on human and superhuman forces to make homes and cross boundaries" (2006: 54). This theory inspires scholars' interpretation of the importance of religion for refugees and migrants for whom it serves as the dynamics of homemaking and crossing borders (Horstmann and Jung 2015). For North Korean migrants, Christianity appears to still be a new culture rather than a traditional belief. In other words, the migrants' conversion to Christianity is a process of ongoing negotiation and configuration that either relies on or accommodates existing church hierarchy and networks within or beyond which some of them continue to make their home and cross social, cultural, and national boundaries. Christianity and the migrants are both itinerant.

Tweed also takes into account a blind spot that the theory of religion, as confluences of organic-cultural flows, may not be able to fully articulate (2006: 171–178). That is, the agency of individuals. In this spirit, the rest of this concluding chapter is devoted to pondering the meanings and practices of what the manager of the FS claims as the ultimate condition of freedom, through the life trajectory of a North Korean missionary, Mrs Kim, whose devotion was exceptionally influential not only in the FS but also in the North Korean community in Seoul (Figures 7.1 and 7.2).

Pastoral caring and freedom

One afternoon, Mrs Kim asked me to go with her to the village office. She wanted me to persuade the personnel in charge of social welfare to extend her full national insurance coverage. This was in the year the government modified the North Korean migrants' support policy and Mrs Kim had been required, like other migrants, to pay the national insurance fee. While I implored the office worker to reconsider, Mrs Kim sat next me with her head drooping. The office worker politely refused

Figure 7.1   The FS commissioning ceremony at Imjingak
Source: Courtesy of the Author.

Figure 7.2   A decoration with fruits to share after the ceremony
Source: Courtesy of the Author.

her request giving the following reasons: Mrs Kim had been in South Korea for seven years and was earning enough income through formal (i.e., from the FS, her employer) and informal means (e.g., by delivering testimonials in churches or lectures at workshops, not recorded for tax purposes) and her two adult sons did not qualify her for a social welfare extension. We left with no success. Mrs Kim told me in frustration,

> Mr Jung, you know well about my family situation and how hard I work every day without a break. I came to this *Chayu Taehan* (liberal South Korea) to live, but for people like us, although we survived hunger in the North, it is not easy to live here. I don't know what freedom is.

She agreed with the village office worker that it was time for her to live independently like ordinary South Koreans. But it was clear to me that the loss of the full health coverage once granted by the state gave her a feeling of deprivation. I realized that, for her and her migrant peers, benefits given by the state were not considered shameful, as most citizens of Seoul perceive them to be. Rather those benefits are a substantial and symbolic marker signifying that they are "cared for" by the state. Such a feeling of being cared for is different from being passively dependent on a state system. She did not consider that she had abandoned her country, but that her fatherland (i.e., North Korea) had turned its back on her and her family. Her statement "I don't know what freedom is" poses a question that spurs an examination of freedom "as much as a sensation or feeling as an idea" (Humphrey 2005: 2) with regard to her life trajectory and socio-political encounters.

In North Korea, free housing, free medical care, free education for children, and food distribution had once been given to Mrs Kim and other citizens in the name of "Our Dear Father Kim Il-sung." Such "free" packages had begun to wane in socialist North Korea from the mid-1980s and then had all but disappeared after Kim Il-sung's death in 1994. The resultant great famine, the Arduous March (1995–1998), resulted in the deaths of at least one million people. The remaining collective and national strength focused on maintaining governance of the country through the notion of liberty, which, for North Korea, equated to a nationalist independent spirit rallied against the imperial United States under the banner of the Military First Policy. This policy is rooted in *Juche*, which stands for political independence, economic self-sustenance, and self-reliance in defense. The "self" in this principle means the national, and not individual, self.[1] However, Mrs Kim, like her compatriots, survived, not by relying on the state's distribution system, but by relying only on her "self" as a mother of children while her husband kept going to a workplace that provided nothing. Her husband became a "daytime light bulb," a common term given to adult men whose efforts were useless in supporting North Korean households. In her household Mrs Kim was the only substantial breadwinner. She utilized all her social networks and resources including her husband's title (as a high-ranking official at the Office of Railroads), as well as connections with military officials, local authorities, and so on, to make money. By her account she undertook a big business. Engaged in black market dealing in stolen salt, she joined a conspiracy with military officials who were in charge of delivering and distributing the salt to various districts. Such activity, culminating in private, black market sales became widespread throughout her province after the mid-1990s. Her husband and sons were very proud of her ability. Her household and those who collaborated with her became wealthier thanks to her talent in business management, a skill that allowed individual and local levels of economic self-sustenance. In a sense, she felt greater freedom in such economic activities when the country turned out to be a "living hell," but such an underground-reliant freedom was fragile when the national "self-reliance" in defense became stronger.

Eventually she and her family left everything behind for China where she had relatives in the Korean-Chinese Autonomous Prefecture. Her great aunt took her to church a few times, but whenever she attended, she felt that such a place was only for "insane people" whose methods of prayer looked abnormal—shouting, tearful crying, and speaking in tongues, to name a few of the practices she witnessed. But it was when she crossed the nine-fold fenced border from China to Mongolia at night that she knelt down together with five other fellow migrants, including her husband, and prayed "God save us," although she didn't know how to pray. They had to cross 100 km of desert before the sun rose. The sand storms were horrible, but she kept praying while walking until suddenly the wind direction reversed and they were all able to walk better. Her husband recalled with her that "it was strange." She told me that this was the first miracle she had experienced in her life.

While some migrants, like Mrs Kim, testify to "miraculous" experiences, others point out that it was neither map nor compass but only their will to survive that led them to succeed in crossing multiple borders. Both experiences are often dubbed as "perilous journeys for freedom" in the mass media, even though in the migrants' own accounts the main "reason" for coming to South Korea was because "we were not able to live there" (as undocumented border crossers in China) and because of the extreme fear of potential punishment if they were deported back to North Korea. In my extensive interviews with migrants in both China and South Korea, indeed, the term freedom is unclear and is not entirely imagined by migrants as their main reason for border crossing. It is through the language of evangelical faith-based activities and churches that run secret shelters and underground railroads that the migrants come to learn that some forms of freedom, in particular religious freedom, were missing in the North.

At this point, one may recall a recent case of nine young North Korean refugees who were deported to North Korea from Laos by way of China in May 2013. The Laotian government treated the case as human trafficking of under-age North Koreans by South Korean Christian missionaries. The North Korean government also accused the missionaries of luring and kidnapping its citizens. In contrast, the South Korean government and North Korean human rights advocates reproached Laos, China, and North Korea.[2] Not surprisingly, in these uncompromising arguments between state powers, and international human rights and Christian organizations, the young refugees' voices are completely missing,[3] but they appear to be "innocent victims" of either human trafficking or human rights violations. Though the vocabularies used in this case are all associated with "universalized" human rights, we find that these young orphans had no room to choose their destinations whatsoever, but were led by either missionaries or state powers. It is mainly faith-based human rights organizations, like the US-based Defense Forum, that support the shelters and orphanages and also operate the rescue missions. Suzanne Scholte from the Defense Forum reported to news media that her organization had arranged for the adoption of three of the nine children, by families in the United States, before this "accident" occurred.

While some extreme liberals in western societies argue that people should be able to move around without passports, the aforementioned institutions exercise "universal" norms to mobilize undocumented North Korean migrants, including street children, to claim a legal status other than a North Korean one. To be free, for them, comes to mean finding legality through physical movements that are intrinsically associated with politico-ideological loyalty shifts and, often, conversion to Christianity (Jung 2011).

The concept of *chayu*, or freedom, in this book refers to aspirations that, as Arjun Appadurai and Peter van der Veer suggest,[4] are tightly linked to a dialectic, and not a teleological, cultural project of people and ideas interacting to define or empower the capacities to desire and achieve them. The concept of "freedom" is part of a new set of western ideas and knowledge that was enthusiastically imported and translated by local intellectuals and national leaders over the course of modern Korean nation-state building following the Japanese annexation and subsequent national division. As Caroline Humphrey (2005) sheds light on Russian forms of freedom that are all distinct from conventional individual rights-based freedom,[5] I look closely at North Korean migrants' life journeys that are complicatedly intertwined with nation-state and (trans)national religious powers. Interestingly, evangelical Protestantism is a crucial part of how migrants "navigate" where and what freedom should be and look like. My interest lies in Seoul as a spatial context, where the concept of freedom, or *chayu*, is highly contested in an arena where northerners confront contradictory power struggles.

Upon their arrival in Seoul, North Korean migrants are recipients of a "package" of freedoms including a Cold War era liberalism that seems to predetermine their political identity in the name of national security, and a neo-liberal welfare system that positions them as low-income households in the eyes of the government. Socially, migrants are exposed to large numbers of religious institutions and consumerist behaviors that are perceived as unavailable in "communist" North Korea, and competitive job and marriage markets where they learn how to choose or be chosen. Religion is dynamically intertwined with and embedded in the mundane urban lifestyles and imaginations that are construed through and also construe the nature of human–divine networks in megacity Seoul.

Cold War politics, the neo-liberal state, the evangelical church

The number of religious symbols and institutions exploded in post-division Seoul;[6] all religions, including the so-called world religions as well as traditional ones, became prosperous and enriched, and yet Protestantism grew fastest, under the auspices of American churches and in collaboration with the state (Kang 2007). Protestant leaders like Reverend Han Kyŏng-jik and his church received foreign aid that they redistributed to war-scarred people in Seoul. In the same vein, Protestantism provided vocabularies through which traumatic experiences, in particular those suffered at the hand of communists, were recognized and sympathized with as a sign that the sufferers were the chosen people rather than that they had sinned. Victimhood religiosity emerged and replaced earlier notions that viewed as a sin collaboration with imperial Japan (cf. Lim 2012).

Today, at the national level, among the competing forms of narrative about freedom, the winner is Cold War liberalism whereby the privileged right-wing elements and authoritarian regimes place "national security" and "capitalism" above such values as social justice, equality, individual based rights, antidiscrimination, and so on (Kim D. 2001; Lee 2004). The latter values were pursued by progressive religious leaders, intellectuals, and college students who led social movements for political democratization and the human rights of urban laborers, but with more emphasis on the national collective "we" than the individual "I." Anticommunism was a shared tendency and sentiment among both forces and in particular it formed a central core and an irreconcilable ill feeling in nearly all Christian denominations. The term "liberal democracy" has become equivalent to anticommunist nationalism, and evangelical Protestant churches have undertaken to safeguard it as a sacred value. This Korean version of McCarthyism is so rigid and powerful that any rational discussion or self-reflection about it is hardly acceptable (cf. Kant in Laidlaw 2002: 314–315). In Seoul, anti-government protesters, trade-union hunger strikers, anti-development renters, anti-US–South Korea joint military exercise campaign participants, LGBT advocates, and, moreover, unification protestors are still all accused of being "Reds," evil forces threatening national security.

It is crucial to acknowledge that, over time, North Korea and its territory became an ahistorical "evil" Other, dark and frozen, while first generation migrants coming from the territory shortly after national division (1945) and during the Korean War (1950–1953) became objectified as exemplary victims, as well as being marginalized, in the South. There are continuities and differences between these earlier war refugees and the newcomers who have come to the South since the mid-1990s. It is equally crucial to recall the section in Chapter 4 in which I elaborated the significance of the economic crises that hit both North and South Korea after the mid-to-late 1990s, though the degree of severity in each state was immensely different. In the South, the Asian debt crisis forced the state to privatize public enterprises, withdraw regulations for hosting foreign capital, and thus retreat from the market. It was a neo-liberal reform transforming South Korea into a neo-liberal workfare state (Song 2009).[7] Similarly yet differently, when its economic recession began in the mid-to-late 1980s as a consequence of the changing geopolitical climate, involving the collapse of the Soviet Union (Armstrong 2013: 243–281), North Korea enacted the Military First Policy to secure its national sovereignty and recover its control over the people and the ever-growing underground market.

Amid these complex and drastic shifts in both South and North Korea and in China, in 1997 the South Korean government issued the Act for Supporting North Korean Defectors as a result of which North Korean migrants who arrived in the South became only partly supported by the state, and were instead encouraged to assimilate and fit into the neo-liberal market society as part of the vision of a reunified nation-state (Chapter 4). This is not to say that the legacy of Cold War state machinery has weakened. The neo-liberal welfare techniques which governmental and non-governmental organizations practice were oddly fused with preexisting Cold War methods. Evangelical Protestant churches embraced the returning "brothers and sisters" in the name of helping North Koreans and national evangelization.

As discussed in Chapter 4, upon their arrival in South Korea, North Korean migrants are sent to *Taesŏngkongsa* in Seoul, a government interrogation facility where they are questioned by security agents about virtually everything including their previous experiences and the information they have about the North and China. The main purpose of the interrogation is to sort out anyone whose thoughts may be harmful to "liberal democratic basic orders" (Lee 2004).[8]

Soon after interrogation, the migrants are sent to Hanawon, a government facility located one hour south of Seoul where they enter a resettlement program for three months. The area is fenced with barbed wire and secured by armed guards in order to protect the migrants from any attacks by North Korean special forces. Such a highly secured and confined facility is run like a vocational school and a halfway house where the newcomers are taught substantial knowledge and various skills that may be helpful for them to live independently in South Korea (Demick 2009).[9] In both *Taesŏngkongsa* and Hanawon, the major religions of Protestant and Catholic Christianity, and Buddhism offer regular services, but the Protestant programs and extra material support are incomparable to others.[10]

When Mrs Kim was finally released from Hanawon to "real" society in Chunchŏn, a mid-size city an hour south of Seoul, she was not afraid of adjusting to the capitalist way of life. This was mainly because she "used to survive on [her] own in the North where [however] most people [do] what the state government requests [them] to do." She appreciated her previous experience of running a "big business" on her own in the North before fleeing to China. She was neither concerned about the politico-ideological bifurcation (i.e., conservatives vs. progressives) that tends to predispose those migrants with a North Korean religious-political inclination to favor the anticommunist right-wing, nor interested in attending church, a potent social institution through which the migrants could integrate into established social relations in South Korea. Instead, she just worked hard at a shopping center. Whenever she could make it, however, she went to church. It didn't take long before she became disappointed with the discriminatory attitudes of South Korean believers and the pastor's preaching that criminalized non-tithing; "You know we are living day by day, and oftentimes we work on Sunday. How dare the pastor ask us to tithe?" she remarked.

After one year in Chunchŏn she moved her family to Seoul for the better opportunities that are pursued by many North Koreans and found she enjoyed singing hymns at church. She enrolled in a training course at the FS and soon after completing it was hired as a full-time secretary. She was called "big sister" or "aunt" by North Korean FS trainees, and among those who knew her, none would disagree that she was a model North Korean migrant: sincere, cheerful, selfless, and spiritual.

In this period she experienced a transformation by means of her physical movement (from the provincial town to Seoul) and by attending the FS. However there were still hardships. She painfully recalled that she divorced her husband who was unable to adjust to South Korean society and even fell in love with another North Korean woman. She felt guilty seeing her older son hospitalized for a liver disease caused by chronic malnutrition while in the North. Nonetheless, she became more convinced day by day that God was leading her in a certain direction, just as the Bible tells the story of Joseph who was once abandoned but became a leader of Egypt (Genesis 37–47).

She was, however, always very humble regarding her religiosity: "Well, I must say that I don't know how much faith I have. I am still walking step by step to know what faith is. I am just like a kindergartener." She regarded the Christian faith as both a kind of knowledge that she needed to learn and accumulate, and a set of manners she needed to follow. Further, the metaphor of walking step by step signifies that her conversion was seen as a passage and process (Austin-Broos 2003).

As a matter of fact, North Korean migrants, including Mrs Kim, appreciate the usefulness of the quality lectures the FS provides but often become overwhelmed with the sum of elements they are expected to embody to be "the future of the nation." Indeed, they come to acknowledge that what is taught as the normative Seoulite morality and etiquette and as what a "free citizen" should look like is too "perfect" to exist in reality. To be a "superior" citizen one is armed with creative, not conventional, Christian wisdom and God's blessing (cf. Nietzsche), advanced knowledge about finances and business, and proper ways of speaking and behaving that make one an "effective" and "deserving" citizen (Song 2009). In other words, it is not a model Seoul citizen that North Korean migrants are mobilized to follow, but rather a model "North Korean subject" created and projected by the South Korean neo-liberal Christian imaginary.[11] I was often told that "I know all the teachings are very useful, but I have too much of a *headache* (*gori apasŏ*) to follow them" (my emphasis). The term "headache" has multiple connotations in the North Korean language. It could be merely a physical pain, but in most cases we should interpret it in its particular context where it can refer to complex somatic-psychological conditions that hinder the sufferer from thinking, understanding, following, or exercising.[12] Despite such "headache" situations, Mrs Kim appropriated all spiritual and material resources not only for her own career but also for "God's calling," namely, serving "our" people. This is why one of her colleagues from North Korea called her an "iron woman," a sobriquet which is elaborated in the next section.

Religious networking

Mrs Kim's nickname at the FS of "iron woman" may be reminiscent of Soviet-style femininity, but she is indeed a model Protestant lay woman joyfully serving others. One of the former deans of the FS remembered her as one of the most humble, positive, passionate, and innocent North Koreans he had ever met in South Korea. As such, it is no exaggeration to say that she was an "almost" perfect born-again example of the FS mission. She was also proud of herself for working so relentlessly and creatively. In addition to at least five days of working at the FS, she was taking two missionary training programs each week, and occasionally she was asked to mobilize other North Korean migrants to participate in various Protestant events related to North Korean human rights issues. In 2007, those events often ended up becoming part of a political campaign supporting a right-wing candidate for presidential election. She acknowledged that the South Korean political Protestants "utilized" North Korean migrants for demonstrating their politico-ideological orthodoxy—anticommunism.

For her, conversion to Christianity at the FS meant not only belonging to the South Korean Protestant community. This belonging went much further by empowering her to expand her networks across denominations and North–South Korean communities. She was convinced that God had called on her to serve "our people," namely North Korean migrants. As such, her social relationships, what she called *indŏk* (*inbok*) or blessedness with friendly people (which she believed were given by God), with South Korean believers were growing rather than enclosed in the logic of reciprocity. Her relationships were trans-denominational across evangelical mainstream churches, enabling her to receive extra financial support with which she could pay the tuition for additional missionary training programs. On top of that, she mediated between other North Korean migrants and her South Korean supporters. For example, when receiving material donations from some South Korean Protestants she became acquainted with via missionary training programs, she redistributed them to FS trainees or her North Korean neighbors; and South Korean churches and intellectuals asked her to bring or introduce other North Korean migrants to the programs, workshops, and events they organized. As such, what I find significant is that Mrs

Kim is utilizing the same qualities or behaving in the same way in the capitalist South Korean system as she did in North Korea, where she was a successful private, black market businesswoman. To be successful in North Korea it seems she surely must have needed to know people and to network. This makes one wonder to what extent she really had a "transformation" by converting to Christianity, or if she experienced "transference" of her knowledge and skill sets from one environment to another.

There is a significant cultural element that gives the religious networks "meaning" and that element is "suffering" discourses. Experiences of suffering that are narrativized and valued in the evangelical churches are crucial to making Korean evangelical "neo-liberalism" both cooperative with and distinguishable from government-based welfare policies for North Korean migrants. I found that recognition and interpretation of "personal" suffering using Biblical vocabularies became essential and predominant when North Korean converts delivered their conversion narratives in churches. The suffering endured under Kim Jong-il's "dictatorship" and en route to South Korea is so central that "Canaan," Seoul's freedom, is reified as "good" as opposed to the "evil" North Korea. In addition to this reproduction of anticommunist binaries, articulating suffering is itself so significant that it makes the testifier an "innocent" victim "deserving" this-worldly and other-worldly compensations.

I argue that this victim/sufferer consciousness reflects a distinctive form of South Korean urban religiosity developed in the context of post-Korean War Seoul. The explosive growth of Protestant Christianity (and other religions) was made possible through a series of massive conversion campaigns. If we read or listen to any prominent pastors' sermons and even testimonies by lay men and women, from the beginning of the growth onward, experiences of suffering, like physical and psychological illness, familial crises, economic difficulties, political persecution, and so on, are likely to be interpreted as being caused by external and structural forces rather than individual wrongdoings and original sin.[13] That the communists were the cause of the Korean War, a great national tragedy, was a trope that appeared frequently in many sermons in the 1960s and onward, with them presented as the evil cause of suffering family loss, poverty, forced migration, and critical illnesses.[14] Such anticommunism functioned not only to silence and purge pro-Japanese crimes, but also restored and even strengthened the collaborators' domination, which was backed in South Korea by the United States. In the same vein, brutal massacres of people by the Christian militia (i.e., the Sŏbuk Youth

League) before and during the Korean War have never been reflected on or repented for in Christian communities.

Further, what is called hatred spirituality became so predominant that people tended to accuse external satanic forces, equated with the communists, of causing their individual sufferings. Korean churches have played a bulwark anticommunist role in South Korea. Their pivotal role is not only in comforting the war-scarred refugees and urban poor, and collaborating (in)directly with the South's authoritarian regimes (in the late 1980s), but in sacralizing evangelical suffering discourses to the point that no rational reflections or discussions about structural and internal problems have been permitted. This "Reds complex" works very efficiently in reproducing and sustaining the politico-economic hegemonic power structures and hierarchy that are equally central to the operation of a neo-liberal welfare state in which religious organizations are involved, particularly evangelical churches. Overall, I would like to highlight that the understanding of "freedom" and the behavior of "free citizens" that North Korean migrants learn in Seoul in general, and in the FS in particular, are construed through and confused with the enduring anticommunist legacy and forms of neo-liberal knowledge and etiquette that tend to both weigh on and empower the migrants in "choosing" their present and future trajectories.

I have tried to unfold the characteristics of "freedom" as experienced and exercised by North Korean migrants in Seoul. Mrs Kim's discontent with the limited health care system, coupled with lamentations over "present" hardship, suggest a reconsideration of the concept of *chayu taehan* or liberal/free South Korea. Based on her life trajectory, situated in the context of national division and post-Korean War Seoul, I have demonstrated the shifting state support policy, and church involvement in the migrants' reconfiguration of their identities as model "free citizens." I pinpointed the enduring Cold War legacy, neo-liberal welfare policy, and Christian neo-liberalism that are reified in FS programs in the form of a set of "substantial" knowledge, a work ethic represented by the term *sŏngsil* or sincerity, and ways of speaking and behaving in order to fit into the market society with Christian spirituality at its best and most intact.

To better understand the efficacy of the FS, I documented Mrs Kim's individual endeavors that extended her capacity through networking. At this point, I must conclude with her continuing life trajectory, which is related to the contradiction between her lamentations and the greater opportunities she has generated through the FS and across churches, classes, and professions. In sum, I share with you my surprise when

I first heard that she has since moved to Canada, and is currently taking a seminary course while serving as a missionary for "our people" (North Korean "refugees") in her town. Her refugee claim was accepted a few years ago. As some may be aware, she was one of those North Korean migrants who took another underground railroad out of South Korea and, pretending they had come from North Korea, went directly to a western country where they could claim refugee status and become naturalized. I was told that the migrants expected a better welfare system on which they could rely in countries like Canada.

In Seoul, to be "free citizens" North Korean migrants are expected to become independent with minimum governmental subsidy and absorb the principles of the neo-liberal welfare state, whereas in churches, for example the FS, they are mobilized to convert to neo-liberal Christian ideal citizens. It is crucial to acknowledge that Korean neo-liberal Christianity coupled with enduring Cold War binaries (suffering as an asset, free South vs. evil North, etc.) tends to offer them additional opportunities by providing not only meanings to their life history but also faith-based human and divine networks that cater to their social and spiritual needs in living in and moving around liberal urban spaces. Mrs Kim's case suggests both the ambiguity and possibility of exercising freedom in Seoul. Her last email, received only a few weeks ago in response to a question I had asked about freedom read, "When being free means free from ideological and mental bondage and servility, and enjoying everyday life according to one's own will and demands, I think I have acquired freedom."[15]

She also implied that she experiences economic difficulties in Canada, as she indicated that she is not satisfied in her material life. She was clear to articulate, though, that she lives with a thankful heart and satisfaction as a Christian who tries to "empty myself" and who follows Jesus as a role model. Her latter account reminds me of Philippians 2: 5–8:

> Let this mind be in you which was also in Christ Jesus, who, being in the form of God, did not consider it robbery to be equal with God, but made Himself of no reputation, taking the form of a bondservant, and coming in the likeness of men. And being found in appearance as a man, He humbled Himself and became obedient to the point of death, even the death of the cross.
>
> (Philippians 2: 5–8, New King James Version)

Further, I recalled our conversation on the bus heading back from visiting her son, who had chronic liver disease, in hospital. I asked her if she could state that her conversion to Christianity was completed or not. It was an odd question, but her answer was so right that it contributed to the primary hypothesis of this book: "I am still trying to accept Christianity which is, however, ambiguous for me." Since then, I have witnessed her devotion to North Korean newcomers, her sons, missionary training programs, and the work of the FS, and as of today, she continues to dedicate herself to "our people" in Canada. Conversion is, for her, a series of endless journeys and crossings in corporeal and cosmic senses.

The journeys of the migrants like Mrs Kim that I have followed so far draw me to my primary concerns, which are not theoretical but empirical: that is, envisioning the reunification of two Koreas. I have documented that North Korean migrants are subjectified as first unifiers, acting as a metaphorical litmus test of the "future of the (Korean) nation," as the FS motto holds. This set of future-oriented aspirations, projected onto the migrants and that they also hold themselves, becomes more diverse and dynamic than solidly fixed as they interact with a wider range of human, institutional, and spiritual beings over time and across place, and with the practices and efforts they make to realize the diversifying trajectories of life. However, popular representations of current North Korean migrants' socio-economic adjustment in the South have hardly helped us remain affirmative in envisioning the future. This is mainly because they are depicted as suffering from much higher unemployment and school drop-out rates, as well as having lower household incomes than those of average South Koreans. With little doubt this kind of quantitative study lacks a deeper relativist understanding of the research subjects. Instead, my ethnographic and historical approaches attend to the migrant individuals' life trajectories that vary in scale and scope, and are spatio-temporally in flux.

In order to better discuss the possible future, let us recall the earlier sketch of *P'asongsik*, the commissioning ceremony of the FS, that took place in Imjingak resort at the northernmost point of South Korea facing the inter-Korean borderline. As *P'asongsik* implied, the migrants were empowered to imagine a predestined return to their home region in North Korea in order to save the souls of their relatives and neighbors and restore the economy with advanced capitalism. Such religious and national aspiration was oddly complicated by the tears of those who felt the traumatic guilt of leaving their families behind in the North. We did not linger so long as to recognize that the inter-Korean ceasefire line is thicker and more heavily armed than the Sino–North Korean border and more difficult to cross than the Gobi desert or the tropical forests of the Mekong river region that they had already crossed at the risk of their lives. The ceasefire line denotes the tragedy of family separation for the first generation of North Korean war refugees whose devotion was pivotal to the growth of evangelical Protestantism. Now its meaning is likely projected to North Korean newcomers such as the trainees of the FS. In other words, *P'asongsik* is emblematic of a historically constructed evangelical yearning for crossing, or in more vigorous terms, for national evangelization. This desire to cross northward has gradually faded as the first generation aged, but in recent years it has again been radically pursued by many new North Korean converts in collaboration with larger transnational evangelical networks.

My extended project with North Korean migrants beyond the FS site suggests that one of the most controversial anti-North Korean direct-actions to have taken place in recent years in the inter-Korean border area is the balloon-leaflet campaign. North Korean activists led this campaign in collaboration with and with support from evangelical individuals and organizations, and domestic and international right-wing organizations as well. The balloons they sent toward the North carried bags filled with tens of thousands of leaflets that articulate anti-Kim Jong-un slogans and images, often including one US dollar note and various goods such as socks, instant noodles, USB drives, CDs, DVDs, and so on. My research has shown that evangelicals contribute the most to the campaign; the Defense Forum, a US-based faith-based organization, has supported the campaign both materially and morally in the name of human rights and freedom of expression, while some of the leaflets show that evangelical perspectives and vocabulary are essential in portraying Kim Il-sung and his *Juche* ideology as delusional and amounting to evil idol worship and in rationalizing the polarity between the "dark and poor" North and the "prosperous" South and its advanced allies (Jung 2014).

This form of activism has been criticized partly because the North Korean regime takes firm counteraction against such campaigns and warns of shelling the place where the balloons are launched, and partly because it has directly and indirectly served to revive the notorious "Red complex" that empowers the conservative regime to control those in opposition, as represented by the recent dismissal of the Unified Progressive Party in December 2014 from the soil of South Korea. In November 2013, the current Park Keun-hye regime petitioned the Constitutional Court of Korea to disband the party on account of their supposed pro-North Korea perspectives. Seven out of the eight judges of the court voted for dissolving the party on December 19, 2014. It is an unprecedented case in South Korean history, and Amnesty International criticized the decision, which raised "serious questions as to the authorities' commitment to freedom of expression and association" (LA Times December 19, 2014).

It is significant to note that the migrant activists leading the balloon-leaflet campaign have neither been forced nor mobilized by the state to carry out these sorts of political campaign. Instead, as I have maintained throughout this book, they have been empowered only within the private spaces of non-governmental organizations and, in particular, in evangelical and right-wing ones. Additionally, it is important to mention that conservative broadcasting companies such as Channel A promotes, as marketable commodities, North Korean issues including North Korean migrants' life stories, concepts of femininity, gossip, and even unverifiable information about the Pyongyang regime.

I assert that the balloon-leaflet campaign reflects a present-day South Korean form of neo-liberal governance. Namely, that the state government no longer celebrates North Korean migrants as anticommunist heroes or heroines does not mean that the state draws its power back from identity politics. Instead, the state appears to have been subject to, or is making use of, "an increase in more subtle methods of intervention and technologies of governance based on ideas of 'freedom', 'enterprise', 'management' and the market—all of which function to make the regulatory power of the state more diffuse and less visible" (Cris and Wright 2005: 21). In addition to the consequences of the actions of private individuals and non-governmental and religion-based organizations, we must also pay particular attention to the revival of ideological confrontations that the present-day government has aggravated in recent years. Thus, it is partly true that North Korean migrants are subjectified within the nexus of state–civil society–market to enunciate the legitimacy of neo-liberal orders inflected with the legacy of the Cold War. Their evangelical encounters and conversion processes exhibit such complex operations of power as lived experiences.

With the term "lived experiences," I want to equally highlight that such a nexus of complex powers that the migrants pass through is neither solidly nor homogeneously experienced. In other words, as I have asserted in earlier chapters, North Korean migrants cannot be labeled or categorized as a monolithic, ahistorical group of individuals, nor should evangelical religiosity and networks. Returning to the FS's commissioning ceremony, it is worth elaborating this point. The ceremony, held at the impermeable ceasefire line, seemed so symbolic and touching that many of the northerners were moved to dramatically reaffirm their born-again missionary identity. For some, it might have been an honest expression, but surprisingly, the majority of the migrants enjoyed the *P'asongsik* as if it were a group excursion, marked as unusual only by the official occasions for praying and singing. They convivially took photos before statues in groups of twos and threes and posed next to tall and immobile border guards, not to mention had big smiles on their faces while making a V with their fingers. Indeed, unlike the South Koreans who were involved, including myself, who perceived the inter-Korean borderline as a powerful symbol of national division, the migrants tended to consider the inter-Korean physical border less real and more purely symbolic if not entertaining. Indeed, for them the Sino–North Korean border is more real mainly because of their physical experience of crossing.

Ultimately, the reunification should be understood as equivalent to a diversification rather than a homogenization of the culture of two Koreas. The evangelical tendency to look down upon local people and cultures in mission fields is not constructive to this end and North Korean migrants' conversion processes often reflect how South Korean-centric church hierarchy can be an obstacle in realizing religious and political aspirations related to a healing of the national divide. Thus, it is, perhaps, an unintended and underappreciated consequence of the inclusion of North Korean migrants in the South Korean church that has created a "God given opportunity" for the church to reflect on and reform religiosity in practice.

Furthermore, few have disagreed on the important role to be played by North Korean migrants in the processes of reunification and the drive for church restoration in the North. With little doubt, they will mediate future North–South Korean contact and interaction with larger transitional communities. However, I am inclined to assert that their role should not be taken for granted without making careful effort to transcend the enduring Cold War legacy as it is ingrained in aspects of political and evangelical cultures. This suggests that only through processes of negotiation and conversation between migrants and evangelicals will true cultural diversification, worthy of constituting and contributing to healing the trauma of national division, be achieved.

Last but not least, it is about time to resume the inter-Korean talks without any preconditions. Current South Korean President Park Keun-hye once notoriously proposed that "unification is a jackpot" which served to inspire people to imagine unexpected material gain from national reunification. Since then, however, there has been no further action proposed to the North, while a type of McCarthyism has been recently revived to control internal dissidents and opposition to the ruling party in the South. As elaborated in this book, the evangelicals and North Korean migrant activists have been called upon to work toward and pray for the South Korean government and the United States to resume interactions with the North since such contact can only pave the way for further mutual exchanges, changes, and negotiations. It is my hope that this research will contribute to this endeavor and that it inspires continued conversation and discussion and a deeper understanding that leads to improving the capacity of all involved to aspire.

Notes

1   Introduction: North Korean Migrants and Contact Zones

1. It is crucial to note that South Korean economic sanctions, known as the 5.24 Measure, ban both governmental and civil economic exchange between North and South Korea. The 5.24 Measure was initiated as a punitive measure against North Korea in response to the sinking of the Chŏnan, a South Korean navy ship, in the Yellow Sea on March 26, 2010. On May 20, 2010, a South Korean-led international investigation team concluded that a North Korean torpedo sunk the ship. North Korea denied responsibility. As a result, Lee Myung-bak's administration advanced economic sanctions against North Korea on May 24, 2010 (see Suh 2010).
2. As for the notion of a field, in an interview with L. D. Wacquant, Bourdieu defines a field as

   > a network, or a configuration, of objective relations between positions objectively defined, in their existence and in the determinations they impose upon their occupants, agents or institutions, by their present and potential situation in the structure of the distribution of power (or capital) whose possession commands access to the specific profits that are at stake in the field, as well as by their objective relations to other positions (domination, subordination, homology, etc.).
   >
   > (Wacquant 1989: 39)

3. "Alexander Solzhenitsyn—Banquet Speech." Nobelprize.org. June 23, 2010 http://nobelprize.org/nobel_prizes/literature/laureates/1970/solzhenitsyn-speech74-e.html.
4. Obviously I should not generalize this point for all migrants. I observed that the majority of migrants suffer chronic health problems and need full-coverage national insurance. According to the South Korean national insurance policy, full-time employment changes ones insurance coverage to a co-payment system. Those who need special and expensive medical treatment try to maintain a part-time job in order to keep the full-coverage national insurance benefit. Some free medical services provided by megachurches for the poor and old are also critical for North Korean migrants.
5. My unwavering belief lasted until I saw a documentary film made by foreign reporters during the 1980 Kwangju Massacre that took hundreds of lives. The then-President Chŏn Tu-hwan took office through a militant coup d'état.
6. As Timothy Lee briefly points out, the Sinch'ŏn Massacre has received popular attention thanks to Hwang Sŏgyŏng (Hwang Sok-yong)'s novel *Sonnim* (The Guest) in which Hwang indicates that communism and Christianity are all merely guests—foreign elements disturbing a host family (i.e., the Korean nation). In light of the term *sonnim*—which used to be a figurative expression for smallpox, thought, in the local folk religion, to be caused by ghost possession—the guests are also seen as ghosts in need of a healing ritual

to make it leave the patient's body, in this case, the Korean peninsula (see Chapter 2).

7. There is a debate among scholars working on the modern history of Christianity in Korea, whereby not all, but most, Korean scholars tend to emphasize Christian leaders' as well as laypersons' nationalist anti-Japanese movements, while foreign experts are likely to highlight that such interpretation is itself nationalistic. American missionaries persisted in the logic of state–religion separation, and this stance served to collaborate with rather than resisting the colonizers. (see Wells 1990; Park 2003; Lee et al. 2006; Ryu 2008, 2009; Lee 2010).

8. Author's translation. Cited from a film videotaped in 1999 and edited in 2000 by Okedongmu Children Korea, a non-government organization working for North Korean children's famine relief. I worked as a research staff member for this organization at the time.

9. Myung-hee, who was in her mid-30s when we met in 2007, once described the ways that her parents practiced *Juche* Idea:

> My parents were really serious about following the party and the leader comrade [Kim Il Sung]. As they learned, the first thing they did in the morning was clean the portrait of Kim Il Sung on the wall, with what we called "sincerity cloth" which they made themselves with luxurious fabric. While they were doing that, they prayed, "Let me live clean today as the great leader Kim Il Sung teaches us." In schools, they conducted ideology education in order to raise the loyalty of students toward the great leader Kim Il Sung for about 30 minutes before class, including singing songs together.

10. See http://www.voakorea.com/content/article/1943141.html (in Korean) for more detailed information. As of 2011, the number was 1,053, according to the United Nations High Commissioner for Refugees (quoted from Song (2012)).

2   Evangelical Nationalism in Divided Korea

1. CNKR is a Protestant organization founded in April 1999 that is affiliated with the Christian Council of Korea (CCK), the largest association of evangelical churches in South Korea. They claim that the number of North Korean refugees they have brought to the South, directly or indirectly, was more than 500 as of the end of 2006. In 2006, CCK decided to dissolve the CNKR and merge with Save North Korea, another Protestant interdenominational organization founded in 2004 that seeks North Korea's collapse (see www.cnkr.org and www.savenorthkorea.org). Kim Sang-chŏl, the founder of CNKR, who passed away in 2012, was respected as a leader of activism for North Korean human rights. A petition campaign that collected about 11 million signatures and was submitted to the United Nations was one of his achievements that aroused social awareness about North Korean human rights.

2. In rendering the expressions used for these particular people in organizations and mass media related to North Korea, I have decided to use their own terms. CNKR officially translates North Korean migrants as "refugees" in English on their website, www.chnk.org.

3. See Timothy S. Lee (2010), pp. 15–23 for a succinct description about the Great Revival based on the missionaries' memoirs.
4. Yun Ch'i-ho, a prominent Protestant nationalist, thought that "if Christianity were the truth, then it would restore Korean strength and dignity" (Wells 1990: 51). Yun put tremendous efforts toward civilizing Koreans:

> How then, given the present state of our country, can we hope for independence, and even were that attained, how will we be able to defend ourselves against subsequent evils and preserve our land? Thus the pressing need at present is to increase knowledge and experience, teach morality and cultivate patriotism .... There is no other instrument able to educate and renew the people outside the Church of Christ.
>
> (cited in Wells 1990: 51)

5. Meanwhile, some scholars in Asian studies used to assume that Korean history was not distinctive. That is, they regarded its ancient histories as a part of Chinese history, while its modern history followed the Japanese trajectory. Until recent decades, Korean studies had thus been more or less marginalized.
6. Yi Mahn-yol summarizes this declaration as follows:

> [It is] divided into three parts, begins with a confession of faith regarding the one true God and the mission of the people of the land, proffering faith-based reasons for the Korean Protestant church's need to eliminate the division. In the first part, the declaration proposes a theological basis for a "confession of sin regarding the division and hatred." In the second, it proposes five principles of reunification, by adding the principles of "humanitarianism" and "the democratic participation of all members of the nation" to the three—autonomy, peace, and pan-national solidarity—already stated in the July 4 joint declaration.
>
> (2006: 247)

7. One can check the daily status of how many South Koreans are staying or visiting North Korea for various reasons at the official website of the Ministry of Unification, South Korea. During my fieldwork (2006–2007), the average number of South Koreans visiting North Korea for business purposes was around 25,000 per year. However, due mostly to the accelerating political tension between the North and the United States in June 2009, the number decreased remarkably.
8. For a political science approach, see Chae and Kim 2008.
9. See Abelmann 1993, 1995, 1996 and Wells 1995 for the discussions about the concept of *minjung*.
10. Timothy Lee (2006) pinpoints a series of corruption scandals involving Protestant elites, revealing the cozy relationship between politics and religion.
11. In the same article, Timothy Lee ascertains that the emphasis on a revival gathering is not unique to Korean Christianity, but has been widely exercised and mobilized throughout the history of Christianity. Likewise, the Encyclopedia Britannica lists some examples of Protestant movements, such as 18th century Pietism in Europe, Methodism in Britain, and the Great

Awakening in America; later, in the 1950s, Billy Graham would spearhead a world-famous revival movement in the United States.

12. *New York Times*, November 1, 2004.

13. "Church ministers' power much greater than the conglomerates," published in *Hankyore 21* (No. 536. November 24, 2004).

14. A personal conversation with Kenneth Wells, a professor of Korean Christian history in the summer of 2007. In particular, he pointed out that Han Kyŏng-jik, a founder of Yŏngrak Presbyterian Church (the world's largest Presbyterian church), rarely blamed the North Korean regime in the early post-war era. Pastor Han was a key organizer of the Socialist Christianity Party founded in the North after the liberation, but soon his party was dismissed as a result of a series of violent clashes with socialists in the North after which Pastor Han had to migrate southward.

15. Some of these can be listed as follows: major national ceremonies were performed according to Protestant tradition; the army chaplain system and prison chaplain system were established; Christian newspapers, a broadcasting system, and education facilities and programs (e.g., schools, YMCA and YWCA) were built or supported; foreign missionaries were given preferential treatment; substantial aid and goods from the United States were distributed through the Korean Christian Association to individual churches, theological schools, and ministers (see An Jong-chol 2009).

16. From an interview conducted on December 11, 2007, at his office.

17. Cho's charismatic performance has often been circulated as a joke among local Korean anthropologists in religious studies circles. For instance, when foreign scholars came to South Korea with an interest in studying Korean shamanism, it was often suggested that they attend Yoido on Sunday to witness one of the greatest shamans in the country. Likewise, it has become common to acknowledge that characteristics of Korean Christianity have synchronized with Korean local religious traditions.

18. Retrieved from http://www.rapidnet.com/~jbeard/bdm/exposes/cho/general.htm.

19. Porterfield explains that although gospel writers distinguish between exorcism and physical healing,

> it would be a mistake to read into it a Cartesian dichotomy between mind and body or to suggest that the gospel writers viewed demonic possession as a spiritual problem wholly separate from the natural problems to which human beings were heir. From the gospel writers' perspective, sin lay at the root of sickness as the underlying cause of the malevolence to which all kinds of misfortune could be traced; so illness and disability clearly had spiritual implications, either as punishments from God or as manifestations of malevolent spiritual powers lurking about the cosmos.
>
> (2005: 22)

20. Reverend Cho's theology emphasizes that the threefold blessing applies to the complete man: spirit, soul, and body. "The Threefold Blessing is a term which encompasses the complete salvation of mankind" (http://www.yfgc.org/n_english/theology/the_yfgc3.asp).

21. Referring to the Exodus, South Korean people are portrayed as "the chosen" to reveal God's blessing. Interestingly, the evangelical interpretation of

the Exodus event is different to that of Minjung (the people) theology (progressive Protestantism similar to liberation theology). Minjung theologians consider the Exodus as a founding Biblical narrative for Minjung theology (Kim W. 2006), as the story highlights a key aspect: "the suffering of the *minjung* is not the original condition meant for God's people but rather a consequence of the Fall (here interpreted as not from Adam and Eve's sin but from social injustices)" (Chang P. 2006: 207).

3 North Korean Crossing and Christian Encounters

1. James Pearson, "Detained American was missionary dispatched to China," *NK News* (May 6, 2013). http://www.nknews.org/2013/05/detained-american-was-missionary-dispatched-to-china/ (accessed August 1, 2013).
2. Kato Hiroshi (2008) further elaborates his criticism against South Korean missionary efforts aimed at North Korean refugees in China. For example, people who are more successful in the assignments given to them by pastors or missionaries receive tickets to third countries sooner. Specific conditions that North Korean refugees must meet if they are to qualify include the following:

   - Does he/she have enough money (3000 RMB in Chinese currency) to travel to their destination third country?
   - If he/she does not have money, does he/she go to a Christian church in China and eagerly engage in morning and evening prayer services?
   - Does he/she attend Bible study meetings to deepen their understanding of the Bible?
   - Can he/she demonstrate a pattern of giving to the church in China?
   - If he/she wishes to settle in South Korea, will they promise to donate 10 percent of their income when they are?

   The North Korean refugees have no alternative. They must obey the dictates of South Korean pastors or missionaries while they are in China because they need the church's help to hide from Chinese police. If they fail to obey, they are very likely to be ushered out of the shelters. Since they are in such a vulnerable position, they frequently have to obey against their will.
   Korean pastors complain that North Korean refugees are enthusiastic Christians while they are in China, but they quit coming to church after they make it to South Korea. This is no surprise. Most of the refugees had to choose to be Christians in order to survive in China. Thus, they often lose interest once they have the liberty to decide for themselves. Unless one chooses to be a believer, of his or her own free will, this constitutes forced belief. This violates their freedom to believe as their conscience guides them, and thus also violates their human rights.
3. At the same time, the church stands as the most dangerous terrain and into which the border crossers are forbidden to go. Associating with a church is reported to be severe national treason in North Korea (ICG 2006). Many refugees testified to me about their trials in a detention center: "The first question I was asked was 'did you go to church, or receive help from a

missionary'. Second is 'did you meet with a South Korean intelligence agent who was disguised as a tourist or missionary,' and so on" (Author's interview with Mrs. Choi and Yang (pseudonyms) in Seoul, South Korea, March 15, 2007). According to testimonies, the most tragic story often ends with the public executions of converted individuals and the banishment of their family members to an "unlivable" place. However, I know of no one who actually witnessed the execution of Christians in the 2000s.

4. All names in this chapter are pseudonyms.

5. My primary goal for this fieldwork was to obtain first-hand data about North Korean children in China. Between 1998 and 2000, I was part of a research team for North Korean Famine Relief that was associated with a South Korean NGO and sponsored by the Korean research foundation, Asan Foundation. In order to meet the children, our team members asked South Korean Protestant Church networks in China to help us, because they were running and supporting many secret shelters and churches for North Korean refugees. In addition to the children, therefore, I was able to meet and talk with Korean-Chinese pastors, South Korean missionaries, North Korean adults, and young North Korean wanderers in China. This chapter is based on experiences and reflections I had in the border area in 2000.

6. "Introduction: Refugees and Religion" in *Building Noah's Ark for Refugee, Migrants and Religious Communities,* edited by Alexander Horstmann and Jin-Heon Jung (2015).

7. Chung (2004) describes a secret shelter as follows:

> July 2004, in an ordinary looking 3-bedroom apartment on the 6th floor [in a building] in Yenji, China, eight boys and one girl live quietly almost invisible even to next door neighbors. A 19-year-old boy named Hyun, from Hoeryŏng, has been staying in this secret shelter for 5 years. He crossed the Sino-Korean border in January 1999 when the famine in North Korea was extremely severe. He and his friends wake up at 4:30 every morning for their first daily routine—an hour and a half long "dawn-prayer." It goes on until 6:00 and after breakfast, clean-up, and a short break, they continue with a three-hour-long morning Bible-study until lunch-time. In the afternoon, they resume their Bible-studies, occasionally learning survival Chinese which they never get a chance to practice in the shelter. After dinner, an "evening-prayer" follows and they are tested on the daily memorization of Bible verses. It usually takes about three hours. They all go to bed at 9:30.

8. Recent studies on faith-based organizations' involvement in humanitarian activities for refugees point out that proselytization violates international human rights principles, and that evangelical groups undertaking humanitarian activities with a missionary message tend to annoy other faith-based agencies as well (see De Cordier 2009; Ferris 2005).

9. For example, "Amnesty International Report 2007" (2007), the International Crisis Group's *Perilous Journeys: The Plight of North Koreans in China and Beyond* (2006), the Congressional Research Service's *North Korean Refugees in China and Human Rights Issues: International Response and US Policy Options* (2007) to name a few among the human rights reports.

10. During fieldwork in the summer of 2000, I went to the church every Sunday and there met with a group on summer mission trips from a Korean-Canadian church, as well as an individual South Korean missionary who was seeking to bring single North Korean young men or women to secret chapels far away from the border area. The latter missionary told me that he was working to discipline and send young North Korean people back to the North as Christian missionaries.

11. The US Commission on International Religious Freedom (USCIRF) stresses in a recently published report entitled *A Prison without Bars* (2008) that based on interviews with former North Korean security agents, the North Korean government treats "the spread of Protestantism as a specific security threat" with the assumption that "South Korean and American intelligence agencies" were behind its growth (page 34).

12. For instance, when the Bush administration included the North Korean refugee issue as evidence of an "axis of evil," it was to demonize the North Korean regime for both its human rights violations and its nuclear weapons development that were viewed as a cause of global instability. Some critics have stressed that the human rights issue in regards to North Korean refugees has likely been utilized in the context of the political tensions of the surrounding nation-states (e.g., Chung Byung-Ho. 2004; see also CRS Report 2007; International Crisis Group 2006; Hiroshi Kato 2008; USCIRF Report 2008 for further discourses by international human rights organizations regarding this issue).

13. Protestantism had been very popular among ethnic Koreans in northeast China since the early 20th century. Protestant leadership led nationalist enlightenment movements as well as independence movements against imperial Japan up to the end of World War II. However, throughout the Cultural Revolution that took place in China during the 1960–1970s, Korean-Chinese who had been granted "model minority" status voluntarily closed all their churches. While the former East European socialist countries domesticated religious practices (see Hann et al. 2006), and the Chinese government officially let patriotic Protestant churches remain under its control, locals recalled that Christian/religious practice was extinct even in "private" sectors in both the Korean-Chinese community and in North Korea around that time.

14. A "house church" refers to an unregistered church of a small size having less than 20 or so members in the congregation. In the term "Three-Self Patriotic Movement," "three-self" means self-supporting (自立), self-governing (自養), and self-propagating (自養). This three-self movement is intended to promote these principles within the Protestant Church in China. In this respect, outsiders tend to assume that Chinese registered churches are under the control of the Chinese socialist government.

15. Refer to a web document in Korean written by Pak Pi-dŭk, a Korean missionary, at the Society for World Internet Mission website http://china.swim. org.

16. By the term "religious market," I do not intend to support but refer to a theory of religious market which has both gained in popularity and attracted criticism in the sociological study of religion. The theory views the revival of religions in the world, though western Europe could be exceptional as

of today, as equivalent to economic market phenomena mainly in terms of supply and demand and rational choices. Some scholars (e.g., Yang 2006) engaging in post-socialist studies, including Chinese studies, have applied the theory to analyze the growth of religion in China. Due to its founding comparison between market and religion with little substantial data, the theory is equally criticized (see van der Veer 2012).

17. Evangelizing North Korea and North Korean refugees has become the first and foremost mission in South Korean Christianity. Today it is reported that "Christians in South Korea have been among the first to help families in the North." Considering the fact that South Korean missionaries compete to establish secret shelters in China and to aid North Korea in a direct way, I am reminded of the sensitive issue of " 'humanitarian' philanthropies [that] served the vital imperial function" (Thorne 1999: 242).

18. Pastor Chun's activities were featured in the film *Seoul Train* (2003), in which he is depicted guiding North Korean refugees in their escape from China to neighboring countries. See also Tom O'Neill's "Escape from North Korea" in *National Geographic* (February 2009).

19. In 2007 when I went to the Yanbian area, the number of North Korean refugees had declined from about 200,000–300,000 in the 1990s and early 2000s to only 1,000–20,000 according to my local interlocutors. It is hard to obtain reliable demographic data about the number of North Korean refugees. Some data rely on local experts or organizations that have undertaken humanitarian activities in the region for years. According to a recent joint project in Heilongjiang Province in China in 2012 between the Korea Institute for National Unification and the Johns Hopkins School of Public Health, it is estimated that the numbers of North Korean refugees as a whole, female refugees, and children born to female refugees, stood at about 4,326 (minimum 3,047–maximum 5,542), 4,240 (minimum 3,014–maximum 5,575), and 12,735 (minimum 10,770–maximum 14,427), respectively (refer to Korea Institute for National Unification 2013: 386–388 for more information). Although their numbers have declined as of late, more than 65 percent of the all North Korean refugees in northeast China are female.

20. The anecdotes that follow were obtained during a period of field study at a village in Jilin province, China, July 2007. All names are pseudonyms.

21. In fact, I felt that she was asking me for help, but the local common rule in "meeting" the refugees had changed. Namely, for a temporal visitor like me, it was not recommended one offer actual cash directly to North Korean care receivers to whom one was introduced by a local caregiver like Pastor Chang. I was introduced to Pastor Chang's church by the pastor of a larger church, a Mr Kwon in Yanji, who was sponsoring Chang's church. Accordingly, I was expected to donate to Pastor Kwon, who requested that I not give anything to Chang in person. The way that Pastor Kwon was taking care of a sister church, i.e. Chang's church, represented a changing method for managing a shelter in the area. In the same vein, when I met with North Korean individuals through another local informant organization, I was requested not to give cash but only a gift or meal to the interviewees.

22. According to an agreement between the city police department and the village headman, all North Korean women were permitted to live in this

village on the condition they paid a seasonal registration fee (about 400 RMB Chinese currency, approximately 58 USD) every three months. Moreover, their half North Korean and half Chinese children were registered as legal Chinese residents under their father's family line. The particular case of this village was not officially reported to the provincial government, but operated as a hidden local policy within its regional sovereignty. Although one may find this village to be a unique example of trying to improve the conditions of North Korean women, what needs to be considered is that this predominantly Han-Chinese village claimed their North Korean women as property they had purchased on the marriage market, and so some of my local interlocutors regarded the aforementioned registration fee as a kind of property tax. This localized case was a product of Han-Chinese male dominated gender hierarchy in the framework of the extended family structure. Despite having a somewhat better degree of status than North Korean women not married to Chinese men, North Korean women's freedom was continually restricted—they were not allowed to visit neighboring towns but had to remain within the village boundary.

4   Heroes and Citizens: Becoming North Koreans in the South

1. North Korean defector Kim Kwang-ho family, who had resettled in South Korea in August 2009, returned to North Korea in January 2013 and held a press conference with the North Korean Central Broadcasting System. However his family fled the North again with the rest of his family members, but all of them were arrested in China. He and his wife and daughter, who have South Korean citizenship, were deported to South Korea, while other family members were sent back to North Korea. His wife and he were recently sentenced to three-and-a-half years imprisonment for violating National Security Law in South Korea by providing information about the Hanawon facility and a list of North Korean migrants to the North Korean government (Yŏnhapnews, January 24, 2013 and Voice of America, December 20, 2013).
2. Parekh stresses that "If we are to develop a coherent political structure for a multicultural society, we need to appreciate the importance of both unity and diversity and establish a satisfactory relationship between them" (2000: 114).
3. This volume is part of "cultural studies of the person" (page 6) based on the theories of L. S. Vygotsky and M. M. Bakhtin.
4. Byung-Ho Chung addresses "the military regimes in the South, which lacked political legitimacy and publicly displayed the border crossers as proof of their success, while the conservative political groups in the United States and Japan used them as proof of their moral superiority to the communist regimes" (2008: 5).
5. Lee Ung-pyŏng received the highest cash compensation according to the compensation system at the time, which as you shall see changed to a long-term support system.
6. Lee died from hepatic insufficiency in 2002 at the age of 48. He allegedly worked very hard, but collapsed one day due to an unexpected illness. It was

reported that before his death he often said "I have lived in Seoul more than a third of my entire life, but I haven't fully assimilated in South Korean society yet—just like oil is floating on the water." In the meantime, one of his acquaintances later testified that he had been consumed with guilt because his family was left behind and punished cruelly for his defection from the North.

7. This is important for further discussions of citizenship; as Foucauldian theory reminds us, we need to understand theories and practices of citizenship as developed by nation-states and as a set of political mechanisms controlling and regulating the "level, type, and range of societal membership" (Rocco 2004: 15).

8. Some Korean scholars tend to only consider the northerners who came to the South after the Korean War, and often divide them into two groups: one being those who came to the South before the end of the 1980s, and the other being those who came to the South after the 1990s.

9. Social discrimination by southerners toward northerners accompanied the emergence of the two nations, based on cultural biases that had been present even in the Chosŏn Dynasty period prior to modern Korea. Historical records show that few bureaucrats from northern provinces were able to achieve the higher positions, which were generally occupied by southerners. See Sun Joo Kim (2009) for more detailed history about that period. The cultural biases of South Koreans toward northerners in my project, however, are not merely bounded to the region but rather are a modern product constructed and inflected by the Cold War legacy and class distinction.

10. See also Kim Kwi-ok (1999, 2004), and Kim Sung-nae (1989, 2001) for more ethnographic discussions on similar issues.

11. In such an authoritarian period, the term human rights (*inkwŏn*) was equated to the position of anti-government pro-democracy movements and thus utilized to mean pro-North Korea in South Korea. Even today, domestic human rights activists working for laborers, homeless people, sexual minorities, immigrant workers and so on often encounter these anticommunist reactions in the field.

12. These Korean diasporas are those whose massive migrations first took place under the Japanese colonial force and their lives as ethnic minorities were also influenced by the Cold War. Since the Korean War (1950–1953), the number of other groups and individuals that emigrated as laborers to Germany, the United States, the Middle East, Latin America, etc. increased as the developmental state mobilized. Also, hundreds of thousands of children were sent as adoptees to western countries after the war and during the industrialization period. In 2009, the Korean diaspora numbered approximately 6.8 million across the world (Ministry of Foreign Affairs and Trade 2009).

13. Paik Hak-soon (2009) stresses that the Sunshine Policy stems from Kim Daejung's three principles of reunification—independence, peace, and democracy. And his ideal form of a reunified nation is one nation, one state, and two regional governments. Kim's idea, however, is not distinctive but is seen as succeeding that of the previous Kim Young-sam regime, whose unification

policy was a revised version of *Hanminjok kongdongch'e t'ongil pangan* (pro-posal for founding Unitary State Korea), which the Roh Tae-woo regime proposed in 1988. Yet Kim Dae-jung actually put into practice the idea with the Sunshine Policy. His, as well as previous South Korean proposals for the unification, is slightly different from the North Korean model which claims one nation, two states, and two regional governments. The North has taken this proposal for founding the Democratic Federal Republic of Koryo (DFRK, *Koryŏ yŏnbangje*), as its official policy, which has allegedly been submitted and revised by Kim Il-sung since 1980. Find more detailed infor-mation on the DFRK at: http://www.uriminzokkiri.com/newspaper/english/reunification/KoRyo.htm.

14. At the airport they may see, but it is unlikely that they can read, "Welcome to Korea!" The sign written in English represents part of the changing culture in South Korea that they have not yet been exposed to. The airport is a space of "betwixt and between" for them to enter into another stage in their life.
15. Adult North Korean interviewees in particular made this point. But young adults who have little and received benefits from the state in the North did not show this attitude.
16. Hankyoreh 21 (1999).
17. Due to my personal situation (married and a full-time staff member of a NGO), I did not stay at Hanawon all the time, but visited a few times a month. Instead, three young civilians serving as full-time teachers at the Hanadool school stayed on the weekdays.
18. From an interview with Mr Kim in 2002, an official from the Ministry of Unification, who was dispatched to Hanawon for about a year.
19. The concept of freedom is controversial in liberal and neo-liberal capitalist society; Marx makes the distinction between negative freedom from positive freedom. Basically, freedom is declared to be essential to human beings not only in Marxist theory but also in the US Declaration of Independence. Ideal freedom is neutral and universal. In reality, however, an individual's free-dom is restricted in favor of economic growth in a capitalist society. In the developmental states, other restrictions are applied; for example, laborers' freedom to form trade unions has been strictly oppressed by militant regimes for decades in South Korea (see Janelli and Janelli 1993; Kwon 2000; Koo 2001; Moon 2005). Even in a liberal capitalist state, laborers are "free to sell labor power," but not free to live without selling the labor unless they have enough economic capital. Neo-liberal norms of good citizenship emphasize productivity through labor power and the autonomous individual as the machinery of governmentality.
20. On February 4, 2007, Korean newspapers presented the then living condi-tions of the Kim Man-chŏl family who sailed down to the South as a family unit in 1987. All his children were grown up and living relatively well, but Kim himself had lost all his money by being deceived by a South Korean he came to know at church and was living in a makeshift house in a rural area. By the year of 2007, it was reported that 21.5 percent of North Korean migrants were victims of frauds in South Korea, 43 times higher than 0.5 per-cent of South Korean (see *Chosun Ilbo*, *Daily Hankyoreh*, *Segye Ilbo*, and *Dong-a Ilbo*, for example, on February 4, 2007).

5   The Freedom School

1. This tendency seems to have multiple roots: a militant method in education that stresses the mental/spiritual armament along with physical punishments; a forced ethnic consciousness that intends to homogenize Korean bodies; and obviously the nature of evangelical Christianity in attaching great importance to the faith.

2. Anthropological methodology suggests that an ethnographer participate and observe not only in public time and space, but also in private or informal time and space in order to better understand the ways in which a particular group of people produces subcultures (Denzin 2000).

3. According to van Gennep, Victor Turner elaborates "three phases in a rite of passage: separation, transition, and incorporation", claimed to be present in almost all types of rites. The first phase of separation includes "symbolic behavior which represents the detachment of the ritual subjects from their previous social statues to a new state or condition." In the phase of transition, "margin" or "limen" (threshold), the ritual subjects pass through a period and area of ambiguity." The third phase "includes symbolic phenomena and actions which represent the return of the subjects to their new, relatively stable, well-defined position in the total society" (1979: 16).

4. South Korean governmental support programs for North Korean migrants are being modified almost every year. Although it has been developed as a long-term (circa five years) aid project in recent years, the main purpose is to quickly train the migrants as independent citizens. For more information on the South Korean social welfare system, see Chapter 4.

5. *Inminbok* is often translated as a "Mao jacket" in English, but following the North Korean meaning, I call it "people's clothing" instead.

6. Kim Min-sŏk, "Migŭgi molgo-on Yi Woong-pyŏng daeryŏng pyŏlse" (Colonel Lee Ung-pyŏng who came with MIG jet fighter died), JoongAng Ilbo, May 6, 2002, 22.

7. Only two months after his death, however, the single largest number (468) of migrants, divided into two groups, arrived in the South. It was planned and organized by a number of civil organizations. The CNKR, the evangelical organization I mentioned in Chapter 2, was one of them. This "planned defection"—Reverend Ch'un Ki-won called it a "planned entry"—angered the North and perplexed the South too. And two months after the incident, the US Senate passed the North Korean Human Rights Act, which the South Korean government, liberal/progressive camps, and the North Korean regime did not welcome at all.

6   Narrativization of Christian Passage

1. Aihwa Ong (2003) traces the lives of Cambodian refugees who migrated from camps in neighboring countries to the United States where they converted to Mormonism in their effort to obtain spiritual, emotional, and material resources. At the same time the Hmong community underwent generational contestations between young Christian converts and the older generation who maintained Buddhist traditions and values. Daphne N. Winland (1994)

observed Hmong Christian women whose conversion and affiliation with the Christian church has not kept them from also maintaining their traditional values, practices, and rituals.

2. Otherwise, she would be stigmatized in the South. One of the deep-seated prejudices that South Koreans hold about refugees from the North is that northerners migrate to the South to evade prosecution for serious crimes committed in North Korea. This fuels the negative cultural perception that North Koreans are criminals. In more explicitly aggressive language, some believe that one who was a traitor to North Korea could just as easily one day become a traitor to South Korea (see Kang 2006 for similar accounts).

3. Whereas recognition of the inherent dignity and of the equal and inalienable rights of all members of the human family is the foundation of freedom, justice, and peace in the world, anthropologists tend to be particularly critical of this "universalization" of such concepts and suggest that generalizing terms like "human rights" be understood as a product of a particular time and place (see Messer 1993; Asad 2003; and others for more discussion about the Universal Declaration of Human Rights).

4. This part of the history of Korean diasporas requires further study. It may not be an exaggeration to say that by the 1980s, the majority of ethnic Koreans in China and Japan considered North Korea, rather than South Korea, to be their motherland. The national division generated internal conflicts within each Korean diasporic community according to which side was supported (i.e., North or South). Those who chose North Korea did so not only because of their birthplace or places of family origin. Rather, they did so because of the actual support systems North Korea initiated in the 1950s. For example, during that time Koreans in Japan were welcomed to return to North Korea and they also received financial support for building schools for Korean children in Japan (see Ryang 1997, 2008 for more anthropological understandings of Koreans in Japan). Meanwhile, in the 1960s and 1970s, when China was experiencing famine and the Cultural Revolution, about 100,000 pregnant Korean-Chinese women were welcomed into North Korean hospitals to deliver their babies. They were able to return to China with free food and baby goods. Several middle-aged Korean-Chinese people I met in China in 2000 showed a strong sense of family obligation to help North Korean border crossers and the country they considered their real homeland.

5. A part of this section previously appeared in an essay published in a Korean journal, Jung, Jin-Heon. 2013. "Narrativization of Religious Conversion: "Christian Passage" of North Korean Refugees in South Korea," *Hankukŏnŏmunhwahak*, 50: 269–288.

6. Statistics regarding North Korean border crossers in China are not considered accurate. Good Friends, a Korean Buddhist organization running underground research and aid activities, has provided reliable data since the mid-1990s. This organization's activities are relatively invisible and non-religious in comparison with Protestant ones, which are nearly always provided through individual churches.

7. For western audiences the scenes she describes in the labor camp may recall Auschwitz during World War II, especially as reported by Jeff Jacoby of the *Boston Globe*, who compares North Korea as a whole to Auschwitz based on

testimonies about "gas chambers, poisoned food, torture, the murder of whole families, [and] massive death tolls" (Jacoby 2004).

7   Conclusion: Free to Be

1. See Kwon & Chung (2012) and Cumings (2004) for extended discussions about the nature of North Korea and its history.
2. For example, Suzanne Scholte, the president of the North Korean Freedom Coalition and the Defense Forum Foundation, US-based international human rights organizations that are involved in the "rescue" projects, accuses Laos, China, and North Korea of human rights violations.
3. Liisa Malkki (1995) pioneered criticism of the tendency to regard refugees as nameless, passive, and mere victims in refugee camps and aid projects.
4. E-document "Comparative study of urban aspirations in mega-cities," http://www.mmg.mpg.de/research/all-projects/comparative-study-of-urban-aspirations-in-mega-cities/.
5. In anthropology, Malinowski spent a great deal of his later career on elaborating freedom as "a gift of culture" in *Freedom and Civilization* (1947), and recently James Laidlaw (2002) and Joel Robbins (2007) have discussed how the concept was defined and developed by such intellectuals as Kant, Durkheim, Weber, Foucault, etc., and how their ideas have been construed with and affected one another and the field of anthropology, and yet how anthropology could and should contribute to developing the studies of freedom and ethics in light of cultural reproduction and changes.
6. Seoul has witnessed various battles of different forms of freedom and liberty that people wanted to exercise and implement. Hegelian dialectical freedom might be better understood through the lens of religion. By the end of the Chosŏn Dynasty (1392–1897), inside the capital fortress no religious symbols other than the Royal Ancestors' Shrine (the Jongmyo), and its associated rituals were allowed. Greater numbers of Buddhist and shamanistic temples and shrines, and more "freedom to worship" existed outside the walls than inside (Walraven 2000). Self-converted Catholic Christians and other domestic religious rebellions aimed at the capital were severely and brutally persecuted. When the Hermit Kingdom opened its ports to foreign forces, the establishment of religious or faith-based institutions in the inner city signified the beginning of modernity. Churches, schools, and hospitals built by American Protestant missionaries, and Shinto shrines of the colonizing Japanese manifested new social orders which the local people either resisted or obeyed. For some Korean Christians the former places were meant to be a practiced place, in Michel de Certeau's term (1984: 117), where they worshipped God and prayed for national liberation of their own free will, while the latter meant national humiliation and religious sin.
7. Jesook Song (2009) convincingly examines how the South Korean neoliberal welfare state emerged without the experience of a classical liberal state, and concentrated its energies on such neo-liberal measures as employability, rehabilitation capacity, flexibility, self-sufficiency, and self-entrepreneurship. Civil societies that mainly originated from and were

associated with religious organizations, among which the Anglican Church was relatively more active, collaborated in quasi-governmental homeless relief activities. Similarly, the liberals supported neo-liberal reform in terms of liberation and democratization as opposed to preceding developmentalist regimes. However, Song has paid less attention to the complex responses and reactions of the faith based right wing that I want to highlight in this book in terms of religious neo-liberalism.

8. Recently some newspapers reported the human rights violation case of a young woman who was kept and interrogated without legal protection for about six months in solitary confinement at the South Korean interrogation facility. Though she was born and raised in North Korea, she was eventually found to be a Chinese-North Korean. At the interrogation facility she was threatened and assaulted, eventually confessing that her brother was a North Korean spy. Her brother had come to South Korea in 2004, had been naturalized, and had been working as a government contract employee since 2011 (Park H. 2013). The trial of her brother for spying as been ongoing since May 2013. This case represents the purpose of extensive interrogation— sorting out non-North Koreans (e.g., mainly Korean-Chinese) and North Korean secret agents; possible human rights violations could occur under the shadow of national security.

9. How to drive a car, how to sew, how to cook, how to speak standard South Korean (i.e., Seoulite dialect), how to use ATMs, how to shop, etc. are among the subjects introduced along with history, the legal system, human rights, etc. to name a few. My interlocutors also received medical treatments and psychological therapy as necessary.

10. Other priests and clerics who provide services to migrants in these facilities are often jealous of Protestant churches' support programs and see them as a model to follow. This is similar to what Alexander Horstmann (2011) witnessed in refugee camps on the Thai–Burmese border, where Protestant missionaries from different denominations, as well as Buddhist and Muslim-based aid organizations are competing and mimicking one another's mission techniques.

11. See Jang (2008, in Korean) for a critical discussion on religion's place in the neo-liberal regime, and Hackworth (2012) on religious neo-liberalism in the United States.

12. The North Korean migrant's term "headache" may sound similar to the English use of "headache" when saying "something is such a headache," but the former is likely related to the migrants' traumatic experiences.

13. I found differences in addressing conversion experiences between American missionaries' descriptions of the 1903 Wonsan Great Revival and the 1907 Pyongyang Great Revival, and domestic Korean modes since the Korean War (1950–1953). While the former weighed the repentance of personal wrong-doings and original sin as the beginning of the conversion process, the latter spend much more on recounting suffering caused by mainly external structural problems.

14. In the same vein, neo-Confucian patriarchy is often accused of causing housewives to suffer personal identity or familial crises (Chong 2008).

As such, an ample number of conversion narratives delivered in churches exhibit a dominant tendency in that repentance of sins or wrongdoings is less articulated than telling her/his suffering experiences as a critical turning point toward God.

15. Email received on June 13, 2013, my translation.

Bibliography

Abelmann, Nancy. 1993. "'Minjung' Theory and Practice." In *Cultural Nationalism in East Asia: Representation and Identity*, edited by Harumi Befu, 139–165. Berkeley: Center for East Asian Studies, University of California.

Abelmann, Nancy. 1995. "Minjung Movements and the Minjung: Organizers and Farmers in a 1980s Farmers' Movement." In *South Korea's Minjung Movement: The Culture and Politics of Dissidence*, edited by Kenneth M. Wells, 119–153. Honolulu: University of Hawai'i Press.

Abelmann, Nancy. 1996. *Echoes of the Past, Epics of Dissent: A South Korean Social Movement*. Berkeley: University of California Press.

Abelmann, Nancy. 2003. *The Melodrama of Mobility; Women, Talk, and Class in Contemporary South Korea*. Honolulu: University of Hawai'i Press.

Agier, Michel. 2008. *On the Margins of the World: The Refugee Experience Today*. Malden, MA: Polity Press.

Allport, Gordon W. 1954. *The Nature of Prejudice*. New York: Perseus Books.

American Anthropological Association (AAA). 1947. "Statement on Human Rights." *American Anthropologist*, 49(4): 539–543.

American Anthropological Association (AAA). 1999. Declaration on Anthropology and Human Rights Committee for Human Rights. Available online http://www.aaanet.org/stmts/humanrts.htm

Amnesty International. 2007. "Amnesty International Report 2007." Available online http://archive.amnesty.org/report2007/eng/Homepage.html (accessed August 14, 2013).

Armstrong, Charles K. 2013. *Tyranny of the Weak: North Korea and the World, 1950–1992*. Studies of the Weatherhead East Asian Institute, Columbia University. New York: Cornell University.

An, Jong-chol. 2009. "Munmyŏng kaehwa esŏ pan'gong ŭro: Yi Sŭng-man kwa Kaesin'gyo ŭi kwan'gye ŭi pyŏnhwa, 1912–1950 (From Enlightenment to Anti-Communism: The Relationship between Syngman Rhee and Christianity, 1921–1950)." *Tongbanghakchi*, 145: 189–225.

Anagnost, Ann. 1997. *National Past-Time: Narrative, Representation, and Power in China*. Durham: Duke University Press.

Anderson, Benedict. 1983. *Imagined Communities: Reflections on the Origin and Spread of Nationalism*. London: Verso.

Appadurai, Arjun. 1996. *Modernity at Large: Cultural Dimensions of Globalization*. Minneapolis, London: University of Minnesota Press.

Appadurai, Arjun. 2004. "The Capacity to Aspire: Culture and the Terms of Recognition." In *Culture and Public Action*, edited by V. Rao and M. Walton, 59–84. Stanford, CA: Stanford University Press.

Asad, Talal. 1993. *Genealogies of Religion: Discipline and Reasons of Power in Christianity and Islam*. Baltimore: Johns Hopkins University Press.

Asad, Talal. 2003. *Formations of the Secular: Christianity, Islam, Modernity*. Stanford, CA: Stanford University Press.

Asad, Talal. 2006. "Trying to Understand French Secularism." In *Political Theologies: Public Religions in a Post Secular World*, edited by Hent de Vries and Lawrence E. Sullivan, 494–526. New York: Fordham University Press.

Askins, Kye and Rachel Pain. 2011. "Contact Zones: Participation, Materiality, and the Messiness of Interaction." *Environment and Planning D: Society and Space*, 29: 803–821.

Austin-Broos, Diane. 2003. "The Anthropology of Conversion: An Introduction." In *The Anthropology of Religious Conversion*, edited by Andrew Buckser and Stephen D. Glazier, 1–12. Lanham, MD, Oxford: Rowman & Littlefield.

Bauman, Zygmunt. 2003. *City of Fears, City of Hopes*. London: Goldsmiths College.

Becci, Irene. 2013. "Religious Involvements in a Post-Socialist Urban Space in Berlin." In *Topographies of Faith: Religion in Urban Spaces*, edited by Irene Becci, Marian Burchardt and José Casanova, 149–166. Leiden, Boston: Brill.

Berdahl, Daphne. 1999. *Where the World Ended: Re-Unification and Identity in the German Borderland*. Berkeley, CA: University of California Press.

Berdahl, Daphne. 2005. "The Spirit of Capitalism and the Boundaries of Citizenship in Post-Wall Germany." *Comparative Studies in Society and History*, 47(2): 235–251.

Black, Richard. 2001. "Fifty Years of Refugee Studies: From Theory to Policy," *International Migration Review*, 35(1): 57–78. Special Issue: UNHCR at 50: Past, Present and Future of Refugee Assistance.

Blair, William Newton and Bruce F. Hunt. 1977. *The Korean Pentecost and the Sufferings Which Followed*. Edinburgh, Carlisle, Penn: The Banner of Truth Trust.

Bleiker, Roland. 2005. *Divided Korea: Toward a Culture of Reconciliation*. Minneapolis: University of Minnesota Press.

Boas, Frederick S. 1896 [1940]. *Shakespeare and His Predecessors*. London: J. Murray.

Bourdieu, Pierre. 1977. *Outline of a Theory of Practice*. Cambridge, MA: Cambridge University Press.

Brain, James 2006. "The Ugly Americans Revisited." In *Talking about People: Readings in Contemporary Cultural Anthropology*, edited by W. Haviland, R. Gordon and L. Vivanco, 4th Ed., 247–250 New York: McGraw-Hill.

Bruner, Edward M. 1986. "Experience and Its Expressions." In *The Anthropology of Experience*, edited by Victor W. Turner and Edward M. Bruner, 3–30. Urbana and Chicago: University of Illinois Press.

Buckser, Andrew and Stephen D. Glazier. 2003. *The Anthropology of Religious Conversion*. Lanham, MD, Oxford: Rowman & Littlefield.

Burdick, John. 1993. *Looking for God in Brazil: The Progressive Catholic Church in Urban Brazil's Religious Arena*. Berkeley: University of California Press.

Buswell, Jr., Robert E. and Lee Timothy S. eds. 2006. *Christianity in Korea*. Honolulu: University of Hawai'i Press.

Cannell, Fenella ed. 2006. *The Anthropology of Christianity*. Durham: Duke University Press.

Casanova, José. 1994. *Public Religions in the Modern World*. Chicago: The University of Chicago Press.

Certeau, Michel de. 1984. *The Practice of Everyday Life*. Berkeley, CA: University of California Press.

Chae, Haesook and Steven Kim. 2008. "Conservatives and Progressives in South Korea." *Washington Quarterly*, 31(4): 77–95.

Chang Kyu-sik. 2006. "kunsachŏngkwŏnki hankuk kyohoewa kukka kwŏnlyŏk (Official English Title: Church and State During the Military Regime: Alliance of Church and State and the Overcoming of the Past)." *Hankuk Kidokkyowa yŏksa* 24: 103–137.

Chang Kyung-Sup. 1999. "Compressed Modernity and Its Discontents: South Korean Society in Transition." *Economy and Society*, 28(1): 30–55.

Chang, Paul Yunsik. 2006. "Carrying the Torch in the Darkest Hours: The Socio-Political Origins of Minjung Protestant Movements." In *Christianity in Korea*, edited by Robert E. Buswell Jr. and Lee S. Timothy, 195–220. Honolulu: University of Hawai'i Press.

Chohan Hye-chŏng (Cho, (Han) Hae-Joang) and Yi U-yŏng, eds. 2000. *T'alpuntan sitae rŭl yŏlmyŏ* (Opening the Era of the Post-Division). Seoul: Samin.

Cho, Hee-Yeon. 2000. "The Structure of the South Korean Developmental Regime and Its Transformation-Statist Mobilization and Authoritarian Integration in the Anticommunist Regimentation." *Inter-Asia Cultural Studies*, 1(3): 408–426.

Cho Yong-gi (Rev. David Yonggi Cho). 2005. *Sŏlkyonŭn naŭi insaeng* (Sermon Is My Life). Seoul: Sŏulmalssŭmsa.

Choe, Hyun. 2007. South Korean Society and Multicultural Citizenship. *Korea Journal*, 47(4): 123–146.

Choi Sŭng-ju, et al. 2005. "Chonggyo hwaltong kwa chonggyo sŏnghyang (Religious Activities and Religious Tendency)." In *Welk'ŏmt'u K'oria*, edited by Chung Byung-Ho et al. Seoul: Hanyang University Press.

Chŏn Hyo-gwan. 2000. "Puntan ŭi ŏnŏ, t'albudan ŭi ŏnŏ: T'ongil tamnon kwa pukhanhak I chaehyŏn ganŭn pukhan ŭ imiji (Division Language of Post-division: The Image of North Korea Represented by Reunification Discourses and North Korean Studies)." In *T'alpuntan sitae rŭl yŏlmyŏ* (Opening the Era of Post-Division), edited by Chohan Hye-chŏng and Yi U-yŏng. Seoul: Samin.

Chong, Kelly H. 2006. "In Search of Healing: Evangelical Conversion of Women in Contemporary South Korea." In *Christianity in Korea*, edited by Robert E. Buswell, and Timothy S. Lee, 351–370. Honolulu: University of Hawai'i Press.

Chong, Kelly H. 2008. *Deliverance and Submission: Evangelical Women and the Negotiation of Patriarchy in South Korea*. Cambridge: Harvard University Asia Center.

Choo, Hae Yeon. 2006. "Gendered Modernity and Ethnicized Citizenship: North Korean Settlers in Contemporary South Korea." *Gender & Society*, 20(5): 576–604.

Chosun Ilbo (Chosun Daily). 2005. "Kim Hong-do moksa 'tsunami hŭisaengjanŭn yesu mitjiannŭn jadŭl' (Rev. Kim Hong-Do 'Tsunami Victims Are Those Who Do Not Believe in Jesus')." January 12. Available online http://www.chosun.com/national/news/200501/200501120300.html (accessed May 15, 2013).

Chu Sŏn-ae. 2008. "Kyohoe ŭi t'albukja sayŏk kaebal (Development of Church Service for North Korean Defectors)." *Kyoyuk Kyohoe*, 369(0): 23–28. Seoul: Changnohoe sinhak taehak kyo Kidokkyo kyoyukwon.

Chung, Byung-Ho. 2000. "North Korean Famine from the Perspective of Center and Periphery." Paper presented at the Korean Specialists Workshop for the Current Culture. University of California-Berkeley Center for Korean Studies.

Chung, Byung-Ho. 2003. "Living Dangerously in Two Worlds: The Risks and Tactics of North Korean Refugee Children in China." *Korea Journal*, 43(3):191–211.

Chung, Byung-Ho. 2004. "Depoliticizing the Politics of North Korean Refugees." Paper presented at the Annual Meeting of the American Anthropological Association, San Francisco, CA, November 17–21.

Chung, Byung-Ho. 2008. "Between Defector and Migrant: Identities and Strategies of North Koreans in South Korea." *Korean Studies*, 32: 1–27.

Chung, Byung-Ho. 2014. "Penetrant Transnational Strategies of North Korean Migrants in South Korea and Beyond." Paper presented at the 7th World Congress of Korean Studies. University of Hawaii, Honolulu, November 7.

Chung Byung-Ho, Jeon Woo-taek, and Chung Jean-Kyung, eds. 2006. *Welk'ŏmt'u K'oria: Pukchosŏn Saramdŭl ŭi Namhansari* (Welcome to Korea: The Life of North Koreans in South Korea). Seoul: Hanyang University Press.

Chung Yong-sup. 2006. *Sokbin Sŏlkyo Kkwakch'an Sŏlkyo* (Meaningless Sermon Meaningful Sermon). Seoul: Taehangidokkyosŏhoy.

Clifford, James. 1994. "Diasporas." *Cultural Anthropology*, 9(3): 302–338.

Clifford, James. 1997. *Routes: Travel and Translation in the Late Twentieth Century*. Cambridge, London: Harvard University Press.

Cohen, Robin. 1997. *Global Diasporas: An Introduction*. Seattle: University of Washington Press.

Cohen, Ronald. 1989. "Human Rights and Cultural Relativism: The Need for a New Approach." *American Anthropologist*, 91(4): 1014–1017.

Coleman, Simon. 2003. "The Faith Movement: A Global Religious Culture?" *Culture and Religion: An Interdisciplinary Journal*, 3(1): 3–19.

Coleman, Simon. 2006. "Materializing the Self: Words and Gifts in the Construction of Charismatic Protestant Identity." In *The Anthropology of Christianity*, edited by Fenella Cannell, 163–184. Durham: Duke University Press.

Comaroff, Jean and John Comaroff. 1991, 1997. *Of Revelation and Revolution: Christianity, Colonialism and Consciousness in South Africa v. I and II*. Chicago: University of Chicago Press.

Comaroff, Jean and John Comaroff. 2003. "Second Comings: Neo-Protestant Ethics and Millennial Capitalism in Africa, and Elsewhere." In *2000 Years and Beyond*, edited by Paul Glifford, David Archard, Trevor A. Hart and Nigel Rapport, 106–126. London, New York: Routledge.

Comaroff, John and Jean Comaroff. 1992. *Ethnography and the Historical Imagination*. Boulder: Westview Press.

Congressional Research Service (CRS). 2007. *North Korean Refugees in China and Human Rights Issues: International Response and US Policy Options*. Washington, DC: Congressional Research Service.

Cowan, Jane K., Marie- Bénédicte Dembour and Richard Wilson eds. 2001. *Culture and Rights: Anthropological Perspectives*. Cambridge: Cambridge University Press.

Cumings, Bruce, Ervand Abrahamian and Moshe Ma'oz eds. 2004. *Investing the Axis of Evil: The Truth about North Korea, Iran, and Syria*. New York, London: New Press.

Cumings, Bruce. 1991. *The Two Koreas: On the Road to Reunification?* Headline Series. New York: Foreign Policy Assn.

Cumings, Bruce. 2004. *North Korea: Another Country*. New York: New Press.

Cumings, Bruce. 2005. *Korea's Place in the Sun: A Modern History*. New York: W. W. Norton.

Cumings, Bruce. 2007. "Kim Jong Il Confronts Bush—and Wins: A New Page in North-South Korean Relations." *Le Monde Diplomatique*, October, and *Japan Focus* on October 9.

De Cordier, B. 2009. "Faith-Based Aid, Globalisation and the Humanitarian Frontline: An Analysis of Western-Based Muslim Aid Organizations." *Disasters*, 33(4): 608–628.

Demick, Barbara. 2009. *Nothing to Envy: Ordinary Lives in North Korea*. New York: Spiegel & Grau.

Denzin, Norman K. and Yvonna S. Lincoln. 2000. *Handbook of Qualitative Research*. Thousand Oaks, CA: Sage Publications, Inc.

Dirks, Nicholas B. 2001. *Castes of Mind: Colonialism and the Making of Modern India*. Princeton, NJ: Princeton University Press.

Donga Ilbo. 2007. "Kwisun20nyŏn Kimmanch'ŏlssi sakip'ihaelo ŏlyŏun saenghwal (20 years after defection, Kim Man-chŏl in a desperate condition due to a fraud)." February 04. Accessed July 13, 2015. http://news.donga.com/Politics_List/3/00/20070204/8403586/1.

Durkheim, Emile. 1965 (1912). *The Elementary Forms of the Religious Life*. (English translation by Joseph Swain: 1915). New York: The Free Press.

Eller, Jack David. 2007. *Introducing Anthropology of Religion: Culture to the Ultimate*. New York and London: Routledge.

Ferris, E. 2005. "Faith-Based and Secular Humanitarian Organizations." *International Review of the Red Cross*, 87(858): 311–325.

Fortier, Anne-Marie. 2000. *Migrant Belongings: Memory, Space, Identity*. Oxford: Berg.

Foucault, Michel. 1994. *The Order of Things: An Archeology of the Human Sciences*. New York: Vintage Books.

Foucault, Michel. 1986. "Of Other Spaces: Utopias and Heterotopias." *Diacritics*, 16(1) (Spring, 1986): 22–27.

Friedman, Milton. 1990 (1979). *Free to Choose: A Personal Statement*. San Diego: Mariner Books.

Geertz, Clifford. 1984. "Distinguished Lecture: Anti Anti-Relativism." *American Anthropologist*, New Series, 86(2): 263–278.

Geertz, Clifford. 1973. "Religion as a Cultural System." In *The Interpretation of Cultures: Selected Essays*, edited by Clifford Geertz, 87–125. New York: Basic Books, Inc.

Gennep, Arnold van. 1960. *The Rites of Passage*. Chicago: University of Chicago Press.

Granovetter, Mark S. 1973. "The Strength of Weak Ties." *American Journal of Sociology*, 78(6): 1360–1380.

Granovetter, Mark S. 1983. "The Strength of Weak Ties: A Network Theory Revisited." *Sociological Theory*, 1(1): 201–233.

Grayson, James Huntley. 2006. "A Quarter-Millennium of Christianity in Korea." In *Christianity in Korea*, edited by Robert E. Buswell Jr. and Lee S. Timothy, 7–25. Honolulu: University of Hawai'i Press.

Grinker, Roy Richard. 1998. *Korea and Its Future: Unification and the Unfinished War*. New York: St. Martin's Press.

Guest, Kenneth J. 2005. "Religion and Transnational Migration in the New Chinatown." In *Immigrant Faiths: Transforming Religious Life in America*, edited by Karen Leonard, 145–164. Walnut Creek, CA: AltaMira.

Gupta, Akhil and James Ferguson. 1992. "Beyond 'Culture': Space, Identity, and the Politics of Difference." *Cultural Anthropology*, 7(1): 6–23.

Habermas, Jürgen. 1996. *Between Facts and Norms: Contributions to a Discourse Theory of Law and Democracy*. Cambridge: Polity Press.

Hackworth, Jason. 2012. *Faith Based: Religious Neoliberalism and the Politics of Welfare in the United States.* Athens: University of Georgia Press.

Haggard, Stephan and Marcus Noland. 2011. *Witness to Transformation: Refugee Insights into North Korea.* Washington, DC: Peterson Institute for International Economics.

Hall, Stuart. 2003. "Cultural Identity and Diaspora." In *Theorizing Diaspora,* edited by J. Braziel and A. Mannur, 233–246. New York: Blackwell.

Han, Ju Hui Judy. 2013. "Beyond Safe Haven: A Critique of Christian Custody of North Korean Migrants in China." *Critical Asian Studies,* 45(4): 533–560.

Han Kyŏng-jik. 1987. *Han Kyŏng-jik sŏlkyo: Korindo chŏn husŏ (Han Kyŏngjik's Sermon: Paul's Letter to the Corinthians).* Seoul: Yemok.

Hankyoreh 21. 1999. "Kukka jŏngbowŏnŭn aknalhaekda." April 22.

Hann, Chris and the "Civil Religion" Group et al. 2006. *The Postsocialist Religious Questions: Faith and Power in Central Asia and East-Central Europe.* Münster: LIT.

Harding, Susan Friend. 1987. "Convicted by the Holy Spirit: The Rhetoric of Fundamental Baptist Conversion." *American Ethnologist,* 14: 167–181.

Harding, Susan Friend. 2000. *The Book of Jerry Falwell: Fundamentalist Language and Politics.* Princeton, Oxford: Princeton University Press.

Harris, Olivia. 2006. "The Eternal Return of Conversion: Popular Christianity in Highland Bolivia." In *The Anthropology of Christianity,* edited by Fenella Cannel, 51–62. Durham: Duke University Press.

Harvey, David. 2005. *A Brief History of Neoliberalism.* Oxford: Oxford University Press.

Hefner, Robert W. ed. 1993. *Conversion to Christianity: Historical and Anthropological Perspectives on a Great Transformation.* Berkeley: University of California Press.

Hiroshi, Kato. 2008. "Japanese Policies on North Korean Refugees and Problems They Encounter When Settling in Japan." Speech delivered at an international conference held at Korea Christian University, Seoul, Korea, April 2. Available online at NorthKoreanRefugees.com http://northkoreanrefugees.com/2008-06-speech.htm (accessed August 15, 2013).

Hobbes, Thomas. 1651. *Leviathan.* Indianapolis: Hackett Publishing Company.

Holland, Dorothy, Debra Skinner, Wiliam Lachicotte Jr., and Carole Cain eds. 1998. *Identity and Agency in Cultural Worlds.* Cambridge, London: Harvard University Press.

Hong Chang-hyŏng, et al. 2005. Oesanghu st'res changae. In *Welk'ŏmt'u K'oria,* edited by Chung Byung-Ho et al. Seoul: Hanyang University Press.

Horstmann, Alexander and Jin-Heon Jung. 2015. "Introduction: Refugees and Religion." In *Building Noah's Ark: Refugees, Migrants and Religious Communities,* edited by Alexander Horstmann and Jin-Heon Jung. New York: Palgrave Macmillan.

Horstmann, Alexander. 2011. "Ethical Dilemmas and Identifications of Faith-Based Humanitarian Organizations in the Karen Refugee Crisis." *Journal of Refugee Studies,* 24(3): 513–531.

Human Rights Without Frontiers (HRWF). 2008. The Role of the EU in North Korea. Available online http://www.hrwf.net

Humphrey, Caroline. 2005. "Alternative Freedoms," *Proceedings of the American Philosophical Society,* 151(1): 1–10.

Hwang Sŏk-yŏng. 1985. *Chang Kil-san 1–12.* Seoul: Changbi Inc.

Hwang Sŏk-yŏng. 2001. *Sonnim* (Guest). Seoul: Changbi Inc.

Hwang Sŏk-yŏng. 2007. *Baridegi*. Seoul: Changbi Inc.

Iannaccone, Laurence R. 1991. "The Consequences of Religious Market Structure: Adam Smith and the Economics of Religion." *Rationality and Society*, 3(2): 156–177.

International Crisis Group (ICG). 2006. *Perilous Journeys: The Plight of North Koreans in China and Beyond*. Seoul, Brussels: International Crisis Group.

Jacoby, Jeff. 2004. "An Auschwitz in Korea." *Boston Globe*, February 8.

Jager, Sheila. 2003. *Narratives of Nation Building in Korea: A Genealogy of Patriotism*. Armonk, New York and London: M. E. Sharpe.

Janelli, Roger L. and Dawnhee Yim Janelli. 1993. *Making Capitalism: The Social and Cultural Construction of a South Korean Conglomerate*. Stanford, CA: Stanford University Press.

Jang, Nam Hyuck. 2004. *Shamanism in Korean Christianity*. Edison, NJ: Jimoondang International.

Jang Sŏk-man. 2008. "Sinjayujuŭiwa chongkyoŭi wich'i (Liberalism and the Position of Religion)." *Chokyomuhwabipyŏng*, 13: 13–34.

Jeon Woo-taek. 1997. "T'albukjadŭl-ŭi chuyo sahoe paegyŏng e ttarŭn chŏgŭng kwa chaa chŏngch'esŏng e kwanhan yŏnku (Study of North Korean Defectors' Adaptation and Self Identity According to Their Major Social Background)." *T'ongilyŏnku*, 1(2): 109–167.

Jeon Woo-taek. 2000. *Saram-ŭi T'ongil ŭl wihayŏ (For People's Unification)*. Seoul, South Korea: Orŭm.

Jeon Woo-taek. 2007. *Saram-ŭi T'ongil ttang- ŭi T'ongil* (Unification of People, Unification of Land). Seoul: Yonsei University Press.

Jeon Woo-taek, Yoon Dŏk-yong and Eom Jin-sŏp. 2003. "T'albukjadŭl-ŭi namhan sahoe chŏgŭng saenghwal silt'ae chosa (Research on the Actual Condition of North Korean Defectors' Adaptation Life in South Korean Society)." *T'ongilyŏnku*, 1(7): 155–208.

Jeon Woo-taek, et al. 2005. Ŭisik kwa saenghwal manjokdo (Consciousness and Satisfaction Level with Life). In *Welk'ŏmt'u K'oria*, edited by Chung Byung-Ho et al. Seoul, South Korea: Hanyang University Press.

Jeung, Russell. 2005. *Faithful Generations: Race and New Asian American Churches*. New Brunswick, NJ, London: Rutgers University Press.

Jin Mi-jŏng, Sun-hyŏng Lee and Chang-dae Kim. 2009. *Talbukin ŭi sahoekwankemang kwa sahoejŏk chabon* (North Korean Defectors' Social Networks and Social Capital). Seoul: Hakjidang.

Jung, Jin-Heon. 2007. "T'alpuntan tamunhwa sitae mainŏrit'i minjokchi: Saet'ŏmin 'uri'rŭl natsŏlge hada (Ethnography in Post-Division Multicultural Era: North Korean Migrants Make 'Us' Unfamiliar)." In *Hankukesŏŭi tamunhwajuŭi hyŏnsil gwa chaengchŏm* (Official English title: Multiculturalism in South Korea: A Critical Review), edited by Oh Kyŏng-sŏk. Seoul: Hanul Ak'ademi.

Jung, Jin-Heon. 2011. "Underground Railroads of Christian Conversion: North Korean Migrants and Evangelical Missionary Networks in Northeast Asia." *Encounters*, 4: 163–188.

Jung, Jin-Heon. 2013. "Narrativization of Religious Conversion: 'Christian Passage' of North Korean Refugees in South Korea." *Hankukŏnŏmunhwahak*, 50: 269–288.

Jung, Jin-Heon. 2014. "Ballooning Evangelism: Psychological Warfare and Christianity in the Divided Korea." *MMG Working Paper* 14–07, Max Planck Institute for the Study of Religious and Ethnic Diversity.

Jung, Jung-Ae, Young-Chul Son and Jeong-Hwa Lee. 2013. "Pukhanit'aljuminŭi t'albuktonggiwa namhansahoe chŏkŭnge kwanhan yŏnku: chŏkŭngyuyŏnsŏngŭi chojŏlhyokwarŭl chungsimŭro (A Study on Defecting Motive and Social Adaptation of North Korean Defectors in South Korea: Focusing on Moderating Effect of Resilience)." *T'ongiljŏngch'aekyŏngu*, 22(2): 215–248.

Kang In-chŏl. 2005. "Hankuk Kaesin'gyo Pan'gongjuŭi ŭi hyŏngsŏng kwa jaesaengsan (Formation and Reproduction of Korean Protestant Anticommunism)." *Yŏksapip'yŏng*, 70: 40–63.

Kang In-chŏl. 2007. *Hankukŭi Kaesinkyowa Pankongjuŭi: Posujŏk Kaesinkyoŭi Chŏngch'ijŏk Haedongjuŭi tamgu (Korean Protestantism and Anti-Communism: The Study of Conservative Protestant Political Behaviorism)*. Seoul: Choonsim.

Kang Ju-wŏn. 2006. "Namhan sahoe ŭi kupyŏl jitki (South Korean Society's Differentiating)." In *Welk'ŏm t'u K'oria: Bukjoseon saramdul ui namhan sari*, edited by Chung Byung-Ho et al. Seoul: Hanyang University Press.

Kang, Myŏng-gyu and Wagner eds. 1990. *Korea and Germany: Lessons in Division*. Seoul: Seoul National University Press.

Keane, Webb. 2006. "Anxious Transcendence." In *The Anthropology of Christianity*, edited by Fenella Cannell. Durham: Duke University Press.

Keane, Webb. 2007. *Christian Moderns: Freedom and Fetish in the Mission Encounter*. Berkeley: University of California Press.

Kelleher, Jr., William F. 2004. *The Troubles in Ballybogoin: Memory and Identity in Northern Ireland*. Ann Arbor: University of Michigan Press.

Kendall, Laurel. 1985. *Shamans, Housewives, and Other Restless Spirits: Women in Korean Ritual Life*. Honolulu: University of Hawaii Press.

Kim, Andrew. 2000. "Korean Religious Culture and Its Affinity to Christianity: The Rise of Protestant Christianity in South Korea." *Sociology of Religion*, 61(2): 117–133.

Kim, Byong-suh. 2006. "Modernization and the Explosive Growth and Decline of Korean Protestant Religiosity." In *Christianity in Korea*, edited by Robert E. Buswell and Timothy S. Lee, 309–329. Honolulu: University of Hawai'i Press.

Kim, Chong Bum. 2006. "Preaching the Apocalypse in Colonial Korea: The Protestant Millennialism of Kil Sŏn-ju." In *Christianity in Korea*, edited by Robert E. Buswell and Timothy S. Lee, 149–166. Honolulu: University of Hawai'i Press.

Kim Dong-chun. 2001. "Hankukŭi uik, Hankukŭi 'chayujuŭija' (Korean Right-Wing, Korean 'Liberalists')." *Sahoipyŏngron* Kyŏulho (Winter issue).

Kim Dŭk-jung. 2009. *Ppalgaengi ŭi t'ansaeng: Yŏsun sagŏn kwa pan'gong kukka ŭi hyŏngsŏng (The Birth of Reds: Yŏsun incident and the Formation of Anticommunist State)*. Seoul: Sŏnin.

Kim Hyŏng-su. 2004. *Mun Ik Hwan Pyŏngjŏn* (Biography of Mun Ik Hwan). Seoul: Silch'ŏnmunhaksa.

Kim Il-sung. 1993. *With the Century* (Vol. 3.1 & Vol. 4.1). E-Library of North Korean official website, http://www.korea-dpr.com/lib/202.pdf

Kim Jong-dae. 2013. "Sŏul pulbada ŏryŏun kkadak (Difficult Reasons to Make Seoul into See of Fire)," *Hankyŏre* (the Hangyoreh), March 15.

Kim Jong-il. 1995. "Giving Priority to Ideological Work Is Essential for Accomplishing Socialism." E-Library of North Korean official website, http://www.korea-dpr.com/lib/101/pdf

Kim Jong-il. 1996. "The Juche Philosophy Is an Original Revolutionary Philosophy." E-Library of North Korean official website, http://www.korea-dpr.com/lib/108.pdf

Kim Kwi-ok. 1999. *Wŏllammin ŭi saenghwal kyŏnghŏm kwa chŏngch'esŏng: Mitŭrobutŏ ŭi Wŏllammin Yŏn'gu* (Life Experiences and Identity of the Wŏllammin: Study of Wŏllammin from Below). Seoul: Seoul University Press.

Kim Kwi-ok. 2004. *Isan'gajok, 'Pan'gongjŏnsa'to 'ppalgaengi'to anin* (Separated Families, Neither 'Anticommunist Fighters' nor 'Communists'). Seoul: Yŏksabip'yŏngsa.

Kim, Samuel S. 2006. *The Two Koreas and the Great Powers.* Cambridge, New York: Cambridge University Press.

Kim, Samuel S. 2007. *North Korean Foreign Relations in the Post-Cold War World.* Carlisle Barracks, PA: U.S. Army War College, Strategic Studies Institute.

Kim, Seong-nae. 1989. "Lamentations of the Dead: The Historical Imagery of Violence on Cheju Island, South Korea." *Journal of Ritual Studies*, 3(2): 251–285.

Kim, Seong-nae. 2001. "Sexual Politics of State Violence: On the Cheju April Third Massacre of 1948." *Taces-Multilingual Journal of Cultural Theory and Translation*, 2: 259–292.

Kim, Sung Gun. 2007. "Korean Protestant Christianity in the Midst of Globalization: Neoliberalism and the Pentecostalization of Korean Churches." *Korea Journal*, 47(4): 147–170.

Kim, Sun Joo. 2009. *Marginality and Subversion in Korea: The Hong Kyŏngnae Rebellion of 1812.* Seattle: University of Washington Press.

Kim Yŏng-su. 2004. "Pukhan it'al chumin ŭi hyŏnhwang kwa jaesahoehwa munje (North Korean Defectors' Present Condition and Problems of Re-socialization)." *Sahoe kwahak yŏn'gu*, 12(1): 118–148.

Kim, Yoon Young. 2009. "Making National Subjects: Education and Adaptation among North Korean Immigrants in South Korea." Ph.D. diss. in Anthropology, University of Hawai'i at Manoa.

Kleinman, Arthur, Veena Das, and Margaret Lock, eds. 1997. *Social Suffering.* Berkeley: University of California Press.

Koo, Hagen. 2001. *Korean Workers: The Culture and Politics of Class Formation.* Ithaca, London: Cornell University Press.

Korea Institute for National Unification. 2013. *Pukhan in'gwŏn paeksŏ 2013* (*White Paper on Human Rights in North Korea 2013*). Seoul: Korea Institute for National Unification.

Kwon, Heonik and Byung-Ho Chung. 2012. *North Korea: Beyond Charismatic Politics.* Plymouth: Rowman & Littlefield Publishers.

Kwon, Hyŏk-bŏm. 2000. *Minjokjuŭi wa paljŏnŭi hwansang* (*Nationalism and Illusion of Development*). Seoul: Sol.

Kwon, Insook. 2000. "Militarism in My Heart: Militarization of Women's Consciousness and Culture in South Korea." Ph.D. diss., Worcester, MA: Clark University.

Laidlaw, James. 2002. "For an Anthropology of Ethics and Freedom," *Journal of the Royal Anthropological Institute*, 8(2): 311–332.

Lankov, Andrei. 2006. "Bitter Taste of Paradise: North Korean Refugees in South Korea." *Journal of East Asian Studies*, 6(1): 105–137.

Lankov, Andrei. 2013. *The Real North Korea: Life and Politics in the Failed Stalinist Utopia.* Oxford and New York: Oxford University Press.

Lee Chang-hyŏn and Sŏng-jun Kim 2007. "Puk'anit'aljoomin ŭi namhan pangson suyong t'ŭksŏng kwa midiŏ kyoyuk ŭi panghyang (The Educational Direction for and the Characteristics of North Korean Migrant Attitude toward South Korean Mass Media)." *Puk'an yŏnku hakhoebo*, 11(2): 197–323.

Lee, Hyo-chae. 1977. "Protestant Missionary Work and the Enlightenment of Korean Women." *Korea Journal*, 17(11): 33–50.

Lee Jong-rok. 2006. "Miguk kwa Hankuk ŭi posu jŏk Kidokkyo: Miguk kwa Hankuk ŭi up'a pikyowa sŏngsŏjŏk pip'an (American and Korean Conservative Protestantism: Comparison of Christian Right-Wings in Korea and the United State and Biblical Criticism)." *Tamnon* 201, 9(4): 259–301.

Lee Kŭm-hee. 2007. *Kŭmhee ŭi yŏhaeng: Aoji esŏ Sŏul kkaji 7,000km* (Kŭmhee's Journey: From Aoji to Seoul 7,000km). Seoul: Mindŭlle.

Lee Sŏng-taek. 2004. "Hankuk sahoeŭi chayuminjujuŭi tamronkwa minjujŏk kongkohwa iron (Liberal Democratic Discourses and Democratic Solidification Theory of Korean Society)." *Sahoewa iron*, 5: 237–281.

Lee Sang-soo. 1992. "Wŏlnam Kwisun yongsa ŭi sam, kŭ bit kwa kŭrimja (North Korean Defector's Life, Its Ray and Shadow)." *Sahoep'yŏngnon*, 92(3): 232–239.

Lee, Soo-Jung. 2006. "Making and unmaking the Korean national division: Separated families in the Cold War and post-Cold War eras." Ph.D. diss., University of Illinois at Urbana-Champaign.

Lee, Timothy S. 2010. *Born Again: Evangelicalism in Korea.* Honolulu: University of Hawai'i Press.

Lee U-yŏng. 2003. "Pukhanitaljuminŭi chiyŏksahoe chŏngch'ak (North Korean Migrants' Regional Society Settlement)," *Yŏnkuch'ongsŏ* (Research Paper Series) 03–02, Seoul: Tongilyŏnkuwŏn (Korea Institute for National Unification).

Leonard, Karen I. 2005. "Introduction." In *Immigrant Faiths: Transforming Religious Life in America*, edited by Karen Leonard, Alex Stepick and Manuel A. Vasquez, 11–38. Walnut Creek, CA: AltaMira.

Lester, Rebecca J. 2005. *Jesus in Our Womb: Embodying Modernity in a Mexican Convent.* Berkeley: University of California Press.

Lim, Jie-Hyun. 2012. "Victimhood Nationalism in the Post-Totalitarian Historiography. On the Third Republic of Poland and the Sixth Republic of Korea," Paper presented at the 9th European Social Science History Conference Glasgow, Scotland, UK, April 12.

Lyon-Callo, Vincent. 2004. *Inequality, Poverty, and Neoliberal Governance: Activist Ethnography in the Homeless Sheltering Industry.* Toronto: University of Toronto Press, Higher Education Division.

Mahmood, Saba. 2001. "Feminist Theory, Embodiment, and the Docile Agent: Some Reflections on the Egyptian Islamic Revival." *Cultural Anthropology*, 16(2): 202–236.

Mahmood, Saba. 2005. *Politics of Piety: The Islamic Revival and the Feminist Subject.* Princeton, NJ: Princeton University Press.

Mahmood, Saba. 2006. Secularism, Hermeneutics, and Empire: The Politics of Islamic Reformation. *Public Culture*, 18(2): 323–247.

Malinowski, Bronislaw. 1992 [1948]. *Magic, Science and Religion and Other Essays*. Prospect Heights, IL: Waveland Press Inc.

Malinowski, Bronislaw. 1960 [1947]. *Freedom and Civilization*. Bloomington: Indiana University Press.

Malkki, Liisa. 1995. *Purity and Exile: Violence, Memory, and National Cosmology among Hutu Refugees in Tanzania*. Chicago: University of Chicago Press.

Malkki, Liisa. 1996. "Speechless Emissaries: Refugees, Humanitarianism, and Dehistoricization." *Cultural Anthropology*, 11(3): 377–404.

Martin, David. 2002. *Pentecostalism: The World Their Parish*. Oxford, Malden, MA: Wiley-Blackwell.

Messer, Ellen. 1993. "Anthropology and Human Rights." *Annual Review of Anthropology*, 22: 221–249.

Meyer, Birgit. 1999. *Translating the Devil: Religion and Modernity among the Ewe in Ghana*. Trenton, NJ: Africa World Press.

Meyer, Birgit and Peter Pels eds. 2003. *Magic and Modernity: Interfaces of Revelation and Concealment*. Stanford, CA: Stanford University Press.

Moon Jiyoung. 2006. "Hankukŭi minjuhwa wa chayujuŭi: Chayujuŭijŏk minjuhwa chŏnmangŭi ŭimiwa hangye (Korean Democratization and Liberalism: Meaning and Limit of Liberalist Democratization Prospect)." *Sahŏiyŏnku*, 11: 75–111.

Moon, S. Sang-Cheol. 2003. "The Protestant Missionary Movement in Korea: Current Growth and Development." *International Bulletin of Missionary Research*, 32(2): 59–64.

Moon, Seung-sook. 2005. *Militarized Modernity and Gendered Citizenship in South Korea*. Durham, NC: Duke University Press.

Myers, B. R. 2010. *The Cleanest Race: How North Koreans See Themselves – And Why It Matters*. Brooklyn, NY: Melville House.

Nock, Arthur Darby. 1933. *Conversion: The Old and the New in Religion from Alexander the Great to Augustine of Hippo*. Oxford: Oxford University Press.

O'Neill, Tom. 2009. "Escape from North Korea." *National Geographic*, February. Available online http://ngm.nationalgeographic.com/2009/02/north-korea/oneill-text (accessed August 15, 2013).

Ong, Aihwa. 1996. "Cultural Citizenship as Subject-Making: Immigrants Negotiate Racial and Cultural Boundaries in the United States." *Current Anthropology*, 37(5): 737–762.

Ong, Aihwa. 2003. *Buddha Is Hiding: Refugees, Citizenship, the New America*. Berkeley, London: University of California Press.

Orta, Andrew. 2004. *Catechizing Culture: Missionaries, Aymara, and the "New Evangelization."* New York: Columbia University Press.

Osnos, Evan. 2008. "Jesus in China: Christianity's Rapid Rise." *Chicago Tribune*, June 22.

Paik Hak-soon. 2009. "Kim Tae-chung chŏngbu wa No Mu-hyŏn chŏngbu ŭi taebukchŏngch'aek pigyo (Comparison between Kim Da-jung and Roh Moo-hyun Governments' North Korean Policies)." *Sejong chŏngch'aekyŏnku*, 5(1): 277–354.

Palais, James B. 1998 "Nationalism: Good or Bad?" In *Nationalism and the Construction of Korean Identity*, edited by Hyung Il Pai and Timothy R. Tangherlini, 214–228. Berkeley: Center for Korean Studies, Institute of East Studies, University of California, Berkeley.

Palmer, Spencer J. 1986. *Korea and Christianity: The Problem of Identification with Tradition*. Monograph series/Royal Asiatic Society, Korea Branch 2. Seoul, South Korea: Published for the Royal Asiatic Society.

Parekh, Bhikhu. 2000. *Rethinking Multiculturalism: Cultural Diversity and Political Theory*. Basingstoke: Macmillan Press.

Park, Chung-shin. 2003. *Protestantism and Politics in Korea*. Seattle: University of Washington Press.

Park Heung-soon. 2006. *P'osŭt'ŭk'olloniŏl sŏngsŏ haesŏk* (Postcolonial Bible Interpretation). South Korea: Yeyŏngbiaenpi.

Park Hyŏn-chŏng. 2013. "Inkwŏnŭn hapdongsimmun centŏr muntŏkŭl nŏmch'I mothaetta (Human Rights Was Unable to Pass over the Threshold of Korean Joint Interrogation Center)." *Hankŏrye 21*, May 13.

Park Myŏng-su. 2009. "Tachonggyo sahoe esŏ ŭi Hankuk Kaesin'gyo wa kukka kwŏllyŏk (Korean Protestantism and National Power in the Plural Religious Context)." *Chonggyo yŏnku*, 54: 1–37.

Park Pi-dŭk. 1999. "21segiro hyanghanŭn Chungguk Chosŏnjok kyohoe (The Korean-Chinese Church in China toward the 21st Century)." *Chungguk Kyohoe wa Sŏnkyo*, 6: 126–135. E-article at the Society for World Internet Mission (SWIM). Available online http://china.swim.org/kr/info/info1/list4/main1.html (accessed August 15, 2013).

Park Sun-yŏng. 2006. "Sŏngjang palyuk – saengmurhak jŏk yŏnku (Growth and Development-Biological Study)." In *Welk'ŏm t'u K'oria: Bukjoseon saramdul ui namhan sari*, edited by Chung Byung-Ho et al. Seoul: Hanyang University Press.

PBS Wide Angle. 2009. Crossing Heaven's Border. A documentary film.

Pearson, James. 2013. "Detained American Was Missionary Dispatched to China," NK News (6 May). Available online http://www.nknews.org/2013/05/detained-american-was-missionary-dispatched-to-china/ (accessed August 1, 2013).

Pels, Peter. 1997. "The Anthropology of Colonialism: Culture, History, and the Emergence of Western Governmentality." *Annual Review of Anthropology*, 26: 163–183.

Pels, Peter. 1998. *A Politics of Presence: Contacts between Missionaries and Waluguru in Late Colonial Tanganyika*. Studies in Anthropology and History, 22. Amsterdam: Harwood Academic Publishers.

Porterfield, Amanda. 2005. *Healing in the History of Christianity*. Oxford: Oxford University Press.

Powles, Julia. 2004. "Life History and Personal Narrative: Theoretical and Methodological Issues Relevant to Research and Evaluation in Refugee Contexts." Working Paper No. 106, UNHCR (e-article, http://www.refworld.org/pdfid/4ff2a61c2.pdf, accessed on September 3, 2013)

Pratt, Mary Louise. 1992. *Imperial Eyes: Travel Writing and Transculturation*. New York, London: Routledge.

Pukhanit'aljuminjiwŏnjaedan (North Korean Refugees Foundation). 2013. *2012 Pukhanit'aljumin silt'aechosa (2012 Report on the Actual Condition of North Korean Refugees in South Korea)*. Seoul: Pukhanit'aljuminjiwŏjaedan.

Rajaram, Prem Kumar. 2002. "Humanitarianism and Representations of the Refugee." *Journal of Refugee Studies*, 15(3): 247–264.

Rambo, Lewis R. 1993. *Understanding Religious Conversion*. New Haven & London: Yale University Press.

Robbins, Joel. 2004. *Becoming Sinners: Christianity and Moral Torment in a Papua New Guinea Society*. Berkeley: University of California Press.

Robbins, Joel. 2007. "Between Reproduction and Freedom: Morality, Value, and Radical Cultural Change." *Ethnos*, 72(3): 293–314.

Rocco, R. 2004. "Transforming Citizenship: Membership, Strategies of Containment and the Public Sphere in Latino Communities." *Latino Studies*, 2: 4–25.

Rogers, Douglas 2005. "Introductory Essay: The Anthropology of Religion after Socialism." *Religion, State and Society*, 33(1): 5–18.

Rosaldo, Renato ed. 2003. *Cultural Citizenship in Island Southeast Asia: Nation and Belonging in the Hinterlands*. Berkeley: University of California Press.

Rosaldo, Renato. 1989. *Culture and Truth: The Remaking of Social Analysis*. Boston: Beacon Press.

Rosaldo, Renato. 1994. "Cultural Citizenship and Educational Democracy." *Cultural Anthropology*, 9(3): 402–411.

Roy, Sanjay K. 2001. *Refugees and Human Rights: Social and Political Dynamics of Refugee Problem in Eastern and North-Eastern India*. Jaipur: Rawat Publications.

Ryang, Sonia. 1997. *North Koreans in Japan: Language, Ideology, and Identity*. Boulder: Westview Press.

Ryang, Sonia. 2008. *Writing Selves in Diaspora: Ethnography of Autobiographics of Korean Women in Japan and the United States*. Lanham, MD, Plymouth: Lexington Books.

Ryang, Sonia. 2012. *Reading North Korea: An Ethnological Inquiry*. Cambridge, MA: Harvard University Asia Center.

Ryu, Dae Young. 2008. "The Origin and Characteristics of Evangelical Protestantism in Korea at the Turn of the Twentieth Century." *Church History: Studies in Christianity and Culture*, 77(2): 371–398.

Ryu, Dae Young. 2009. *Hankuk kŭnhyŏndaesa wa Kidokkyo (Korean Modern History and Christianity)*. Seoul: p'urŭnyŏksa.

Ryu, Paul K. 1965. "Legal Education in the Far East." *Seoul Law Journal*, 71(1): 117–128.

Said, Edward. 1979. *Orientalism*. New York: Vintage Books.

Tudela, Sampson Vera Elisa. 2000. *Colonial Angels: Narratives of Gender and Spirituality in Mexico 1580–1750*. Austin: University of Texas Press.

Schepher-Hughes, Nancy. 1994. "Embodied Knowledge: Thinking with the Body in Critical Medical Anthropology." *Assessing Cultural Anthropology*, 229: 229–242.

Shin, Eun-hee. 2005. "Kidokkyowa chuch'esasangkwaŭi taehwa: saenmyŏngjuŭi tamunhwa t'ongillon (The Dialogue between Christianity and Juche Idea: Theory of Vitalism Multicultural Unification)." *Minjoksasangyŏnku*, 13.

Shin, Gi-wook. 2006. *Ethnic Nationalism in Korea: Genealogy, Politics, and Legacy*. Stanford, CA: Stanford University Press, Studies of the Walter H. Shorenstein Asia-Pacific Research Center.

Shore, Cris and Susan Wright. 2005 [1997]. "Policy: A New Field of Anthropology." In *Anthropology of Policy: Perspectives on Governance and Power*, edited by Cris Shore and Susan Wright, 3–30. London, New York: Routledge.

Solzhenitsyn, Alexander. 1974. "Alexander Solzhenitsyn – Banquet Speech." Nobelprize.org. June 23, 2010. Available online http://nobelprize.org/nobel_prizes/literature/laureates/1970/solzhenitsyn-speech74-e.html

Song, Jesook. 2006. "Family Breakdown and Invisible Homeless Women: Neoliberal Governance during the Asian Debt Crisis in South Korea, 1997–2001." *Positions: East Asia Cultures Critique*, 14(1): 37–65.

Song, Jesook. 2009. *South Koreans in Debt Crisis: The Creation of a Neoliberal Welfare State*. Durham: Duke University Press.

Song ŭi-dal. 1996. "Panisang saengkyekonlan chetochŏk changch'i p'ilyo (More than half (of North Koreans in the South) suffering poverty, necessary of a systematic (social welfare) program)." Chosun ilpo, February 07. Accessed July 13, 2015. http://srchdb1.chosun.com.access.yonsei.ac .kr:8080/pdf/i_archive/read_body.jsp?Y=1996&M=02&D=07&ID=9602070502.

Song Yŏng-hun. 2012. "Haeoe talbukiju hyŏnsangŭi hyŏnhwangkwa jaenjŏm (The Present Condition and Issue of the Phenomenon of Overseas North Korean Defection)." Paper presented at Jeju Peace Institute Forum, November 9.

Steinberg, Mark and Catherine Wanner eds. 2008. *Religion, Morality and Community in Post-Soviet Societies*. Washington, DC: Bloomington: Indiana University Press.

Stromberg, Peter G. 1993. *Language and Self-Transformation: A Study of the Christian Conversion Narrative*. Cambridge [England], New York, NY: Cambridge University Press.

Suh, Jae-jean. 2002. "North Korean Defectors: Their Adaptation and Resettlement." *East Asian Review*, 14(3): 67–86.

Suh, Jae-Jung. 2010. "Race to Judge, Rush to Act: The Sinking of the Cheonan and the Politics of National Insecurity." *Critical Asian Studies*, 42(3): 403–424.

Thorne, Susan. 1999. *Congregational Missions and the Making of an Imperial Culture in Nineteenth-Century England*. Stanford, CA: Stanford University Press.

Turner, Victor. 1979. *Process, Performance, and Pilgrimage: A Study in Comparative Symbology*. New Delhi: Concept Publishing Company.

Tweed, Thomas A. 2006. *Crossing and Dwelling: A Theory of Religion*. Cambridge, London: Harvard University Press.

The United States Commission on International Religious Freedom (USCIRF). 2008. *A Prison without Bars: Refugee and Defector Testimonies of Severe Violations of Freedom of Religion or Belief in North Korea*.

van den Berghe, Pierre. 2006. "The Modern State: Nation-Builder or Nation Killer?" In *Talking about People: Readings in Contemporary Cultural Anthropology*, edited by W. Haviland, R. Gordon and L. Vivanco, 4th Ed., 209–217. New York: McGraw-Hill.

van der Veer, Peter ed. 1996. *Conversion to Modernities: The Globalization of Christianity*. New York: Routledge.

van der Veer, Peter. 2007. "Global Breathing: Religious Utopias in India and China." *Anthropological Theory*, 7(3): 315–328.

van der Veer, Peter. 2012. "Market and Money: A Critique of Rational Choice Theory." *Social Compass*, 59(2): 183–192.

van der Veer, Peter and Arjun Appadurai. "Comparative Study of Urban Aspirations in Mega-Cities," E-document of research project description, Available online http://www.mmg.mpg.de/research/all-projects/comparative-study-of-urban-aspirations-in-mega-cities/

van der Veer, Peter and Hartmut Lehmann eds. 1999. *Nation and Religion: Perspectives on Europe and Asia*. Princeton, NJ: Princeton University Press.

Verdery, Katherine. 1996. *What Was Socialism? And What Comes Next?* Princeton, NJ: Princeton University Press.

Vertovec, Steven. 2007. "Super-Diversity and Its Implications." *Ethnic and Racial Studies*, 30(6): 1024–1054.

Wacquant, Loic J. D. 1989. "Towards a Reflexive Sociology: A Workshop with Pierre Bourdieu." *Sociological Theory*, 7(1): 26–63.

Walraven, Boudewijin. 2000. "Religion and the City: Seoul in the Nineteenth Century." *The Review of Korean Studies*, 3: 178–206.

Wanner, Catherine. 2007. *Communities of the Converted: Ukrainians and Global Evangelism.* Ithaca, NY: Cornell University Press.

Weber, Max. 1963. *The Sociology of Religion.* Boston: Beacon Press.

Wells, Kenneth M. 1990. *New God, New Nation: Protestants and Self-Reconstruction nationalism in Korea 1896–1937.* Honolulu: University of Hawaii Press.

Wells, Kenneth M. ed. 1995. *South Korea's Minjung Movement: The Culture and Politics of Dissidence.* Honolulu: University of Hawai'i Press.

Whiteman, Darrell L. 2004. "Part II: Anthropology and Mission: The Incarnational Connection." *International Journal of Frontier Missions*, 21(2): 79–88.

Wiegele, Katharine L. 2005. *Investing in Miracles: El Shaddai and the Transformation of Popular Catholicism in the Philippines.* Honolulu: University of Hawaii Press.

Wightman, Jill. 2007. "New Bolivians, New Bolivia: Pentecostal Conversion and Neoliberal Transformation in Contemporary Bolivia." Ph.D. diss. in Anthropology, University of Illinois at Urbana-Champaign.

Wikan, Unni. 2002. *Generous Betrayal: Politics of Culture in the New Europe.* Chicago, London: University of Chicago Press.

Wilson, Richard ed. 1997. *Human Rights, Culture & Context.* London: Pluto Press.

Wilson, Richard A. and Jon P. Mitchell, eds. 2003. *Human Rights in Global Perspective: Anthropological Studies of Rights, Claims and Entitlements.* London: Routledge.

Wimmer, Andreas. 2009. "Herder's Heritage and the Boundary-Making Approach: Studying Ethnicity in Immigrant Societies." *Sociological Theory*, 27(3): 244–270.

Winland, Daphne N. 1994. "Christianity and Community: Conversion and Adaptation among Hmong Refugee Women," *The Canadian Journal of Sociology*, 19(1): 21–45.

Yang, Fenggang. 1999. "Religious Conversion and Identity Construction: A Study of a Chinese Christian Church in the United States." Ph.D. diss., The Catholic University of America.

Yang, Fenggang. 2006. "The Red, Black, and Gray Markets of Religion in China." *Sociological Quarterly*, 47(1): 93–122.

Yang Kye-min and Chung Jean-kyung. 2008. *Sahoe t'onghapŭl wihan chŏngsonyŏn tamunhwakyoyuk hwalsŏnghwa pangan yŏnku* (Research for Promoting Multicultural Education for Social Integration of Youth). Seoul: Hankukch'ŏngsonyŏnyŏnkuwon.

Yi Mahn-yol. 1981. *Hankuk Kidokkyo wa yŏksa ŭisik* (Korean Protestantism and Historical Consciousness). Seoul, South Korea: Chisik sanŏpsa.

Yi Mahn-yol. 2006. "Korean Protestants and the Reunification Movement." In *Christianity in Korea*, edited by Robert E. Buswell and Timothy S. Lee, 238–257. Honolulu: University of Hawai'i Press.

Yi Su-wŏn. 2011. "Pukhan chuch'esasanghaksŭpch'ekeŭl chongkyosŏng yŏnku: Kidokkyo chongkyo hwaldong kwaŭi pikyorŭl jungsimŭro (A Study about Religious Trait of Juche Ideology Learning System in North Korea: Focused on Comparison with Christian Religious Activities)." *T'ongilmujeyŏnku*, 55: 311–343.

Yoon In-jin. 2009. *Pukhanijumin: Saenghwalkwa ŭisik, kŭriko Chŏnch'akjiwŏn chŏngch'aek* (North Korean Migrants: Life, Consciousness, and Settlement Support Policy). Seoul: Chipmuntang.

Yoon In-Jin, and Chang-Kyu Lim. 2007. "Social Adjustments of North Korean Migrants in South Korea." Paper presented at the American Sociological Association Conference, New York, August 11–14.

Yoon Yŏ-sang. 2001. "Pukhan it'al chumin chiwŏn chŏngch'aek hyŏnhwang kwa kaesŏn pangan (The Present Conditions of Support System and Alternatives for North Korean Migrants)." *Hankuk chŏngch'aek hakhoe Fall Semester Conference Papers*, 279–318.

Yoon Yŏ-Sang. 2002. "Pukhan it'al chumin hyŏnhwang kwa Min'gwan hyŏmnyŏk pangan (Conditions of North Korean Migrants and the Civil–Government Cooperation Plan)." *Tong'ilmunjeyŏn'gu* [Unification Research] 24: 65–101.

Yoon Yŏ-sang. 2003. "Pukhan it'al chumin kŭpchŭng e ttarŭn chŏngch'aek taean (Policy Options to the Rapid Increase of North Korean Migrants)." *Kukkachŏllyak*, 9(1): 65–88.

Yun, Sŏng-bŏm. 1964. *Kidokkyo wa hankuk sasang* (Christianity and Korean Thought). Seoul: Christian Literature Society.

Index

Note: Locators followed by 'n' refer to notes section.

Printed in the USA
CPSIA information can be obtained
at www.ICGtesting.com
LVHW012305250923
759328LV00006B/70